The World's Best Poetry

Volume VII

Descriptive and Narrative

Poetry Anthology Press

The World's Best Poetry

Volume   I   Home and Friendship
   II   Love
   III   Sorrow and Consolation
   IV   The Higher Life
   V   Nature
   VI   Fancy and Sentiment
   VII   Descriptive and Narrative
   VIII   National Spirit
   IX   Tragedy and Humor
   X   Poetical Quotations; General Indexes

Supplement   I   Twentieth Century English and American Verse, 1900-1929
   II   Twentieth Century English and American Verse, 1930-1950
   III   Critical Companion

Survey of American Poetry

Volume   I   Colonial Period, 1607-1765
   II   Revolutionary Era, 1766-1799
   III   Early 19th Century, 1800-1829
   IV   First Great Period, 1830-1860
   V   Civil War and Aftermath, 1861-1889
   VI   Twilight Interval, 1890-1912
   VII   Poetic Renaissance, 1913-1919
   VIII   Interval Between World Wars, 1920-1939
   IX   World War II and Aftermath, 1940-1950
   X   Midcentury to Present; General Indexes

The World's Best Poetry

Volume VII

Descriptive and Narrative

Edited by Bliss Carman

Prepared by
The Editorial Board, Granger Book Co., Inc.

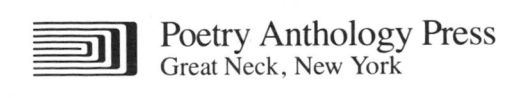 Poetry Anthology Press
Great Neck, New York

TABLE OF CONTENTS.

INTRODUCTORY ESSAY:

   "What 's the Use of Poetry?"

                                          PAGE

      By *Richard Le Gallienne* ix

DESCRIPTIVE POEMS:

   Personal: Rulers; Statesmen; Warriors 3
      Great Writers 37
      Miscellaneous 110
   Nature and Art 124
   Places 160

NARRATIVE POEMS:

   Greece: Rome 261
   Norseland: Germany 284
   The Orient: Spain: France 305
   England: Scotland 352
   America 433

INDEX: Authors and Titles 441

Preface

The publications of **Poetry Anthology Press** constitute a comprehensive conspectus of international verse in English designed to form the core of a library's poetry collection. Covering the entire range of poetic literature, these anthologies encompass all topics and national literatures.

Each collection, published in a multivolume continuing series format, is devoted to a major area of the whole undertaking and contains complete author, title, and first line indexes. Biographical data is also provided.

The World's Best Poetry, with coverage through the 19th century, is topically classified and arranged by subject matter. Supplements keep the 10 volume foundation collection current and complete.

Survey of American Poetry is an anthology of American verse arranged chronologically in 10 volumes. Each volume presents a significant period of American poetic history, from 1607 to date.

"WHAT 'S THE USE OF POETRY?"

BY RICHARD LE GALLIENNE.

" And idly tuneful, the loquacious throng
    Flutter and twitter, prodigal of time,
And little masters make a toy of song
    Till grave men weary of the sound of rhyme."
        —WILLIAM WATSON, in " Wordsworth's Grave."

THERE is no doubt that many—one might almost say most—people are firmly convinced that they do not care for poetry. They have no use for it, they tell you. Either it bores them, as a fantastic, highflown method of saying something that, to their way of thinking, could be better said in plain prose, or they look upon it as the sentimental nonsense of the moonstruck and lovesick young,—a kind of intellectual " candy " all very well for women and children, but of no value to grown men with the serious work of the world on their shoulders.

It is not at all difficult to account for, and, indeed, to sympathize with, this attitude. To begin with, of course, there is a large class outside our present consideration which does not care for poetry, simply because it does not care for any literature whatsoever.

Serious reading of any kind does not enter into

its scheme of life. Beyond the newspapers and magazines and an occasional novel of the hour, idly taken up and indifferently put aside, it has no literary needs. With this listless multitude we have not to concern ourselves, but rather with that sufficiently heterogeneous body known as the reading public, the people for whom Mr. Carnegie builds libraries, and the publishers display their wares. Of course, among these there must necessarily be a considerable percentage temperamentally unappreciative of poetry,—just as there are numbers of people born with no ear for music, and numbers, again, born with no color-sense. The lover of poetry is no less born than the poet himself. Yet, as the poet is made as well as born, so is his reader; and there are many who really love poetry without knowing it, but who think they do not care for it,—either because they have contracted a wrong notion of what poetry is, or because they have some time or other made a bad start with the wrong kind.

I am convinced that one widespread provocative of the prevailing impression of the foolishness of poetry is the mediocre magazine verse of the day. In an age when we go so much to the magazines for our reading, we may rely on finding there the best work being done in every branch of literature except—the highest. The best novelists, the best historians, and the best essayists write for the magazines; but the best poets must be looked for in their high-priced volumes, and a magazine reader must rely for his verse on lady amateurs and tuneful college boys. Thus he too

often approaches poetry not through the great
masters, but through—the little misses; and he
forms his naturally contemptuous notion of
poetry from feeble echoes and insipid imitations.
No wonder, therefore, that he should refuse to
waste his good eyesight on anything in the shape
of verse, and should conceive of poetry as a mild
mental dissipation for young ladies, a sickly
sweetmeat made of molasses and moonshine.

If the magazine editors of the world would only
bind themselves to publish no verse except the
best, and, failing to obtain a contemporary sup-
ply of the best, would fill their spare corners of
space with reprints of the old fine things, I am
convinced that they would do a great deal toward
rectifying this widespread misconception of an
art which, far from being trivial and superficial,
is, of all the arts, the most serious and most vi-
tally human. I am not saying that all poetry is
for all readers. There is a section of poetry
which has been called " poet's poetry," which, of
necessity, can appeal only to those in whom the
sense of beauty and verbal exquisiteness has become specialized. Spenser and Keats, for example, are poets of the rainbow. For the average
reader their poems are the luxuries rather than
the necessities of literature,—though, in making
a distinction so rough and ready, it must not be
forgotten that beauty, happily, is becoming more
and more a general necessity; nor must it be forgotten, either, that rainbows, refined and remote
as they are, belong also to the realities. It is *the
reality of poetry* that I wish, if possible, to bring

home to readers in this article. " Some flowers,"
says George Meredith, " have roots deep as oaks."
Poetry is one of those flowers, and, instead of its
being a superficial decoration of life, it is, rightly
understood, the organic expression of life's deepest meaning, the essence in words of human
dreams and human action. It is the truth of life
told beautifully,—and yet truthfully.

There is only one basis for the longevity of human forms. That basis is reality. No other form
of human expression has continued with such per-
sistent survival from the beginning until now as
poetry,—from " The Iliad " to " The Absent-
Minded Beggar." It and the wild flowers, for
all their adventurous fragility, are as old, and no
less stable, than the hills, and for the same reason,
—because they are no less real. The world is apt
to credit prose with a greater reality than poetry;
but the truth is that the prose of life is real only
in proportion as it is vitalized by that spirit of
poetry that breathes in all created things. Life
exacts practical reasons for the survival of all its
forms of expression, and, unless poetry served
some practical purpose of existence, it would long
since have perished. It is because poetry has a
practical work to do in the world that it con-
tinues, and will continue, to exist; because it is
one of the motive forces of the universe,—life's
motive meaning, one might almost say,—the nerve
force of existence. A great man has defined it
as " the finer spirit of all knowledge," and the
phrase, though limited, may help us to a broader
and deeper apprehension of poetry, and help us

to say, too, that poetry is the finer spirit of all
impulse, the finer meaning of all achievement.
There is no human interest desiring to be displayed in all its essential vividness that does not
realize the value of a poetical expression.

Those who would depreciate the power of poetry
in the sternest practical affairs have only to be re-
minded how much modern imperialism owes to
Rudyard Kipling; and it is by no means trivial
to remark that the most successful advertisements
have been in verse. So soon as " poetry," so
called, really is poetry, its appeal is immediately
admitted and its force undeniably felt. It is the
false poets who account for the false ideas of
poetry. One has only to confront a " practical
man " with the real thing to convince him that,
without realizing it, he has cared a great deal
about poetry all his life. Probably he has imagined that this great stumbling-block has been
the verse. " Why not say it in plain English? " he
has impatiently exclaimed,—thinking all the time
of bad verse, of lifeless, contorted rhyming, and
of those metrical inanities of the magazines; and
yet, when you bring him a verse that is really
alive, in which the metre is felt to be the very life-
beat of the thought, you don't find him asking to
have it turned into prose. How about " Manda-
lay " in prose, for example, or that old bugle-call
of Scott's?—

> " Sound, sound the clarion, fill the fife !
> To all the sensual world proclaim,
> One crowded hour of glorious life
> Is worth an age without a name "—

or Tennyson's " Tears, idle tears," or Coleridge's

> " He prayeth best who loveth best
> All things, both great and small ;
> For the dear God, who loveth us,
> He made and loveth all "—

or " The quality of mercy is not strained," or " Under the greenwood tree," or Mr. Swinburne's—

> " Ask nothing more of me, sweet ;
> All I can give you I give.
> Heart of my heart, were it more,
> More would be laid at your feet :
> Love that should help you to live,
> Song that should spur you to soar."

In all these cases the verse is immediately felt to be the very life of the expression,—for the reason that it echoes in words the life-rhythms to which, unconsciously, all such human emotions keep time. Say it in prose! Can you say a trumpet in prose, or a tear, or a butterfly? If you can, your prose is really poetry, and will be found to be eloquent with sunken rhythms, not immediately obvious to the ear and eye.

The first thing to realize about poetry is that the metre is the meaning,—even more than the words. In Tennyson's sad " Tears, idle tears," for example, it is not so much the words that are accountable for the wistful sorrow of the general effect as the sad, rain-like melody mysteriously charging the words with sorrow, like some beautiful interpretative voice; and it is this subtly mimetic quality, endlessly adaptable, which is the *raison d'être* of metre, and the secret of its power over mankind.

Perhaps it may help us to attempt here a definition of poetry,—though it is a bold, even foolhardy thing to do, for there has never yet been a definition of poetry that satisfied any one but the man who made it. We may recall one fashionable in its day,—Matthew Arnold's " Poetry is a criticism of life." That a poet should have made such a harrowing definition is amazing, though one, of course, understands it, in the light of the fact that the inspiration of Matthew Arnold's muse was almost entirely that of a philosophical criticism of life. Far from being a *criticism* of life, poetry is much more like a *re-creation* of it. It *is* life—in words. But let me timidly launch my own definition :

Poetry is that impassioned arrangement of words, whether in verse or prose, which embodies the exaltation, the beauty, the rhythm, and the pathetic truth of life.

There is a motive idealism behind all human action of which most of us are unconscious, or to which we ordinarily give but little thought, a romance of impulse, which is the real significance of human effort. The walls of Thebes were built to music, according to the old story,—but so were the walls of every other city that has ever been built. The sky-scrapers of New York are soaring to music also,—a masterful music of the future, which not all can hear, and of which, perhaps, the music-makers themselves are most ignorant of all. Once more, in Emerson's immortal phrase, the

builders are building better than they know,—
these ruthless speculators and stern business men,
who are the last to suspect themselves of the
poetry which they involuntarily serve.

Human life, in the main, is thus unconsciously
poetical, and moves to immortal measures of a
mysterious spiritual music. It is this impassioned exaltation, this strange rhythm, this spiritual beauty,—" the finer spirit " of life,—which
the poet seizes on and expresses, and therewith
also that pathos which seems to inhere in all
created things. We read him because he gives
that value of life which we feel belongs to it, but
for which we are unable to find the words ourselves. How often one has heard people say, on
reading a poem: " Why, that is just what I have
always felt, but could never express! "—and the
exclamation was obviously a recognition of *the
truth* of the poem. The poet had made a true ob-
servation, and recorded it with all the vividness of
truth. It is the business of the poet to be all the
time thus recording, and re-creating, life in all its
manifestations, not only for those who already
possess something of the poetic vision, yet lack the
poetic utterance, but also for those who need to be
awakened to the ideal meanings and issues of life.
Poetry is thus seen to be a kind of lay religion,
revealing and interpreting the varied beauty and
nobility of life.

But a better way than theorizing to show the
" use "—the sweet uses—of poetry is to call up
the names of some of the great poets, and ponder
what they have meant, and still mean, in the life

of humanity,—Dante, Milton, and Wordsworth,
for example, and to them we might add Tennyson,
Browning, and Matthew Arnold. How much
these six poets alone have meant to the graver life
of humanity: the life of religion, of thought, of
conduct! Particularly with regard to the four
poets of the last century we are compelled to note
how, far more than any professed teachers and
thinkers, they were the teachers and thinkers of
their age, and did indeed mould the thought of
their century. For how many have Wordsworth's
" Prelude," Tennyson's " In Memoriam," Browning's " Rabbi Ben Ezra," and Matthew Arnold's
" Empedocles " been literally sacred books, books
of daily exercise and meditation,—to name only a
few of their more typical poems. They are well
worn to-day, but think what forces in the world
these lines of Wordsworth have been:

> " The world is too much with us ; late and soon,
> Getting and spending, we lay waste our powers :
> Little we see in nature that is ours ;
> We have given our hearts away, a sordid boon ! "

Tennyson says:—

> " Are God and Nature then at strife,
> That Nature lends such evil dreams ?
> So careful of the type she seems,
> So careless of the single life ;
>
> " That I, considering everywhere
> Her secret meaning in her deeds,
> And finding that of fifty seeds
> She often brings but one to bear,
>
> " I falter where I firmly trod,
> And, falling with my weight of cares
> Upon the great world's altar-stairs
> That slope through darkness up to God,

> " I stretch lame hands of faith, and grope
> And gather dust and chaff, and call
> To what I feel is Lord of all,
> And faintly trust the larger hope."

I quote this from Matthew Arnold:

> " Is it so small a thing
> To have enjoyed the sun,
> To have lived light in the spring,
> To have loved, to have thought, to have done ;
> To have advanced true friends, and beat down
> baffling foes ;
> That we must feign a bliss
> Of doubtful future date,
> And, while we dream on this,
> Lose all our present state,
> And relegate to worlds yet distant our repose ? "

These lines, and many more like them that one could quote, have done definite spiritual service for mankind, have inspired countless men and women with new faith, new hope, and new fortitude, and will remain permanent springs of sustenance for the human spirit.

Again, the mere mention of such names as Goethe, Byron, and Shelley carries with it their tremendous significance in the " practical " life of the modern world. When we think of such figures as occur over and over again in the history of poetry, we realize that Tennyson's " one poor poet's scroll " that " shook the world " was no mere boyish inflation of the poet's mission. That sad musical poet, Arthur O'Shaughnessy, said no more than the truth when he sang,—in verse like the motion of moonlight on water:

" We are the music-makers,
    And we are the dreamers of dreams,
  Wandering by lone sea breakers,
    And sitting by desolate streams;
  World-losers and world-forsakers,
    On whom the pale moon gleams:
  Yet we are the movers and shakers
    Of the world for ever, it seems."

To realize what a sheerly political force poetry
has been in America alone one has only to recall
the poems of Whittier and Lowell, Poe and Longfellow, and Julia Ward Howe's immortal " Battle
Hymn of the Republic."

But, apart from such strenuous and stern services, how many other services no less valuable
has poetry rendered to mankind,—services of joy
and universal sympathy! The poet, often so sad
himself, sings all men's joys and sorrows as if
they were his own, and there is nothing that can
happen to us, nothing we can experience, no stroke
of fate, and no mood of heart or mind that we
can not find expressed and interpreted for us
somewhere in some poet's book. Take but one
poet,—Robert Burns, for instance,—and think of
the immense addition to the sum total of human
pleasure and human consolation that his handful
of Scotch songs has made. Who asks, " What 's
the use of poetry?" when he joins in " Auld Lang
Syne," and feels his heart stirred to its tearful
depths with the sentiment of human brotherhood,
and the almost tragic dearness of friends. And
who that has ever been in love has not once in
his life felt the brotherly hand of a fellow experience in—

> " Had we never loved sae kindly,
> Had we never loved sae blindly,
> Never met,—or never parted,—
> We had ne'er been broken-hearted,"

and been consoled somehow with that mysterious consolation which belongs to the perfect
expression of sorrow?

If the simple songs of a Scotch peasant have
been of so much " use " to the world, what of that
lordly pleasure-house of Shakespeare? Think of
the boundless universe of mere delight that has
written over its door, " The Works of Shakespeare,"—the laughter, the wisdom, the beauty,
the all-comprehending humanity.

If it be of no use to make men happy, to quicken
in them the joy of life, to heighten their pleasures,
to dry their tears, to bind up their wounds; if it
be of no use to teach them wisdom, to open their
eyes, to purify and direct their spirits, to gird
them to fight, to brace them to endure, to teach
them to be gentle, then, indeed, we may ask,
" What 's the use of poetry? " but, while poetry
can do all these things, I think it must be allowed
by the most practical that it has a very important
part to play in the work of the world.

To end, as I began, with that practical man
who imagines that he does not care for poetry, I
gave one or two explanations of his distaste,—
but there is one other important one that must
not be forgotten. He begins too often with
" Paradise Lost,"—I mean that he too often at-
tempts some tough classic, before he is ready for
it, and, because he cannot read Milton with

pleasure, imagines that he does not care for poetry at all. Thus he finds himself bewildered by the insipid magazine muses on the one hand and the unscalable immortals on the other. Too many make the famous Mr. Boffin's mistake of beginning the study of English literature with Gibbon's " Decline and Fall "; and what wonder if a man beginning the study of English poetry with Browning's " Sordello " should imagine, like Douglas Jerrold in the story, either that his mind was failing him, or that there was something radically wrong with the poet! Actually a man may love poetry very deeply, and care nothing at all for " Paradise Lost." He may also find nothing for him in Homer or Æschylus or Dante or Goethe. The great architectural works of such masters may seem too godlike and grim for his gentler human need. But give him a handful of violets from Ophelia's grave, or a bunch of Herrick's daffodils, or take him out under the sky where Shelley's lark is singing, or try him with a lyric of Heine's, or some ballad of

> ". . . old, unhappy, far-off things,
> And battles long ago,"

and you will see whether or not he loves poetry.

The mistake is in thinking that all poetry is for all readers. On the contrary, the realm of poetry is as wide as the world, for the very reason that each man may find there just what he needs, and leave the rest. The thing is to discover the poetry that was meant for us, and perhaps the best way to do that is to turn over the pages of some well-made selection, and see where our eyes get caught and held. Palgrave's "Golden Treasury" is, of course, the classical anthology, a little volume filled with the purest gold of English lyrical poetry.* If a man should read in that for an hour, and find nothing to his taste, it is to be feared that he was born deaf to the sweet rippling of the Pierian spring. But, as I have said, I believe that few have been so hardly treated by nature. "A poet died young in every one of us," said some one. I think he did not so much die as fall asleep, nor is he so fast asleep but that the right song sung right would awaken him.

What is the use of poetry? It is just the whole use of living,—and let any one who doubts it enter the garden for himself.

> " Ay, come ye hither to this pleasant land,
>   For here in truth are vines of Engaddi,
> Here golden urns of manna to thy hand,
>   And rocks whence honey flows deliciously ;
>   Udders from which comes frothing copiously
> The milk of life, ears filled with sweetest grains,
>   And fig trees knowing no sterility ;
> Here Paradisal streams make rich the plains,
> Oh ! come and bathe therein, ye world-worn
>   weary swains."

Richard Le Gallienne

---

* The "Golden Treasury," when it was published—more than forty years ago—was certainly the finest anthology that had been made in England ; and it still holds its place as a very choice collection of British poets—small and select.

The World's
Best Poetry

Volume VII

Descriptive and Narrative

DESCRIPTIVE POEMS.

I.

PERSONAL: RULERS; STATESMEN; WARRIORS.

TO THE SPRING.

FROM " HYMNES OF ASTRÆA, IN ACROSTICKE VERSE."

E arth now is green, and heaven is blue,
L ively Spring which makes all new,
I olly Spring, doth enter;
S weet young sun-beams do subdue
A ngry, agèd Winter.

B lasts are mild, and seas are calm,
E very meadow flows with balm,
T he Earth wears all her riches;
H armonious birds sing such a psalm,
A s ear and heart bewitches.

R eserve (sweet Spring) this Nymph of ours,
E ternal garlands of thy flowers,
G reen garlands never wasting:
I n her shall last our state's fair Spring,
N ow and for ever flourishing,
A s long as Heaven is lasting.

SIR JOHN DAVIES.

TO MARY STUART.

ALL beauty, granted as a boon to earth,
That is, has been, or ever can have birth,
Compared to hers, is void, and Nature's care
Ne'er formed a creature so divinely fair.

In spring amidst the lilies she was born,
And purer tints her peerless face adorn;
And though Adonis' blood the rose may paint,
Beside her bloom the rose's hues are faint:

With all his richest store Love decked her eyes;
The Graces each, those daughters of the skies,
Strove which should make her to the world most
        dear,
And, to attend her, left their native sphere.

The day that was to bear her far away,—
Why was I mortal to behold that day?
O, had I senseless grown, nor heard, nor seen!
Or that my eyes a ceaseless fount had been,
That I might weep, as weep amidst their bowers
The nymphs, when winter winds have cropped
        their flowers,
Or when rude torrents the clear streams deform,
Or when the trees are riven by the storm!
Or rather, would that I some bird had been
Still to be near her in each changing scene,
Still on the highest mast to watch all day,
And like a star to mark her vessel's way:
The dangerous billows past, on shore, on sea,
Near that dear face it still were mine to be!

O France! where are thy ancient champions
gone,—
Roland, Rinaldo?—is there living none
Her steps to follow and her safety guard,
And deem her lovely looks their best reward,—
Which might subdue the pride of mighty Jove
To leave his heaven, and languish for her love?
No fault is hers, but in her royal state,—
For simple Love dreads to approach the great;
Le flies from regal pomp, that treacherous snare,
Where truth unmarked may wither in despair.

Wherever destiny her path may lead,
Fresh-springing flowers will bloom beneath her
tread,
All nature will rejoice, the waves be bright,
The tempest check its fury at her sight,
The sea be calm: her beauty to behold,
The sun shall crown her with his rays of gold,—
Unless he fears, should he approach her throne
Her majesty should quite eclipse his own.

From the French of PIERRE DE RONSARD.
Translation of LOUISE STUART COSTELLO.

TO THE LORD-GENERAL CROMWELL.

CROMWELL, our chief of men, who through a cloud,
Not of war only, but detractions rude,
Guided by faith and matchless fortitude,
To peace and truth thy glorious way hast
ploughed,
And on the neck of crownèd fortune proud

Hast reared God's trophies, and his work pursued,
While Darwen stream, with blood of Scots inbued,
And Dunbar field resounds thy praises loud,
And Worcester's laureate wreath. Yet much re-
    mains
To conquer still; Peace hath her victories
No less renowned than War: new foes arise,
Threatening to bind our souls with secular chains:
Help us to save free conscience from the paw
Of hireling wolves, whose gospel is their maw.

MILTON.

O, BREATHE NOT HIS NAME!

ROBERT EMMET.

O, BREATHE not his name! let it sleep in the shade,
Where cold and unhonored his relics are laid;
Sad, silent, and dark be the tears that we shed,
As the night-dew that falls on the grave o'er his
    head.

But the night-dew that falls, though in silence
    it weeps,
Shall brighten with verdure the grave where he
    sleeps;
And the tear that we shed, though in secret it
    rolls,
Shall long keep his memory green in our souls.

THOMAS MOORE.

CHARLES XII.

FROM "THE VANITY OF HUMAN WISHES."

On what foundations stands the warrior's pride,
How just his hopes, let Swedish Charles decide:
A frame of adamant, a soul of fire,
No dangers fright him, and no labors tire;
O'er love, o'er fear, extends his wide domain,
Unconquered lord of pleasure and of pain.
No joys to him pacific sceptres yield,
War sounds the trump, he rushes to the field;
Behold surrounding kings their power combine,
And one capitulate, and one resign;
Peace courts his hand, but spreads her charms in
    vain;
" Think nothing gained," he cries, " till naught
    remain,
On Moscow's walls till Gothic standards fly,
And all be mine beneath the polar sky."
The march begins in military state,
And nations on his eye suspended wait;
Stern famine guards the solitary coast,
And winter barricades the realms of frost.
He comes, nor want nor cold his course delay;
Hide, blushing glory, hide Pultowa's day!
The vanquished hero leaves his broken bands,
And shows his miseries in distant lands;
Condemned a needy supplicant to wait,
While ladies interpose and slaves debate.
But did not chance at length her error mend?
Did no subverted empire mark his end?

Did rival monarchs give the fatal wound,
Or hostile millions press him to the ground?
His fall was destined to a barren strand,
A petty fortress, and a dubious hand;
He left the name, at which the world grew pale,
To point a moral or adorn a tale.

DR. SAMUEL JOHNSON.

NAPOLEON.

" Tu domines notre âge ; ange ou démon, qu'importe ! "

ANGEL or demon! thou—whether of light
The minister, or darkness—still dost sway
This age of ours; thine eagle's soaring flight
Bears us, all breathless, after it away.
The eye that from thy presence fain would
stray
Shuns thee in vain; thy mighty shadow thrown
Rests on all pictures of the living day,
And on the threshold of our time alone,
Dazzling, yet sombre, stands thy form, Napoleon!

Thus, when the admiring stranger's steps ex-
plore
The subject-lands that 'neath Vesuvius be,
Whether he wind along the enchanting shore
To Portici from fair Parthenope,
Or, lingering long in dreamy revery,
O'er loveliest Ischia's od'rous isle he stray,
Wooed by whose breath the soft and am'rous
sea
Seems like some languishing sultana's lay,
A voice for very sweets that scarce can win its
way:

Him, whether Pæstum's solemn fane detain,
    Shrouding his soul with meditation's power;
Or at Pozzuoli, to the sprightly strain
    Of tarantella danced 'neath Tuscan tower,
    Listening, he while away the evening hour;
Or wake the echoes, mournful, lone, and deep,
    Of that sad city, in its dreaming bower
By the volcano seized, where mansions keep
The likeness which they wore at that last fatal
        sleep;

Or be his bark at Posilippo laid,
    While as the swarthy boatman at his side
Chants Tasso's lays to Virgil's pleasèd shade,—
    Ever he sees throughout that circuit wide,
    From shaded nook or sunny lawn espied,
From rocky headland viewed, or flow'ry shore,
    From sea and spreading mead alike descried,
The Giant Mount, tow'ring all objects o'er,
And black'ning with its breath th' horizon ever-
        more!

From the French of VICTOR HUGO.
Translation from FRASER'S MAGAZINE.

NAPOLEON.

FROM "CHILDE HAROLD," CANTO III.

THERE sunk the greatest, nor the worst of men,
Whose spirit antithetically mixed
One moment of the mightiest, and again
On little objects with like firmness fixed,
Extreme in all things! hadst thou been betwixt,

Thy throne had still been thine, or never been;
For daring made thy rise as fall: thou seek'st
Even now to reassume the imperial mien,
And shake again the world, the Thunderer of the
    scene!

Conqueror and captive of the earth art thou!
She trembles at thee still, and thy wild name
Was ne'er more bruited in men's minds than now
That thou art nothing, save the jest of Fame,
Who wooed thee once, thy vassal, and became
The flatterer of thy fierceness, till thou wert
A god unto thyself: nor less the same
To the astounded kingdoms all inert,
Who deemed thee for a time whate'er thou didst
    assert.

O more or less than man—in high or low,
Battling with nations, flying from the field;
Now making monarchs' necks thy footstool, now
More than thy meanest soldier taught to yield:
An empire thou couldst crush, command, re-
    build,
But govern not thy pettiest passion, nor,
However deeply in men's spirits skilled,
Look through thine own, nor curb the lust of
    war,
Nor learn that tempted Fate will leave the loftiest
    star.

Yet well thy soul hath brooked the turning tide
With that untaught innate philosophy,
Which, be it wisdom, coldness, or deep pride,
Is gall and wormwood to an enemy.

When the whole host of hatred stood hard by,
To watch and mock thee shrinking, thou hast
    smiled
With a sedate and all-enduring eye,—
When Fortune fled her spoiled and favorite
    child,
He stood unbowed beneath the ills upon him piled.

Sager than in thy fortunes; for in them
Ambition steeled thee on too far to show
That just habitual scorn which could contemn
Men and their thoughts; 't was wise to feel, not
    so
To wear it ever on thy lip and brow,
And spurn the instruments thou wert to use
Till they were turned unto thine overthrow;
'T is but a worthless world to win or lose;
So hath it proved to thee, and all such lot who
    choose.

If, like a tower upon a headlong rock,
Thou hadst been made to stand or fall alone,
Such scorn of man had helped to brave the
    shock;
But men's thoughts were the steps which paved
    thy throne,
Their admiration thy best weapon shone;
The part of Philip's son was thine, not then
(Unless aside thy purple had been thrown)
Like stern Diogenes to mock at men;
For sceptred cynics earth were far too wide a den.

But quiet to quick bosoms is a hell,
And *there* hath been thy bane; there is a fire

And motion of the soul which will not dwell
In its own narrow being, but aspire
Beyond the fitting medium of desire;
And, but once kindled, quenchless evermore,
Preys upon high adventure, nor can tire
Of aught but rest; a fever at the core,
Fatal to him who bears, to all who ever bore.

This makes the madmen who have made men
    mad
By their contagion! Conquerors and Kings,
Founders of sects and systems, to whom add
Sophists, Bards, Statesmen, all unquiet things
Which stir too strongly the soul's secret springs,
And are themselves the fools to those they fool;
Envied, yet how unenviable! what stings
Are theirs! One breast laid open were a school
Which would unteach mankind the lust to shine
    or rule.

Their breath is agitation, and their life
A storm whereon they ride, to sink at last,
And yet so nursed and bigoted to strife,
That should their days, surviving perils past,
Melt to calm twilight, they feel overcast
With sorrow and supineness, and so die;
Even as a flame, unfed, which runs to waste
With its own flickering, or a sword laid by,
Which eats into itself, and rusts ingloriously.

He who ascends to mountain-tops shall find
The loftiest peaks most wrapt in clouds and
    snow;

He who surpasses or subdues mankind
Must look down on the hate of those below.
Though high above the sun of glory glow,
And far beneath the earth and ocean spread,
Round him are icy rocks, and loudly blow
Contending tempests on his naked head,
And thus reward the toils which to those summits
   led.

LORD BYRON.

ON THE MONUMENT ERECTED TO MAZZINI AT GENOA.

ITALIA, mother of the souls of men,
   Mother divine,
Of all that served thee best with sword or pen,
   All sons of thine,

Thou knowest that here the likeness of the best
   Before thee stands:
The head most high, the heart found faithfulest,
   The purest hands.

Above the fume and foam of time that flits,
   The soul, we know,
Now sits on high where Alighieri sits
   With Angelo.

Nor his own heavenly tongue hath heavenly
   speech
   Enough to say
What this man was, whose praise no thought may
   reach,
   No words can weigh.

Since man's first mother brought to mortal birth
    Her first-born son,
Such grace befell not ever man on earth
    As crowns this One.

Of God nor man was ever this thing said:
    That he could give
Life back to her who gave him, that his dead
    Mother might live.

But this man found his mother dead and slain,
    With fast-sealed eyes,
And bade the dead rise up and live again,
    And she did rise:

And all the world was bright with her through
      him:
    But dark with strife,
Like heaven's own sun that storming clouds bedim,
    Was all his life.

Life and the clouds are vanished; hate and fear
    Have had their span
Of time to hurt and are not: He is here
    The sunlike man.

City superb, that hadst Columbus first
    For sovereign son,
Be prouder that thy breast hath later nurst
    This mightier One.

Glory be his forever, while this land
    Lives and is free,
As with controlling breath and sovereign hand
    He bade her be.

Earth shows to heaven the names by thousands
    told
  That crown her fame:
But highest of all that heaven and earth behold
  Mazzini's name.

          ALGERNON CHARLES SWINBURNE.

GEORGE WASHINGTON.

By broad Potomac's silent shore
  Better than Trajan lowly lies,
  Gilding her green declivities
With glory now and evermore;
Art to his fame no aid hath lent;
His country is his monument.
          ANONYMOUS.

WASHINGTON.

[From " Under the Elm," read at Cambridge, July 3,
1875, on the Hundredth Anniversary of Washington's
taking Command of the American Army.]

BENEATH our consecrated elm
A century ago he stood,
Famed vaguely for that old fight in the wood,
Which redly foamèd round him but could not over-
    whelm
The life foredoomed to wield our rough-hewn
    helm.
From colleges, where now the gown
To arms had yielded, from the town,

Our rude self-summoned levies flocked to see
The new-come chiefs and wonder which was he.
No need to question long; close-lipped and tall,
Long trained in murder-brooding forests lone
To bridle others' clamors and his own,
Firmly erect, he towered above them all,
The incarnate discipline that was to free
With iron curb that armed democracy.

    .   .   .   .   .   .

Haughty they said he was, at first, severe,
But owned, as all men owned, the steady hand
Upon the bridle, patient to command,
Prized, as all prize, the justice pure from fear,
And learned to honor first, then love him, then
    revere.
Such power there is in clear-eyed self-restraint,
And purpose clean as light from every selfish
    taint.

Musing beneath the legendary tree,
The years between furl off: I seem to see
The sun-flecks, shaken the stirred foliage through,
Dapple with gold his sober buff and blue,
And weave prophetic aureoles round the head
That shines our beacon now, nor darkens with
    the dead.
O man of silent mood,
A stranger among strangers then,
How art thou since renowned the Great, the Good,
Familiar as the day in all the homes of men!
The wingèd years, that winnow praise and blame,
Blow many names out: they but fan to flame
The self-renewing splendors of thy fame.

    .   .   .   .   .   .

O, for a drop of that terse Roman's ink
Who gave Agricola dateless length of days,
To celebrate him fitly, neither swerve
To phrase unkempt, nor pass discretion's brink,
With him so statuelike in sad reserve,
So diffident to claim, so forward to deserve!
Nor need I shun due influence of his fame
Who, mortal among mortals, seemed as now
The equestrian shape with unimpassioned brow,
That paces silent on through vistas of acclaim.
What figure more immovably august
Than that grave strength so patient and so pure,
Calm in good fortune, when it wavered, sure,
That soul serene, impenetrably just,
Modelled on classic lines, so simple they endure?
That soul so softly radiant and so white
The track it left seems less of fire than light,
Cold but to such as love distemperature?
And if pure light, as some deem, be the force
That drives rejoicing planets on their course,
Why for his power benign seek an impurer
    source?
His was the true enthusiasm that burns long,
Domestically bright,
Fed from itself and shy of human sight,
The hidden force that makes a lifetime strong,
And not the short-lived fuel of a song.
Passionless, say you? What is passion for
But to sublime our natures and control,
To front heroic toils with late return,
Or none, or such as shames the conqueror?
That fire was fed with substance of the soul,
And not with holiday stubble, that could burn

Through seven slow years of unadvancing war,
Equal when fields were lost or fields were won,
With breath of popular applause or blame,
Nor fanned nor damped, unquenchably the same,
Too inward to be reached by flaws of idle fame.

Soldier and statesman, rarest unison;
High-poised example of great duties done
Simply as breathing, a world's honors worn
As life's indifferent gifts to all men born;
Dumb for himself, unless it were to God,
But for his barefoot soldiers eloquent,
Tramping the snow to coral where they trod,
Held by his awe in hollow-eyed content;
Modest, yet firm as Nature's self; unblamed
Save by the men his nobler temper shamed;
Not honored then or now because he wooed
The popular voice, but that he still withstood;
Broad-minded, higher-souled, there is but one
Who was all this, and ours, and all men's,—
    Washington.

Minds strong by fits, irregularly great,
That flash and darken like revolving lights,
Catch more the vulgar eye unschooled to wait
On the long curve of patient days and nights,
Rounding the whole life to the circle fair
Of orbed completeness; and this balanced soul,
So simple in its grandeur, coldly bare
Of draperies theatric, standing there
In perfect symmetry of self-control,
Seems not so great at first, but greater grows
Still as we look, and by experience learn

How grand this quiet is, how nobly stern
The discipline that wrought through life-long
    throes
This energetic passion of repose.
A nature too decorous and severe
Too self-respectful in its griefs and joys
For ardent girls and boys,
Who find no genius in a mind so clear
That its grave depths seem obvious and near,
Nor a soul great that made so little noise.
They feel no force in that calm, cadenced phrase,
The habitual full-dress of his well-bred mind,
That seems to pace the minuet's courtly maze
And tell of ampler leisures, roomier length of
    days.
His broad-built brain, to self so little kind
That no tumultuary blood could blind,
Formed to control men, not amaze,
Looms not like those that borrow height of haze:
It was a world of statelier movement then
Than this we fret in, he a denizen
Of that ideal Rome that made a man for men.

.   .   .   .   .

Placid completeness, life without a fall
From faith or highest aims, truth's breachless
    wall,
Surely if any fame can bear the touch,
His will say " Here! " at the last trumpet's call,
The unexpressive man whose life expressed so
    much.

             JAMES RUSSELL LOWELL.

DANIEL WEBSTER.

WHEN, stricken by the freezing blast,
  A nation's living pillars fall,
How rich the storied page, how vast,
  A word, a whisper, can recall!

No medal lifts its fretted face,
  Nor speaking marble cheats your eye;
Yet, while these pictured lines I trace,
  A living image passes by :

A roof beneath the mountain pines;
  The cloisters of a hill-girt plain;
The front of life's embattled lines;
  A mound beside the heaving main.

These are the scenes: a boy appears;
  Set life's round dial in the sun,
Count the swift arc of seventy years,
  His frame is dust; his task is done.

Yet pause upon the noontide hour,
  Ere the declining sun has laid
His bleaching rays on manhood's power,
  And look upon the mighty shade.

No gloom that stately shape can hide,
  No change uncrown his brow; behold!
Dark, calm, large-fronted, lightning-eyed,
  Earth has no double from its mould!

Ere from the fields by valor won
  The battle-smoke had rolled away,
And bared the blood-red setting sun,
  His eyes were opened on the day.

His land was but a shelving strip,
  Black with the strife that made it free;
He lived to see its banners dip
  Their fringes in the western sea.

The boundless prairies learned his name,
  His words the mountain echoes knew;
The northern breezes swept his fame
  From icy lake to warm bayou.

In toil he lived; in peace he died;
  When life's full cycle was complete,
Put off his robes of power and pride,
  And laid them at his Master's feet.

His rest is by the storm-swept waves,
  Whom life's wild tempests roughly tried,
Whose heart was like the streaming caves
  Of ocean, throbbing at his side.

Death's cold white hand is like the snow
  Laid softly on the furrowed hill;
It hides the broken seams below,
  And leaves the summit brighter still.

In vain the envious tongue upbraids;
  His name a nation's heart shall keep,
Till morning's latest sunlight fades
  On the blue tablet of the deep!

OLIVER WENDELL HOLMES.

WILLIAM LLOYD GARRISON.

" Some time afterward, it was reported to me by the city officers that they had ferreted out the paper and its editor; that his office was an obscure hole, his only visible auxiliary a negro boy, and his supporters a few very insignificant persons of all colors."—*Letter of* H. G. OTIS.

In a small chamber, friendless and unseen,
   Toiled o'er his types one poor, unlearned young
     man;
The place was dark, unfurnitured, and mean:
   Yet there the freedom of a race began.

Help came but slowly; surely no man yet
   Put lever to the heavy world with less:
What need of help? He knew how types were
     set,
   He had a dauntless spirit, and a press.

Such earnest natures are the fiery pith,
   The compact nucleus, round which systems
     grow:
Mass after mass becomes inspired therewith,
   And whirls impregnate with the central glow.

O Truth! O Freedom! how are ye still born
   In the rude stable, in the manger nursed!
What humble hands unbar those gates of morn
   Through which the splendors of the New Day
     burst!

What! shall one monk, scarce known beyond his
     cell,
   Front Rome's far-reaching bolts, and scorn her
     frown?

Brave Luther answered Yes; that thunder's swell
    Rocked Europe, and discharmed the triple
      crown.

Whatever can be known of earth we know,
    Sneered Europe's wise men, in their snail-
      shells curled;
No! said one man in Genoa, and that No
    Out of the dark created this New World.

Who is it will not dare himself to trust?
Who is it hath not strength to stand alone?
Who is it thwarts and bilks the inward Must?
    He and his works, like sand, from earth are
      blown.

Men of a thousand shifts and wiles, look here!
    See one straightforward conscience put in pawn
To win a world; see the obedient sphere
    By bravery's simple gravitation drawn!

Shall we not heed the lesson taught of old,
    And by the Present's lips repeated still,
In our own single manhood to be bold,
    Fortressed in conscience and impregnable will?

We stride the river daily at its spring,
    Nor, in our childish thoughtlessness, foresee
What myriad vassal streams shall tribute bring.
    How like an equal it shall greet the sea.

O small beginnings, ye are great and strong,
    Based on a faithful heart and weariless brain!
Ye build the future fair, ye conquer wrong,
    Ye earn the crown, and wear it not in vain.

                JAMES RUSSELL LOWELL.

HENRY WARD BEECHER.

His tongue was touched with sacred fire,
  He could not rest, he must speak out,
  When Liberty lay stabbed, and doubt
Stalked through the night in vestments dire,—

When slaves uplifted manacled hands,
  Praying in agony and despair,
  And answer came not anywhere,
But gloom through all the stricken lands,—

His voice for freedom instant rang,
  " For shame!" he cried; "spare thou the rod;
  All men are free before their God!"
The dragon answered with its fang.

'T is brave to face embrasured death
  Hot belching from the cannon's mouth,
  Yet brave it is, for North or South,
And Truth, to face the mob's mad breath.

So spake he then,—he and the few
  Who prized their manhood more than praise;
  Their faith failed not of better days
After the nights of bloody dew.

England's great heart misunderstood:
  She looked upon her child askance;
  But heard his words and lowered her lance,
Remembering her motherhood.

Majestic Liberty, serene
    Thou frontest on the chaste white sea!
    Quench thou awhile thy torch, for he
    Lies dead on whom thou once did lean.

Thy cause was ever his,—the slave
    In any fetters was his friend;
    His warfare never knew an end;
    Wherever men lay bound he clave.

CHARLES HENRY PHELPS.

ABRAHAM LINCOLN.

FOULLY ASSASSINATED APRIL 14, 1865.*

You lay a wreath on murdered Lincoln's bier,
    You, who with mocking pencil wont to trace,
Broad for the self-complacent British sneer,
    His length of shambling limb, his furrowed face,

His gaunt, gnarled hands, his unkempt, bristling
            hair,
    His garb uncouth, his bearing ill at ease,
His lack of all we prize as debonair,
    Of power or will to shine, of art to please;

You, whose smart pen backed up the pencil's
            laugh,
    Judging each step as though the way were
            plain,
Reckless, so it could point its paragraph
    Of chief's perplexity, or people's pain:

* This tribute appeared in the London *Punch*, which, up
to the time of the assassination of Mr. Lincoln, had ridi-
culed and maligned him with all its well-known powers of
pen and pencil.

Beside this corpse, that bears for winding-sheet
  The Stars and Stripes he lived to rear anew,
Between the mourners at his head and feet,
  Say, scurrile jester, is there room for *you?*

Yes: he had lived to shame me from my sneer,
  To lame my pencil, and confute my pen;
To make me own this hind of princes peer,
  This rail-splitter a true-born king of men.

My shallow judgment I had learned to rue,
  Noting how to occasion's height he rose;
How his quaint wit made home-truth seem more
    true;
    How, iron-like, his temper grew by blows.

How humble, yet how hopeful, he could be;
  How in good fortune and in ill, the same;
Nor bitter in success, nor boastful he,
  Thirsty for gold nor feverish for fame.

He went about his work,—such work as few
  Ever had laid on head and heart and hand,—
As one who knows, where there 's a task to do,
  Man's honest will must Heaven's good grace
    command;

Who trusts the strength will with the burden
    grow,
  That God makes instruments to work his will,
If but that will we can arrive to know,
  Nor tamper with the weights of good and ill.

So he went forth to battle, on the side
    That he felt clear was Liberty's and Right's,
As in his peasant boyhood he had plied
    His warfare with rude Nature's thwarting
        mights;

The uncleared forest, the unbroken soil,
    The iron-bark, that turns the lumberer's axe,
The rapid, that o'erbears the boatman's toil,
    The prairie, hiding the mazed wanderer's tracks,

The ambushed Indian, and the prowling bear,—
    Such were the deeds that helped his youth to
        train:
Rough culture, but such trees large fruit may
        bear,
    If but their stock be of right girth and grain.

So he grew up, a destined work to do,
    And lived to do it: four long-suffering years'
Ill-fate, ill-feeling, ill-report, lived through,
    And then he heard the hisses change to cheers,

The taunts to tribute, the abuse to praise,
    And took both with the same unwavering
        mood;
Till, as he came on light, from darkling days,
    And seemed to touch the goal from where he
        stood,

A felon hand, between the goal and him,
    Reached from behind his back, a trigger prest,
And those perplexed and patient eyes were dim,
    Those gaunt, long-laboring limbs were laid to
        rest!

The words of mercy were upon his lips,
  Forgiveness in his heart and on his pen,
When this vile murderer brought swift eclipse
  To thoughts of peace on earth, good-will to men.

The Old World and the New, from sea to sea,
  Utter one voice of sympathy and shame:
Sore heart, so stopped when it at last beat high;
  Sad life, cut short just as its triumph came!

A deed accurst! Strokes have been struck before
  By the assassin's hand, whereof men doubt
If more of horror or disgrace they bore;
  But thy foul crime, like Cain's, stands darkly
    out.

Vile hand, that brandest murder on a strife,
  Whate'er its grounds, stoutly and nobly striven;
And with the martyr's crown crownest a life
  With much to praise, little to be forgiven.

                                        TOM TAYLOR.

O CAPTAIN! MY CAPTAIN!

O Captain! my Captain! our fearful trip is done,
The ship has weathered every rack, the prize we
      sought is won,
The port is near, the bells I hear, the people all
      exulting,
While follow eyes the steady keel, the vessel grim
      and daring;
    But O heart! heart! heart!
      O the bleeding drops of red,
        Where on the deck my Captain lies,
        Fallen cold and dead.

O Captain! my Captain! rise up and hear the
 bells;
Rise up—for you the flag is flung—for you the
 bugle trills,
For you bouquets and ribboned wreaths—for you
 the shores a-crowding,
For you they call, the swaying mass, their eager
 faces turning;
 Here Captain! dear father!
 This arm beneath your head!
  It is some dream that on the deck
  You 've fallen cold and dead.

My Captain does not answer, his lips are pale and
 still,
My father does not feel my arm, he has no pulse
 nor will,
The ship is anchored safe and sound, its voyage
 closed and done,
From fearful trip the victor ship comes in with
 object won;
 Exult O shores, and ring O bells!
 But I, with mournful tread,
  Walk the deck my Captain lies,
  Fallen cold and dead.

WALT WHITMAN.

ON THE LIFE-MASK OF LINCOLN.

THIS bronze doth keep the very form and mould
Of our great martyr's face. Yes, this is he:
That brow all wisdom, all benignity;
That human, humorous mouth; those cheeks
 that hold

Like some harsh landscape all the summer's gold;
  That spirit fit for sorrow, as the sea
  For storms to beat on; the lone agony
  Those silent, patient lips too well foretold.
Yes, this is he who ruled a world of men
  As might some prophet of the elder day,—
  Brooding above the tempest and the fray
With deep-eyed thought and more than mortal
  ken.
  A power was his beyond the touch of art
  Of armèd strength: his pure and mighty heart.
             RICHARD WATSON GILDER.

THE HAND OF LINCOLN

Look on this cast, and know the hand
  That bore a nation in its hold:
From this mute witness understand
  What Lincoln was,—how large of mould

The man who sped the woodman's team,
  And deepest sunk the ploughman's share,
And pushed the laden raft astream,
  Of fate before him unaware.

This was the hand that knew to swing
  The axe—since thus would Freedom train
Her son—and made the forest ring,
  And drove the wedge, and toiled amain.

Firm hand, that loftier office took,
  A conscious leader's will obeyed,
And, when men sought his word and look,
  With steadfast might the gathering swayed.

No courtier's toying with a sword,
  Nor minstrel's, laid across a lute;
A chief's, uplifted to the Lord
  When all the kings of earth were mute!

The hand of Anak, sinewed strong,
  The fingers that on greatness clutch;
Yet, lo! the marks their lines along
  Of one who strove and suffered much.

For here in knotted cord and vein
  I trace the varying chart of years;
I know the troubled heart, the strain,
  The weight of Atlas—and the tears.

Again I see the patient brow
  That palm erewhile was wont to press;
And now 't is furrowed deep, and now
  Made smooth with hope and tenderness.

For something of a formless grace
  This moulded outline plays about;
A pitying flame, beyond our trace,
  Breathes like a spirit, in and out,—

The love that cast an aureole
  Round one who, longer to endure,
Called mirth to ease his ceaseless dole,
  Yet kept his nobler purpose sure.

Lo, as I gaze, the statured man,
  Built up from yon large hand, appears:
A type that Nature wills to plan
  But once in all a people's years.

What better than this voiceless cast
  To tell of such a one as he,
Since through its living semblance passed
  The thought that bade a race be free!

EDMUND CLARENCE STEDMAN.

ABRAHAM LINCOLN.

FROM THE HARVARD COMMEMORATION ODE.

July 21, 1865.

LIFE may be given in many ways,
  And loyalty to Truth be sealed
As bravely in the closet as the field,
    So bountiful is Fate;
    But then to stand beside her,
    When craven churls deride her,
To front a line in arms and not to yield,
    This shows, methinks, God's plan
    And measure of a stalwart man,
    Limbed like the old heroic breeds,
    Who stand self-poised on manhood's solid
        earth,
  Not forced to frame excuses for his birth,
Fed from within with all the strength he needs.

Such was he, our Martyr-Chief,
  Whom late the Nation he had led,
  With ashes on her head,
Wept with the passion of an angry grief:
Forgive me, if from present things I turn

To speak what in my heart will beat and burn,
And hang my wreath on his world-honored urn.
Nature, they say, doth dote,
And cannot make a man
Save on some worn-out plan,
Repeating us by rote:
For him her Old-World moulds aside he threw,
And choosing sweet clay from the breast
Of the unexhausted West,
With stuff untainted shaped a hero new,
Wise, steadfast in the strength of God, and true.
How beautiful to see
Once more a shepherd of mankind indeed,
Who loved his charge, but never loved to lead;
One whose meek flock the people joyed to be,
Not lured by any cheat of birth,
But by his clear-grained human worth,
And brave old wisdom of sincerity!
They knew that outward grace is dust;
They could not choose but trust
In that sure-footed mind's unfaltering skill,
And supple tempered will
That bent like perfect steel to spring again and
thrust.
His was no lonely mountain-peak of mind,
Thrusting to thin air o'er our cloudy bars,
A sea-mark now, now lost in vapors blind;
Broad prairie rather, genial, level-lined,
Fruitful and friendly for all human kind,
Yet also nigh to heaven and loved of loftiest stars.
Nothing of Europe here,
Or, then, of Europe fronting mornward still,
Ere any names of Serf and Peer

Could Nature's equal scheme deface;
Here was a type of the true elder race,
And one of Plutarch's men talked with us face to
     face.
I praise him not; it were too late;
And some innative weakness there must be
In him who condescends to victory
Such as the Present gives, and cannot wait,
    Safe in himself as in a fate.
      So always firmly he:
      He knew to bide his time,
      And can his fame abide,
Still patient in his simple faith sublime,
    Till the wise years decide.
    Great captains, with their guns and drums,
      Disturb our judgment for the hour,
      But at last silence comes;
  These all are gone, and, standing like a tower,
  Our children shall behold his fame,
    The kindly-earnest, brave, foreseeing man,
Sagacious, patient, dreading praise, not blame,
New birth of our new soil, the first American.
             JAMES RUSSELL LOWELL.

ALBERT, PRINCE CONSORT OF ENGLAND.

FROM " IDYLS OF THE KING."

DEDICATION.

THESE to His Memory—since he held them dear,
Perchance as finding there unconsciously
Some image of himself—I dedicate,
I dedicate, I consecrate with tears—
These Idyls.

And indeed He seems to me
Scarce other than my own ideal knight,
" Who reverenced his conscience as his king;
Whose glory was, redressing human wrong;
Who spake no slander, no, nor listened to it;
Who loved one only and who clave to her—"
Her—over all whose realms to their last isle,
Commingled with the gloom of imminent war,
The shadow of His loss moved like eclipse,
Darkening the world. We have lost him: he is
   gone:
We know him now: all narrow jealousies
Are silent; and we see him as he moved,
How modest, kindly, all-accomplished, wise,
With what sublime repression of himself,
And in what limits, and how tenderly;
Not swaying to this faction or to that:
Not making his high place the lawless perch
Of winged ambitions, nor a vantage-ground
For pleasure; but through all this tract of years
Wearing the white flower of a blameless life,
Before a thousand peering littlenesses,
In that fierce light which beats upon a throne,
And blackens every blot: for where is he,
Who dares foreshadow for an only son
A lovelier life, a more unstained, than his?
Or how should England dreaming of *his* sons
Hope more for these than some inheritance
Of such a life, a heart, a mind as thine,
Thou noble Father of her Kings to be,
Laborious for her people and her poor—
Voice in the rich dawn of an ampler day—
Far-sighted summoner of War and Waste

To fruitful strifes and rivalries of peace—
Sweet nature gilded by the gracious gleam
Of letters, dear to Science, dear to Art,
Dear to thy land and ours, a Prince indeed,
Beyond all titles, and a household name,
Hereafter, through all times, Albert the Good!

Break not, O woman's-heart, but still endure;
Break not, for thou art Royal, but endure,
Remembering all the beauty of that star
Which shone so close beside Thee, That ye made
One light together, but has passed and left
The Crown of lonely splendor.
                              May all love,
His love, unseen but felt, o'ershadow Thee.
The love of all Thy sons encompass Thee,
The love of all Thy daughters cherish Thee,
The love of all Thy people comfort Thee,
Till God's love set Thee at his side again!

                              ALFRED, LORD TENNYSON.

I.

PERSONAL: GREAT WRITERS.

TO VIRGIL.

[Written at the request of the Mantuans for the Nineteenth Centenary of Virgil's death, B. C. 19.]

I.

ROMAN Virgil, thou that singest
　　Ilion's lofty temples robed in fire,
Ilion falling, Rome arising,
　　wars, and filial faith, and Dido's pyre;

II.

Landscape-lover, lord of language
　　more than he that sang the Works and Days,
All the chosen coin of fancy
　　flashing out from many a golden phrase;

III.

Thou that singest wheat and woodland,
　　tilth and vineyard, hive and horse and herd;
All the charm of all the Muses
　　often flowering in a lonely word;

37

IV.

Poet of the happy Tityrus
    piping underneath his beechen bowers;
Poet of the poet-satyr whom
    the laughing shepherd bound with flowers;

V.

Chanter of the Pollio, glorying
    in the blissful years again to be,
Summers of the snakeless meadow,
    unlaborious earth and oarless sea;

VI.

Thou that seëst Universal
    Nature moved by Universal Mind;
Thou majestic in thy sadness
    at the doubtful doom of human kind;

VII.

Light among the vanish'd ages;
    star that gildest yet this phantom shore;
Golden branch amid the shadows,
    kings and realms that pass to rise no more;

VIII.

Now thy Forum roars no longer,
    fallen every purple Cæsar's dome—
Tho' thine ocean-roll of rhythm
    sound for ever of Imperial Rome—

IX.

Now the Rome of slaves hath perished,
  and the Rome of freemen holds her place,
I, from out the Northern Island
  sundered once from all the human race,

X.

I salute thee, Mantovano,
  I that loved thee since my day began,
Wielder of the stateliest measure
  ever moulded by the lips of man.

ALFRED, LORD TENNYSON.

IN A COPY OF OMAR KHAYYÁM

THESE pearls of thought in Persian gulfs were
    bred,
Each softly lucent as a rounded moon;
The diver Omar plucked them from their bed,
Fitzgerald strung them on an English thread.

Fit rosary for a queen, in shape and hue,
When Contemplation tells her pensive beads
Of mortal thoughts, forever old and new.
Fit for a queen? Why, surely then for you!

The moral? Where Doubt's eddies toss and
    twirl
Faith's slender shallop till her footing reel,
Plunge: if you find not peace beneath the whirl,
Groping, you may like Omar grasp a pearl.

JAMES RUSSELL LOWELL.

TO MADAME DE SEVIGNÉ

PLAYING BLIND-MAN'S-BUFF.

You charm when you talk, walk, or move,
  Still more on this day than another:
When blinded—you 're taken for Love;
  When the bandage is off—for his mother!

MATHIEU DE MONTREUIL.

GEORGE SAND.

TRUE genius, but true woman! dost deny
Thy woman's nature with a manly scorn,
And break away the gauds and armlets worn
By weaker women in captivity?
Ah, vain denial! that revolted cry
Is sobbed in by a woman's voice forlorn;
Thy woman's hair, my sister, all unshorn,
Floats back dishevelled strength in agony,
Disproving thy man's name; and while before
The world thou burnest in a poet-fire,
We see thy woman-heart beat evermore
Through the large flame. Beat purer, heart, and
    higher,
Till God unsex thee on the heavenly shore,
Where unincarnate spirits purely aspire.

ELIZABETH BARRETT BROWNING.

TO VICTOR HUGO.

VICTOR in poesy! Victor in romance!
Cloud-weaver of phantasmal hopes and fears!
French of the French and lord of human tears!
Child-lover, bard, whose fame-lit laurels glance,
Darkening the wreaths of all that would advance
Beyond our strait their claim to be thy peers!
Weird Titan, by thy wintry weight of years
As yet unbroken! Stormy voice of France,
Who does not love our England, so they say;
I know not! England, France, all men to be,
Will make one people, ere man's race be run;
And I, desiring that diviner day,
Yield thee full thanks for thy full courtesy
To younger England in the boy, my son.
ALFRED, LORD TENNYSON.

ON A BUST OF DANTE.

SEE, from this counterfeit of him
Whom Arno shall remember long,
How stern of lineament, how grim,
The father was of Tuscan song!
There but the burning sense of wrong,
Perpetual care, and scorn, abide—
Small friendship for the lordly throng,
Distrust of all the world beside.

Faithful if this wan image be,
No dream his life was—but a fight;

Could any Beatrice see
A lover in that anchorite?
To that cold Ghibeline's gloomy sight
Who could have guessed the visions came
Of beauty, veiled with heavenly light,
In circles of eternal flame?

The lips as Cumæ's cavern close,
The cheeks with fast and sorrow thin,
The rigid front, almost morose,
But for the patient hope within,
Declare a life whose course hath been
Unsullied still, though still severe,
Which, through the wavering days of sin,
Kept itself icy-chaste and clear.

Not wholly such his haggard look
When wandering once, forlorn, he strayed,
With no companion save his book,
To Corvo's hushed monastic shade;
Where, as the Benedictine laid
His palm upon the pilgrim guest,
The single boon for which he prayed
The convent's charity was rest.

Peace dwells not here—this rugged face
Betrays no spirit of repose;
The sullen warrior sole we trace,
The marble man of many woes.
Such was his mien when first arose
The thought of that strange tale divine—
When hell he peopled with his foes,
The scourge of many a guilty line.

War to the last he waged with all
The tyrant canker-worms of earth;
Baron and duke, in hold and hall,
Cursed the dark hour that gave him birth;
He used Rome's harlot for his mirth;
Plucked bare hypocrisy and crime;
But valiant souls of knightly worth
Transmitted to the rolls of time.

O time! whose verdicts mock our own,
The only righteous judge art thou;
That poor, old exile, sad and lone,
Is Latium's other Virgil now.
Before his name the nations bow;
His words are parcel of mankind,
Deep in whose hearts, as on his brow,
The marks have sunk of Dante's mind.

THOMAS WILLIAM PARSONS.

HANS CHRISTIAN ANDERSEN.

1805–1875.

A BEING cleaves the moonlit air,
  With eyes of dew and plumes of fire,
New-born, immortal, strong and fair;
    Glance ere he goes!
His feet are shrouded like the dead,
  But in his face a wild desire
Breaks like the dawn that flushes red,
    And like a rose.

The stars shine out above his path,
  And music wakes through all the skies;

What mortal such a triumph hath,
  By death set free?
What earthly hands and heart are pure
As this man's, whose unshrinking eyes
Gaze onward through the deep obscure,
  Nor quail to see?

Ah! this was he who drank the fount
  Of wisdom set in speechless things,
Who, patient, watched the day-star mount,
  While others slept.
Ah! this was he whose loving soul
  Found heart-beats under trembling wings,
And heard divinest music roll
  Where wild springs leapt.

For poor dumb lips had song for him
  And children's dreamings ran in tune,
And strange old heroes, weird and dim,
  Walked by his side.
The very shadows loved him well
And danced and flickered in the moon,
And left him wondrous tales to tell
  Men far and wide.

And now no more he smiling walks
  Through greenwood alleys full of sun,
And, as he wanders, turns and talks,
  Though none be there;
The children watch in vain the place
  Where they were wont, when day was done,
To see their poet's sweet worn face,
  And faded hair.

Yet dream not such a spirit dies,
 Though all its earthly shrine decay!
Transfigured under clearer skies,
 He sings anew;
The frail soul-covering, racked with pain,
 And scored with vigil, fades away,
The soul set free and young again
 Glides upward through.

Weep not, but watch the moonlit air!
 Perchance a glory like a star
May leave what hangs about him there,
 And flash on us! . . .
Behold! the void is full of light,
 The beams pierce heaven from bar to bar
And all the hollows of the night
 Grow luminous!

EDMUND GOSSE.

SIR PHILIP SIDNEY.

FROM "AN ELEGY ON A FRIEND'S PASSION FOR HIS
ASTROPHILL."

WITHIN these woods of Arcadia
He chiefe delight and pleasure tooke,
And on the mountaine Parthenie,
Upon the chrystall liquid brooke,
 The Muses met him ev'ry day,
 That taught him sing, to write, and say.

When he descended downe the mount,
His personage seemed most divine,
A thousand graces one might count

Upon his lovely, cheerfull eine;
　To heare him speake and sweetly smile,
　You were in Paradise the while.

A sweet attractive kinde of grace,
A full assurance given by lookes,
Continuall comfort in a face,
The lineaments of Gospell bookes;
　I trowe that countenance cannot lie,
　Whose thoughts are legible in the eie.

Was never eie did see that face,
Was never eare did heare that tong,
Was never minde did minde his grace,
That ever thought the travell long;
　But eies, and eares, and ev'ry thought,
　Were with his sweet perfection caught.

MATTHEW. ROYDEN.

TO THE MEMORY OF BEN JONSON.

THE Muse's fairest light in no dark time,
The wonder of a learnèd age; the line
Which none can pass! the most proportioned
　　wit,—
To nature, the best judge of what was fit;
The deepest, plainest, highest, clearest pen;
The voice most echoed by consenting men;
The soul which answered best to all well said
By others, and which most requital made;
Tuned to the highest key of ancient Rome,
Returning all her music with his own;

In whom, with nature, study claimed a part,
And yet who to himself owed all his art:
Here lies Ben Jonson! every age will look
With sorrow here, with wonder on his book.

JOHN CLEVELAND.

ODE TO BEN JONSON.

Ah Ben!
Say how or when
Shall we, thy guests,
Meet at those lyric feasts,
Made at the Sun,
The Dog, the Triple Tun;
Where we such clusters had
As made us nobly wild, not mad;
And yet each verse of thine
Outdid the meat, outdid the frolic wine.

My Ben!
Or come again,
Or send to us
Thy wit's great overplus;
But teach us yet
Wisely to husband it,
Lest we that talent spend:
And having once brought to an end
That precious stock, the store
Of such a wit, the world should have no more.

ROBERT HERRICK.

ON THE PORTRAIT * OF SHAKESPEARE.

THIS figure, that thou here seest put,
It was for gentle Shakespeare cut;
Wherein the Graver had a strife
With Nature to outdo the life:
O, could he but have drawn his wit
As well in brass, as he hath hit
His face; the Print would then surpass
All that was ever writ in brass.
But since he cannot, Reader, look
Not at his picture, but his book.

BEN JONSON.

TO THE MEMORY OF MY BELOVED MAS-TER, WILLIAM SHAKESPEARE, AND WHAT HE HATH LEFT US.

To draw no envy, Shakespeare, on thy name,
Am I thus ample to thy book and fame;
While I confess thy writings to be such
As neither man nor Muse can praise too much.
. . . . . .
Soul of the age!
The applause, delight, the wonder of our stage!
My Shakespeare, rise! I will not lodge thee by
Chaucer, or Spenser, or bid Beaumont lie
A little further off, to make thee room:
Thou art a monument without a tomb,
And art alive still, while thy book doth live,

* The engraving by Martin Droeshout.

And we have wits to read, and praise to give.
That I not mix thee so, my brain excuses,
I mean with great but disproportioned Muses:
For if I thought my judgment were of years,
I should commit thee surely with thy peers,
And tell how far thou didst our Lyly outshine,
Or sporting Kyd or Marlowe's mighty line.
And though thou had small Latin and less Greek,
From thence to honor thee I will not seek
For names; but call forth thundering Eschylus,
Euripides, and Sophocles to us,
Pacuvius, Accius, him of Cordova dead,
To live again, to hear thy buskin tread,
And shake a stage: or when thy socks were on,
Leave thee alone for the comparison
Of all, that insolent Greece or haughty Rome
Sent forth, or since did from their ashes come.
Triumph, my Britain, thou hast one to show,
To whom all scenes of Europe homage owe.
He was not of an age, but for all time!
And all the Muses still were in their prime,
When, like Apollo, he came forth to warm
Our ears, or like a Mercury, to charm!
Nature herself was proud of his designs,
And joyed to wear the dressing of his lines!
Which were so richly spun, and woven so fit,
As, since, she will vouchsafe no other wit.
The merry Greek, tart Aristophanes,
Neat Terence, witty Plautus, now not please:
But antiquated and deserted lie,
As they were not of nature's family.
Yet must I not give nature all; thy art,
My gentle Shakespeare, must enjoy a part.

For though the poet's matter nature be,
His art doth give the fashion; and, that he
Who casts to write a living line, must sweat
(Such as thine are) and strike the second heat
Upon the Muses' anvil; turn the same,
And himself with it, that he thinks to frame;
Or for the laurel gain a scorn;
For a good poet 's made as well as born.
And such wert thou! Look how the father's face
Lives in his issue, even so the race
Of Shakespeare's mind and manners brightly
      shines
In his well turned and true filed lines:
In each of which he seems to shake a lance,
As brandished at the eyes of ignorance.
Sweet Swan of Avon! what a sight it were
To see thee in our water yet appear,
And make those flights upon the banks of Thames
That so did take Eliza and our James!
But stay, I see thee in the hemisphere
Advanced, and made a constellation there!
Shine forth, thou Star of Poets, and with rage,
Or influence, chide, or cheer the drooping stage
Which since thy flight from hence hath mourned
      like night,
And despairs day, but for thy volume's light!

BEN JONSON.

SHAKESPEARE.

FROM " PROLOGUE."

[Spoken by Mr. Garrick at the opening of the Theatre in
Drury Lane, in 1747.]

WHEN Learning's triumph o'er her barbarous
    foes
First reared the stage, immortal Shakespeare
    rose;
Each change of many-colored life he drew,
Exhausted worlds, and then imagined new:
Existence saw him spurn her bounded reign,
And panting Time toiled after him in vain:
His powerful strokes presiding Truth impressed,
And unresisted Passion stormed the breast.

DR. SAMUEL JOHNSON.

AN EPITAPH ON THE ADMIRABLE DRA-MATIC POET, W. SHAKESPEARE.

WHAT needs my Shakespeare for his honored
    bones,
The labor of an age in pilèd stones?
Or that his hallowed relics should be hid
Under a star-y-pointing pyramid?
Dear son of memory, great heir of fame,
What need'st thou such weak witness of thy
    name?
Thou in our wonder and astonishment
Hast built thyself a livelong monument.

For whilst to the shame of slow-endeavoring art
Thy easy numbers flow, and that each heart
Hath from the leaves of thy unvalued book
Those Delphic lines with deep impression took,
Then thou our fancy of itself bereaving,
Dost make us marble with too much conceiving;
And so sepúlchred in such pomp dost lie,
That kings for such a tomb would wish to die.

MILTON.

SHAKESPEARE.

THE soul of man is larger than the sky,
Deeper than ocean, or the abysmal dark
Of the unfathomed centre. Like that ark,
Which in its sacred hold uplifted high,
O'er the drowned hills, the human family,
And stock reserved of every living kind,
So, in the compass of the single mind,
The seeds and pregnant forms in essence lie,
That make all worlds. Great poet, 't was thy
  art
To know thyself, and in thyself to be
Whate'er love, hate, ambition, destiny,
Or the firm fatal purpose of the heart
Can make of man. Yet thou wert still the same,
Serene of thought, unhurt by thy own flame.

HARTLEY COLERIDGE.

GUILIELMUS REX.

THE folk who lived in Shakespeare's day
And saw that gentle figure pass
By London Bridge, his frequent way—
They little knew what man he was.

The pointed beard, the courteous mien,
The equal port to high and low,
All this they saw or might have seen—
But not the light behind the brow!

The doublet's modest gray or brown,
The slender sword-hilt's plain device,
What sign had these for prince or clown?
Few turned, or none, to scan him twice.

Yet 't was the king of England's kings!
The rest with all their pomps and trains
Are mouldered, half-remembered things—
'T is he alone that lives and reigns!

THOMAS BAILEY ALDRICH.

HIERARCHY OF ANGELS.

MELLIFLUOUS Shakespeare, whose enchanting
        quill
Commanded mirth or passion, was but Will;
And famous Jonson, though his learnèd pen
Be dipped in Castaly, is still but Ben.
Fletcher and Webster, of that learnèd pack
None of the meanest, was but Jack;
Dekker but Tom, nor May, nor Middleton,
And he's but now Jack Ford that once was John.

THOMAS HEYWOOD.

UNDER THE PORTRAIT OF JOHN MILTON.

PREFIXED TO " PARADISE LOST."

THREE Poets, in three distant ages born,
Greece, Italy, and England did adorn.
The first in loftiness of thought surpassed;
The next in majesty; in both the last.
The force of nature could no further go;
To make a third, she joined the former two.

JOHN DRYDEN.

TO MILTON.

" LONDON, 1802."

MILTON! thou shouldst be living at this hour:
England hath need of thee: she is a fen
Of stagnant waters: altar, sword, and pen,
Fireside, the heroic wealth of hall and bower,
Have forfeited their ancient English dower
Of inward happiness. We are selfish men;
Oh! raise us up, return to us again;
And give us manners, virtue, freedom, power.
Thy soul was like a star, and dwelt apart:
Thou hadst a voice whose sound was like the
  sea:
Pure as the naked heavens. majestic, free,
So didst thou travel on life's common way,
In cheerful godliness; and yet thy heart
The lowliest duties on herself did lay.

WILLIAM WORDSWORTH.

WALTON'S BOOK OF LIVES.

FROM " ECCLESIASTICAL SONNETS," PART III.

THERE are no colors in the fairest sky
So fair as these. The feather, whence the pen
Was shaped that traced the lives of these good men
Dropped from an angel's wing. With moistened
    eye
We read of faith and purest charity
In statesman, priest, and humble citizen :
O, could we copy their mild virtues, then
What joy to live, what blessedness to die!
Methinks their very names shine still and bright ;
Apart,—like glow-worms on a summer night ;
Or lonely tapers when from far they fling
A guiding ray ; or seen, like stars on high,
Satellites burning in a lucid ring
Around meek Walton's heavenly memory.

WILLIAM WORDSWORTH.

THE SONNET.

SCORN not the sonnet ; critic, you have frowned,
Mindless of its just honors ; with this key
Shakespeare unlocked his heart ; the melody
Of this small lute gave ease to Petrarch's wound ;
A thousand times this pipe did Tasso sound ;
With it Camoëns soothed an exile's grief ;
The sonnet glittered a gay myrtle leaf
Amid the cypress with which Dante crowned

His visionary brow; a glow-worm lamp,
It cheered mild Spenser, called from fairy-land
To struggle through dark ways; and when a damp
Fell round the path of Milton, in his hand
The thing became a trumpet; whence he blew
Soul-animating strains,—alas! too few.

WILLIAM WORDSWORTH.

CAMP–BELL.

CHARADE.

Come from my first, ay, come!
    The battle-dawn is nigh;
And the screaming trump and the thundering
        drum
    Are calling thee to die!

Fight as thy father fought;
    Fall as thy father fell;
Thy task is taught; thy shroud is wrought;
    So forward and farewell!

Toll ye my second, toll!
    Fling high the flambeau's light,
And sing the hymn for a parted soul
    Beneath the silent night!

The wreath upon his head,
    The cross upon his breast,
Let the prayer be said and the tear be shed,
    So,—take him to his rest!

Call ye my whole,—ay, call
　　The lord of lute and lay;
And let him greet the sable pall
　　With a noble song to-day.

Go, call him by his name!
　　No fitter hand may crave
To light the flame of a soldier's fame
　　On the turf of a soldier's grave.
　　　　　　　WINTHROP MACKWORTH PRAED.

TO THOMAS MOORE.

My boat is on the shore,
　　And my bark is on the sea;
But before I go, Tom Moore,
　　Here's a double health to thee!

Here's a sigh to those who love me,
　　And a smile to those who hate;
And, whatever sky's above me,
　　Here's a heart for every fate:

Though the ocean roar around me,
　　Yet it still shall bear me on;
Though a desert should surround me,
　　It hath springs that may be won.

Were't the last drop in the well,
　　As I gasped upon the brink,
Ere my fainting spirit fell,
　　'T is to thee that I would drink.

With that water, as this wine,
  The libation I would pour
Should be,—Peace with thine and mine,
  And a health to thee, Tom Moore!

LORD BYRON.

SHELLEY.

THE odor of a rose: light of a star:
The essence of a flame blown on by wind,
That lights and warms all near it, bland and kind,
But aye consumes itself, as though at war
With what supports and feeds it;—from afar
It draws its life, but evermore inclined
To leap into the flame that makes men blind
Who seek the secret of all things that are.
Such wert thou, Shelley, bound for airiest goal:
Interpreter of quintessential things:
Who mounted ever up on eagle-wings
Of phantasy: had aimed at heaven and stole
Promethean fire for men to be as gods,
And dwell in free, aerial abodes.

ALEXANDER HAY JAPP.

MEMORABILIA.

AH, did you once see Shelley plain,
  And did he stop and speak to you,
And did you speak to him again?
  How strange it seems, and new!

But you were living before that,
    And also you are living after;
And the memory I started at—
    My starting moves your laughter!

I crossed a moor, with a name of its own
    And a certain use in the world, no doubt,
Yet a hand's-breadth of it shines alone
    'Mid the blank miles round about:

For there I picked up on the heather
    And there I put inside my breast
A moulted feather, an eagle-feather!
    Well, I forget the rest.

ROBERT BROWNING.

BYRON.

FROM "THE COURSE OF TIME," BOOK IV

HE touched his harp, and nations heard en-
    tranced.
As some vast river of unfailing source,
Rapid, exhaustless, deep, his numbers flowed,
And openèd new fountains in the human heart.
Where Fancy halted, weary in her flight,
In other men, his fresh as morning rose,
And soared untrodden heights, and seemed at
    home,
Where angels bashful looked. Others, though
    great,
Beneath their argument seemed struggling; whiles

He, from above descending, stooped to touch
The loftiest thought; and proudly stooped, as
    though
It scarce deserved his verse. With Nature's self
He seemed an old acquaintance, free to jest
At will with all her glorious majesty.
He laid his hand upon " the Ocean's mane,"
And played familiar with his hoary locks;
Stood on the Alps, stood on the Apennines,
And with the thunder talked as friend to friend;
And wove his garland of the lightning's wing,
In sportive twist,—the lightning's fiery wing,
Which, as the footsteps of the dreadful God,
Marching upon the storm in vengeance, seemed;
Then turned, and with the grasshopper, who sung
His evening song beneath his feet, conversed.
Suns, moons, and stars, and clouds his sisters
    were;
Rocks, mountains, meteors, seas, and winds, and
    storms
His brothers, younger brothers, whom he scarce
As equals deemed. All passions of all men,
The wild and tame, the gentle and severe;
All thoughts, all maxims, sacred and profane;
All creeds; all seasons, time, eternity;
All that was hated, and all that was dear;
All that was hoped, all that was feared, by
    man,—
He tossed about, as tempest-withered leaves;
Then, smiling, looked upon the wreck he made.
With terror now he froze the cowering blood,
And now dissolved the heart in tenderness;
Yet would not tremble, would not weep himself;

But back into his soul retired, alone,
Dark, sullen, proud, gazing contemptuously
On hearts and passions prostrate at his feet.
                                    ROBERT POLLOK.

MACAULAY AS POET.

THE dreamy rhymer's measured snore
Falls heavy on our ears no more;
And by long strides are left behind
The dear delights of womankind,
Who wage their battles like their loves,
In satin waistcoats and kid gloves,
And have achieved the crowning work
When they have trussed and skewered a Turk.
Another comes with stouter tread,
And stalks among the statelier dead.
He rushes on, and hails by turns
High-crested Scott, broad-breasted Burns;
And shows the British youth, who ne'er
Will lag behind, what Romans were,
When all the Tuscans and their Lars
Shouted, and shook the towers of Mars.
                            WALTER SAVAGE LANDOR.

ON THE DEPARTURE OF SIR WALTER SCOTT FROM ABBOTSFORD, FOR NAPLES.

A TROUBLE, not of clouds, or weeping rain,
Nor of the setting sun's pathetic light
Engendered, hangs o'er Eildon's triple height:
Spirits of Power, assembled there, complain

For kindred Power departing from their sight;
While Tweed, best pleased in chanting a blithe
    strain,
Saddens his voice again, and yet again.
Lift up your hearts, ye Mourners! for the might
Of the whole world's good wishes with him goes;
Blessings and prayers in nobler retinue
Than sceptred king or laurelled conqueror knows,
Follow this wondrous Potentate. Be true,
Ye winds of ocean, and the midland sea,
Wafting your Charge to soft Parthenope!

                        WILLIAM WORDSWORTH.

TO THE MEMORY OF THOMAS HOOD.

TAKE back into thy bosom, earth,
    This joyous, May-eyed morrow,
The gentlest child that ever mirth
    Gave to be reared by sorrow!
'T is hard—while rays half green, half gold,
    Through vernal bowers are burning,
And streams their diamond mirrors hold
    To Summer's face returning—
To say we're thankful that his sleep
    Shall nevermore be lighter,
In whose sweet-tongued companionship
    Stream, bower, and beam grow brighter!

But all the more intensely true
    His soul gave out each feature
Of elemental love,—each hue
    And grace of golden nature,—

The deeper still beneath it all
    Lurked the keen jags of anguish;
The more the laurels clasped his brow
    Their poison made it languish.
Seemed it that, like the nightingale
    Of his own mournful singing,
The tenderer would his song prevail
    While most the thorn was stinging.

So never to the desert-worn
    Did fount bring freshness deeper
Than that his placid rest this morn
    Has brought the shrouded sleeper.
That rest may lap his weary head
    Where charnels choke the city,
Or where, mid woodlands, by his bed
    The wren shall wake its ditty;
But near or far, while evening's star
    Is dear to heart's regretting,
Around that spot admiring thought
    Shall hover, unforgetting.
                    BARTHOLOMEW SIMMONS.

BURNS.

A POET'S EPITAPH.

STOP, mortal! Here thy brother lies,—
    The poet of the poor.
His books were rivers, woods, and skies,
    The meadow and the moor;
His teachers were the torn heart's wail,
    The tyrant, and the slave,

The street, the factory, the jail,
    The palace,—and the grave!
Sin met thy brother everywhere!
    And is thy brother blamed?
From passion, danger, doubt, and care
    He no exemption claimed.
The meanest thing, earth's feeblest worm,
    He feared to scorn or hate;
But, honoring in a peasant's form
    The equal of the great,
He blessed the steward, whose wealth makes
    The poor man's little more;
Yet loathed the haughty wretch that takes
    From plundered labor's store.
A hand to do, a head to plan,
    A heart to feel and dare,—
Tell man's worst foes, here lies the man
    Who drew them as they are.

                    EBENEZER ELLIOTT.

BURNS.

ON RECEIVING A SPRIG OF HEATHER IN BLOSSOM.

No more these simple flowers belong
    To Scottish maid and lover;
Sown in the common soil of song,
    They bloom the wide world over.

In smiles and tears, in sun and showers,
    The minstrel and the heather,
The deathless singer and the flowers
    He sang of live together.

Wild heather-bells and Robert Burns!
The moorland flower and peasant!
How, at their mention, memory turns
Her pages old and pleasant!

The gray sky wears again its gold
And purple of adorning,
And manhood's noonday shadows hold
The dews of boyhood's morning:

The dews that washed the dust and soil
From off the wings of pleasure,
The sky, that flecked the ground of toil
With golden threads of leisure.

I call to mind the summer day,
The early harvest mowing,
The sky with sun and clouds at play,
And flowers with breezes blowing.

I hear the blackbird in the corn,
The locust in the haying;
And, like the fabled hunter's horn,
Old tunes my heart is playing.

How oft that day, with fond delay,
I sought the maple's shadow,
And sang with Burns the hours away,
Forgetful of the meadow!

Bees hummed, birds twittered, overhead
I heard the squirrels leaping;
The good dog listened while I read,
And wagged his tail in keeping.

I watched him while in sportive mood
    I read " The Twa Dogs' " story,
And half believed he understood
    The poet's allegory.

Sweet day, sweet songs!—The golden hours
    Grew brighter for that singing,
From brook and bird and meadow flowers
    A dearer welcome bringing.

New light on home-seen Nature beamed,
    New glory over Woman;
And daily life and duty seemed
    No longer poor and common.

I woke to find the simple truth
    Of fact and feeling better
Than all the dreams that held my youth
    A still repining debtor:

That Nature gives her handmaid, Art,
    The themes of sweet discoursing;
The tender idyls of the heart
    In every tongue rehearsing.

Why dream of lands of gold and pearl,
    Of loving knight and lady,
When farmer boy and barefoot girl
    Were wandering there already?

I saw through all familiar things
    The romance underlying;
The joys and griefs that plume the wings
    Of Fancy skyward flying.

I saw the same blithe day return,
　　The same sweet fall of even,
That rose on wooded Craigie-burn,
　　And sank on crystal Devon.

I matched with Scotland's heathery hills
　　The sweet-brier and the clover;
With Ayr and Doon, my native rills,
　　Their wood-hymns chanting over.

O'er rank and pomp, as he had seen,
　　I saw the Man uprising;
No longer common or unclean,
　　The child of God's baptizing.

With clearer eyes I saw the worth
　　Of life among the lowly;
The Bible at his Cotter's hearth
　　Had made my own more holy.

And if at times an evil strain,
　　To lawless love appealing,
Broke in upon the sweet refrain
　　Of pure and healthful feeling,

It died upon the eye and ear,
　　No inward answer gaining;
No heart had I to see or hear
　　The discord and the staining.

Let those who never erred forget
　　His worth, in vain bewailings;
Sweet Soul of Song!—I own my debt
　　Uncancelled by his failings!

Lament who will the ribald line
  Which tells his lapse from duty,
How kissed the maddening lips of wine,
  Or wanton ones of beauty;

But think, while falls that shade between
  The erring one and Heaven,
That he who loved like Magdalen,
  Like her may be forgiven.

Not his the song whose thunderous chime
  Eternal echoes render,—
The mournful Tuscan's haunted rhyme,
  And Milton's starry splendor.

But who his human heart has laid
  To Nature's bosom nearer?
Who sweetened toil like him, or paid
  To love a tribute dearer?

Through all his tuneful art, how strong
  The human feeling gushes!
The very moonlight of his song
  Is warm with smiles and blushes!

Give lettered pomp to teeth of Time,
  So " Bonny Doon " but tarry;
Blot out the Epic's stately rhyme,
  But spare his " Highland Mary! "
                JOHN GREENLEAF WHITTIER.

TO BENJAMIN ROBERT HAYDON.

GREAT spirits now on earth are sojourning:
He of the cloud, the cataract, the lake,
Who on Helvellyn's summit, wide awake,
Catches his freshness from Archangel's wing:
He of the rose, the violet, the spring,
The social smile, the chain for Freedom's sake:
And lo! whose steadfastness would never take
A meaner sound than Raphael's whispering.
And other spirits there are, standing apart
Upon the forehead of the age to come;
These, these will give the world another heart,
And other pulses. Hear ye not the hum
Of mighty workings?—
Listen awhile, ye nations, and be dumb.

JOHN KEATS.

ON A PORTRAIT OF WORDSWORTH,

BY B. R. HAYDON.

WORDSWORTH upon Helvellyn! Let the cloud
Ebb audibly along the mountain-wind,
Then break against the rock, and show behind
The lowland valleys floating up to crowd
The sense with beauty. *He*, with forehead bowed
And humble-lidded eyes, as one inclined
Before the sovran thought of his own mind,
And very meek with inspirations proud,—
Takes here his rightful place as poet-priest

By the high-altar, singing prayer and prayer
To the higher Heavens. A noble vision free,
Our Haydon's hand hath flung out from the mist!
No portrait this, with Academic air,—
This is the poet and his poetry.

ELIZABETH BARRETT BROWNING.

THE LOST LEADER.*

Just for a handful of silver he left us,
    Just for a ribbon to stick in his coat—
Found the one gift of which fortune bereft us,
    Lost all the others she lets us devote;
They, with the gold to give, doled him out silver,
    So much was theirs who so little allowed;

---

* This bitter attack, famous for its invective, was made
by Browning (1845) on Wordsworth, after the latter had
accepted the post of Poet Laureate (1843), thus, in Browning's view, deserting the people and selling himself to the
government. Wordsworth's only official poem, however,
was on the installation of Albert, Prince Consort, as
Chancellor of Cambridge University in 1847 ; and in 1850
he died : so that the protest of Browning was not justified.
Indeed, in 1875, Browning himself wrote : " I did in my
hasty youth presume to use the great and venerated per-
sonality of Wordsworth as a sort of painter's model ; one
from which this or the other particular feature may be
selected and turned to account ; had I intended more . . .
I should not have talked about ᐧ handfuls of silver and bits
of ribbon.' These never influenced the change of politics
in the great poet, whose defection, nevertheless . . . was
to my juvenile apprehension, and even mature consideration, an event to be deplored."

How all our copper had gone for his service!
Rags—were they purple, his heart had been
    proud!
We that had loved him so, followed him, honored
    him,
    Lived in his mild and magnificent eye,
Learned his great language, caught his clear ac-
    cents,
    Made him our pattern to live and to die!
Shakespeare was of us, Milton was for us,
    Burns, Shelley, were with us,—they watch from
    their graves!
He alone breaks from the van and the freemen,
    He alone sinks to the rear and the slaves!

We shall march prospering,—not thro' his pres-
    ence;
    Songs may inspirit us,—not from his lyre;
Deeds will be done,—while he boasts his quies-
    cence,
    Still bidding crouch whom the rest bade aspire.
Blot out his name, then, record one lost soul more,
    One task more declined, one more footpath un-
    trod,
One more devil's-triumph and sorrow for angels,
    One wrong more to man, one more insult to
    God!
Life's night begins: let him never come back to us!
    There would be doubt, hesitation, and pain,
Forced praise on our part—the glimmer of twi-
    light,
    Never glad confident morning again!
Best fight on well, for we taught him—strike gal-
    lantly,

Menace our heart ere we master his own;
Then let him receive the new knowledge and wait
    us,
  Pardoned in heaven, the first by the throne!

ROBERT BROWNING.

MEMORIAL VERSES.

APRIL, 1850.

GOETHE in Weimar sleeps, and Greece,
Long since, saw Byron's struggle cease.
But one such death remained to come;
The last poetic voice is dumb—
We stand to-day by Wordsworth's tomb.

When Byron's eyes were shut in death,
We bowed our head and held our breath.
He taught us little; but our soul
Had *felt* him like the thunder's roll.
With shivering heart the strife we saw
Of passion with eternal law;
And yet with reverential awe
We watched the fount of fiery life
Which served for that Titanic strife.

When Goethe's death was told, we said:
Sunk, then, is Europe's sagest head.
Physician of the iron age,
Goethe has done his pilgrimage.
He took the suffering human race,
He read each wound, each weakness clear:
And struck his finger on the place,
And said: *Thou ailest here, and here!*

He looked on Europe's dying hour
Of fitful dream and feverish power;
His eye plunged down the weltering strife,
The turmoil of expiring life—
He said: *The end is everywhere,*
Art still has truth, take refuge there!
And he was happy, if to know
Causes of things, and far below
His feet to see the lurid flow
Of terror, and insane distress,
And headlong fate, be happiness.

And Wordsworth!—Ah, pale ghosts, rejoice!
For never has such soothing voice
Been to your shadowy world conveyed,
Since erst, at morn, some wandering shade
Heard the clear song of Orpheus come
Through Hades, and the mournful gloom.
Wordsworth has gone from us—and ye,
Ah, may ye feel his voice as we!
He too upon a wintery clime
Had fallen—on this iron time
Of doubts, disputes, distractions, fears.
He found us when the age had bound
Our souls in its benumbing round;
He spoke, and loosed our hearts in tears.
He laid us as we lay at birth
On the cool flowery lap of earth,
Smiles broke from us, and we had ease;
The hills were round us, and the breeze
Went o'er the sun-lit fields again;
Our foreheads felt the wind and rain.
Our youth returned; for there was shed

On spirits that had long been dead,
Spirits dried up and closely furled,
The freshness of the early world.

Ah! since dark days still bring to light
Man's prudence and man's fiery might,
Time may restore us in his course
Goethe's sage mind and Byron's force;
But where will Europe's latter hour
Again find Wordsworth's healing power?
Others will teach us how to dare,
And against fear our breast to steel;
Others will strengthen us to bear—
But who, ah! who, will make us feel?
The cloud of mortal destiny,
Others will front it fearlessly—
But who, like him, will put it by?
Keep fresh the grass upon his grave,
O Rotha, with thy living wave!
Sing him thy best! for few or none
Hears thy voice right, now he is gone.

MATTHEW ARNOLD.

FROM "WORDSWORTH'S GRAVE."

POET who sleepest by this wandering wave!
  When thou wast born, what birth-gift hadst
    thou then?
To thee what wealth was that the Immortals gave,
  The wealth thou gavest in thy turn to men?

Not Milton's keen, translunar music thine;
  Not Shakespeare's cloudless, boundless human
    view;

Not Shelley's flush of rose on peaks divine;
  Nor yet the wizard twilight Coleridge knew.

What hadst thou that could make so large amends
  For all thou hadst not and thy peers possessed,
Motion and fire, swift means to radiant ends?—
  Thou hadst for weary feet the gift of rest.

From Shelley's dazzling glow or thunderous haze,
  From Byron's tempest-anger, tempest-mirth,
Men turned to thee and found—not blast and
      blaze,
  Tumult of tottering heavens, but peace on earth.

Nor peace that grows by Lethe, scentless flower,
  There in white languors to decline and cease;
But peace whose names are also rapture, power,
  Clear sight, and love: for these are parts of
      peace.

WILLIAM WATSON.

IN MEMORY OF WALTER SAVAGE LANDOR.

BACK to the flower-town, side by side,
    The bright months bring,
New-born, the bridegroom and the bride,
    Freedom and spring.

The sweet land laughs from sea to sea,
    Filled full of sun;
All things come back to her, being free;
    All things but one.

In many a tender wheaten plot
    Flowers that were dead
Live, and old suns revive; but not
    That holier head.

By this white wandering waste of sea,
    Far north, I hear
One face shall never turn to me
    As once this year:

Shall never smile and turn and rest
    On mine as there,
Nor one most sacred hand be prest
    Upon my hair.

I came as one whose thoughts half linger,
    Half run before;
The youngest to the oldest singer
    That England bore.

I found him whom I shall not find
    Till all grief end,
In holiest age our mightiest mind,
    Father and friend.

But thou, if anything endure,
    If hope there be,
O spirit that man's life left pure,
    Man's death set free,

Not with disdain of days that were
    Look earthward now;
Let dreams revive the reverend hair,
    The imperial brow;

Come back in sleep, for in the life
    Where thou art not
We find none like thee. Time and strife
    And the world's lot

Move thee no more; but love at least
    And reverent heart
May move thee, royal and release
    Soul, as thou art.

And thou, his Florence, to thy trust
    Receive and keep,
Keep safe his dedicated dust,
    His sacred sleep.

So shall thy lovers, come from far,
    Mix with thy name
As morning-star with evening-star
    His faultless fame.

               ALGERNON CHARLES SWINBURNE.

A WELCOME TO "BOZ,"

ON HIS FIRST VISIT TO THE WEST.

COME as artist, come as guest,
Welcome to the expectant West,
Hero of the charmèd pen,
Loved of children, loved of men.
We have felt thy spell for years;
Oft with laughter, oft with tears,
Thou hast touched the tenderest part
Of our inmost, hidden heart.
We have fixed our eager gaze

On thy pages nights and days,
Wishing, as we turned them o'er,
Like poor Oliver, for " more,"
And the creatures of thy brain
In our memory remain,
Till through them we seem to be
Old acquaintances of thee.
Much we hold it thee to greet,
Gladly sit we at thy feet;
On thy features we would look,
As upon a living book,
And thy voice would grateful hear,
Glad to feel that Boz were near,
That his veritable soul
Held us by direct control:
Therefore, author loved the best,
Welcome, welcome to the West.

In immortal Weller's name,
By Micawber's deathless fame,
By the flogging wreaked on Squeers,
By Job Trotter's fluent tears,
By the beadle Bumble's fate
At the hands of vixen mate,
By the famous Pickwick Club,
By the dream of Gabriel Grubb,
In the name of Snodgrass' muse,
Tupman's amorous interviews,
Winkle's ludicrous mishaps,
And the fat boy's countless naps;
By Ben Allen and Bob Sawyer,
By Miss Sally Brass, the lawyer,
In the name of Newman Noggs,

River Thames, and London fogs,
Richard Swiveller's excess,
Feasting with the Marchioness,
By Jack Bunsby's oracles,
By the chime of Christmas bells,
By the cricket on the hearth,
Scrooge's frown and Crotchit's mirth,
By spread tables and good cheer,
Wayside inns and pots of beer,
Hostess plump and jolly host,
Coaches for the turnpike post,
Chambermaids in love with Boots,
Toodles, Traddles, Tapley, Toots,
Jarley, Varden, Mister Dick,
Susan Nipper, Mistress Chick,
Snevellicci, Lilyvick,
Mantalini's predilections,
To transfer his " dem " affections,
Podsnap, Pecksniff, Chuzzlewit,
Quilp and Simon Tappertit,
Weg and Boffin, Smike and Paul,
Nell and Jenny Wren and all,—
Be not Sairy Gamp forgot,—
No, nor Peggotty and Trot,—
By poor Barnaby and Grip,
Flora, Dora, Di, and Gip,
Peerybingle, Pinch, and Pip,—
Welcome, long-expected guest,
Welcome, Dickens, to the West.

In the name of gentle Nell,
Child of light, belovèd well,—
Weeping, did we not behold
Roses on her bosom cold?

Better we for every tear
Shed beside her snowy bier,—
By the mournful group that played
Round the grave where Smike was laid,
By the life of Tiny Tim,
And the lesson taught by him,
Asking in his plaintive tone
God to " bless us every one,"
By the sounding waves that bore
Little Paul to Heaven's shore,
By thy yearning for the human
Good in every man and woman,
By each noble deed and word
That thy story-books record,
And each noble sentiment
Dickens to the world hath lent,
By the effort thou hast made
Truth and true reform to aid,
By thy hope of man's relief
Finally from want and grief,
By thy never-failing trust
That the God of love is just,—
We would meet and welcome thee,
Preacher of humanity:
Welcome fills the throbbing breast
Of the sympathetic West.

W. H. VENABLE.

DICKENS IN CAMP.

ABOVE the pines the moon was slowly drifting,
The river sang below;
The dim Sierras, far beyond, uplifting
Their minarets of snow.

The roaring camp-fire, with rude humor, painted
    The ruddy tints of health
On haggard face and form that drooped and
    fainted
    In the fierce race for wealth;

Till one arose, and from his pack's scant treasure
    A hoarded volume drew,
And cards were dropped from hands of listless
    leisure,
    To hear the tale anew;

And then, while round them shadows gathered
    faster,
    And as the firelight fell,
He read aloud the book wherein the Master
    Had writ of " Little Nell."

Perhaps 't was boyish fancy,—for the reader
    Was youngest of them all,—
But, as he read, from clustering pine and cedar
    A silence seemed to fall:

The fir-trees, gathering closer in the shadows,
    Listened in every spray,
While the whole camp, with " Nell," on English
    meadows
    Wandered and lost their way.

And so in mountain solitudes—o'ertaken
    As by some spell divine—
Their cares dropped from them like the needles
    shaken
    From out the gusty pine.

Lost is that camp, and wasted all its fire;
    And he who wrought that spell?—
Ah, towering pine and stately Kentish spire,
    Ye have one tale to tell!

Lost is that camp! but let its fragrant story
    Blend with the breath that thrills
With hop-vines' incense all the pensive glory
    That fills the Kentish hills.

And on that grave where English oak and holly
    And laurel wreathes intwine,
Deem it not all a too presumptuous folly,—
    This spray of Western pine.

BRET HARTE.

DICKENS.

Chief in thy generation born of men
Whom English praise acclaimed as English born,
With eyes that matched the world-wide eyes of
        morn
For gleam of tears or laughter, tenderest then
When thoughts of children warmed their light, or
        when
Reverence of age with love and labor worn,
Or godlike pity fired with godlike scorn,
Shot through them flame that winged thy swift
        live pen:
Where stars and suns that we beheld not burn,
Higher even than here, though highest was here
        thy place,
Love sees thy spirit laugh and speak and shine
With Shakespeare, and the soft bright soul of
        Sterne,

And Fielding's kindliest might, and Goldsmith's
    grace;
Scarce one more loved or worthier than thine.
ALGERNON CHARLES SWINBURNE.

TO THACKERAY.

O GENTLER Censor of our age!
Prime master of our ampler tongue!
Whose word of wit and generous page
Were never wroth except with Wrong.

Fielding—without the manner's dross,
Scott—with a spirit's larger room,
What Prelate deems thy grave his loss?
What Halifax erects thy tomb?

But, may be, He—who could so draw
The hidden Great, the humble Wise—
Yielding with them to God's good law,
Makes the Pantheon where he lies.
RICHARD MONCKTON MILNES.
(LORD HOUGHTON.)

TENNYSON.

SHAKESPEARE and Milton—what third blazoned
    name
Shall lips of after-ages link to these?
  His who, beside the wild encircling seas,
Was England's voice, her voice with one acclaim,
For three score years; whose word of praise was
    fame,
  Whose scorn gave pause to man's inquities.

What strain was his in that Crimean war?
  A bugle-call in battle; a low breath,
  Plaintive and sweet, above the fields of death!
So year by year the music rolled afar,
From Euxine wastes to flowery Kandahar,
  Bearing the laurel or the cypress wreath.

Others shall have their little space of time,
  Their proper niche and bust, then fade away
  Into the darkness, poets of a day;
But thou, O builder of enduring rhyme,
Thou shalt not pass! Thy fame in every clime
  On earth shall live where Saxon speech has
    sway.

Waft me this verse across the winter sea,
  Through light and dark, through mist and blind-
    ing sleet,
  O wintry winds, and lay it at his feet;
Though the poor gift betray my poverty,
At his feet lay it: it may chance that he
  Will find no gift, where reverence is, unmeet.

                    THOMAS BAILEY ALDRICH.

LACHRYMÆ MUSARUM.

(6TH OCTOBER, 1982.)

Low, like another's, lies the laurelled head:
The life that seemed a perfect song is o'er:
Carry the last great bard to his last bed.
Land that he loved, thy noblest voice is mute.
Land that he loved, that loved him! nevermore

Meadow of thine, smooth lawn or wild seashore,
Gardens of odorous bloom and tremulous fruit,
Or woodlands old, like Druid couches spread,
The master's feet shall tread.
Death's little rift hath rent the faultless lute:
The singer of undying songs is dead.

Lo, in this season pensive-hued and grave,
While fades and falls the doomed, reluctant leaf
From withered Earth's fantastic coronal,
With wandering sighs of forest and of wave
Mingles the murmur of a people's grief
For him whose leaf shall fade not, neither fall.
He hath fared forth, beyond these suns and show-
    ers.
For us, the autumn glow, the autumn flame,
And soon the winter silence shall be ours:
Him the eternal spring of fadeless fame
Crowns with no mortal flowers.

Rapt though he be from us,
Virgil salutes him, and Theocritus;
Catullus, mightiest-brained Lucretius, each
Greets him, their brother, on the Stygian beach;
Proudly a gaunt right hand doth Dante reach;
Milton and Wordsworth bid him welcome home;
Bright Keats to touch his raiment doth beseech;
Coleridge, his locks aspersed with fairy foam,
Calm Spenser, Chaucer suave,
His equal friendship crave:
And godlike spirits hail him guest, in speech
Of Athens, Florence, Weimar, Stratford, Rome.

What needs his laurel our ephemeral tears,
To save from visitation of decay?
Not in his temporal sunlight, now, that bay
Blooms, nor to perishable mundane ears
Sings he with lips of transitory clay;
For he hath joined the chorus of his peers
In habitations of the perfect day:
His earthly notes a heavenly audience hears,
And more melodious are henceforth the spheres,
Enriched with music stolen from earth away.

He hath returned to regions whence he came,
Him doth the spirit divine
Of universal loveliness reclaim.
All nature is his shrine.
Seek him henceforward in the wind and sea,
In earth's and air's emotion or repose,
In every star's august serenity,
And in the rapture of the flaming rose.
There seek him if ye would not seek in vain,
There, in the rhythm and music of the Whole;
Yea, and forever in the human soul
Made stronger and more beauteous by his strain.

For lo! creation's self is one great choir,
And what is nature's order but the rhyme
Whereto the worlds keep time,
And all things move with all things from their
          prime?
Who shall expound the mystery of the lyre?
In far retreats of elemental mind
Obscurely comes and goes
The imperative breath of song, that as the wind

Is trackless, and oblivious whence it blows.
Demand of lilies wherefore they are white,
Extort her crimson secret from the rose,
But ask not of the Muse that she disclose
The meaning of the riddle of her might:
Somewhat of all things sealed and recondite,
Save the enigma of herself, she knows.
The master could not tell, with all his lore,
Wherefore he sang, or whence the mandate sped:
Even as the linnet sings, so I, he said;—
Ah, rather as the imperial nightingale,
That held in trance the ancient Attic shore,
And charms the ages with the notes that o'er
All woodland chants immortally prevail!
And now, from our vain plaudits greatly fled,
He with diviner silence dwells instead,
And on no earthly sea with transient roar,
Unto no earthly airs, he trims his sail,
But far beyond our vision and our hail
Is heard forever and is seen no more.

   No more, O never now,
Lord of the lofty and the tranquil brow
Whereon nor snows of time
Have fallen, nor wintry rime,
Shall men behold thee, sage and mage sublime.
Once, in his youth obscure,
The maker of this verse, which shall endure
By splendor of its theme that cannot die,
Beheld thee eye to eye,
And touched through thee the hand
Of every hero of thy race divine,
Even to the sire of all the laurelled line,

The sightless wanderer on the Ionian strand,
With soul as healthful as the poignant brine,
Wide as his skies and radiant as his seas,
Starry from haunts of his Familiars nine,
Glorious Mæonides.
Yea, I beheld thee, and behold thee yet:
Thou hast forgotten, but can I forget?
The accents of thy pure and sovereign tongue,
Are they not ever goldenly imprest
On memory's palimpsest?
I see the wizard locks like night that hung,
I tread the floor thy hallowing feet have trod;
I see the hands a nation's lyre that strung,
The eyes that looked through life and gazed on
    God.

The seasons change, the winds they shift and
    veer;
The grass of yesteryear
Is dead; the birds depart, the groves decay:
Empires dissolve and peoples disappear:
Song passes not away.
Captains and conquerors leave a little dust,
And kings a dubious legend of their reign;
The swords of Cæsars, they are less than rust:
The poet doth remain.
Dead is Augustus, Maro is alive;
And thou, the Mantuan of our age and clime,
Like Virgil shalt thy race and tongue survive,
Bequeathing no less honeyed words to time,
Embalmed in amber of eternal rhyme,
And rich with sweets from every Muse's hive;
While to the measure of the cosmic rune

For purer ears thou shalt thy lyre attune,
And heed no more the hum of idle praise
In that great calm our tumults cannot reach,
Master who crown'st our immelodious days
With flower of perfect speech.

WILLIAM WATSON.

ROBERT BROWNING.

THERE is delight in singing, though none hear
Beside the singer; and there is delight
In praising, though the praiser sit alone
And see the praised far off him, far above.
Shakespeare is not our poet, but the world's,
Therefore on him no speech! and brief for thee,
Browning! Since Chaucer was alive and hale,
No man hath walked along our roads with step
So active, so inquiring eye, or tongue
So varied in discourse. But warmer climes
Give brighter plumage, stronger wing: the breeze
Of Alpine heights thou playest with, borne on
Beyond Sorrento and Amalfi, where
The Siren waits thee, singing song for song.

WALTER SAVAGE LANDOR.

THE BURIAL OF ROBERT BROWNING.

Upon St. Michael's Isle
They laid him for awhile
That he might feel the Ocean's full embrace,
And wedded be
To that wide sea—

The subject and the passion of his race.
As Thetis, from some lovely underground
Springing, she girds him round
With lapping sound
And silent space:
Then, on more honor bent,
She sues the firmament,
And bids the hovering, western clouds combine
To spread their sabled amber on her lustrous
brine.

It might not be
He should lie free
Forever in the soft light of the sea;
For lo! one came,
Of step more slow than fame,
Stooped over him—we heard her breathe his
name—
And as the light drew back,
Bore him across the track
Of the subservient waves that dare not foil
That veiled, maternal figure of its spoil.

Ah! where will she put by
Her journeying majesty?
She hath left the lands of the air and sun;
She will take no rest till her course be run.
Follow her far, follow her fast,
Until at last,
Within a narrow transept led,
Lo! she unwraps her face to pall her dead.

'T is England who has travelled far,
England who brings
Fresh splendor to her galaxy of Kings.

We kiss her feet, her hands,
Where eloquent she stands;
Nor dare to lend
A wailful choir about the poet dumb
Who is become
Part of the glory that her sons would bleed
To save from scar;
Yea, hers in very deed
As Runnymede,
Or Trafalgar.

MICHAEL FIELD.

JOSEPH RODMAN DRAKE.

DIED IN NEW YORK, SEPTEMBER, 1820.

GREEN be the turf above thee,
Friend of my better days!
None knew thee but to love thee,
Nor named thee but to praise.

Tears fell, when thou wert dying,
From eyes unused to weep,
And long, where thou art lying,
Will tears the cold turf steep.

When hearts, whose truth was proven,
Like thine, are laid in earth,
There should a wreath be woven
To tell the world their worth;

And I, who woke each morrow
To clasp thy hand in mine,
Who shared thy joy and sorrow,
Whose weal and woe were thine,

It should be mine to braid it
    Around thy faded brow,
But I've in vain essayed it,
    And feel I cannot now.

While memory bids me weep thee,
    Nor thoughts nor words are free,
The grief is fixed too deeply
    That mourns a man like thee.

                    FITZ-GREENE HALLECK.

FITZ–GREENE HALLECK.

[Read at the Unveiling of His Statue in Central Park,
                    May, 1877.]

AMONG their graven shapes to whom
    Thy civic wreaths belong,
O city of his love! make room
    For one whose gift was song.

Not his the soldier's sword to wield,
    Nor his the helm of state,
Nor glory of the stricken field,
    Nor triumph of debate.

In common ways, with common men,
    He served his race and time
As well as if his clerkly pen
    Had never danced to rhyme.

If, in the thronged and noisy mart,
    The Muses found their son,
Could any say his tuneful art
    A duty left undone?

He toiled and sang; and year by year
  Men found their homes more sweet,
And through a tenderer atmosphere
  Looked down the brick-walled street.

The Greek's wild onset Wall Street knew,
  The Red King walked Broadway;
And Alnwick Castle's roses blew
  From Palisades to Bay.

Fair City by the Sea! upraise
  His veil with reverent hands;
And mingle with thy own the praise
  And pride of other lands.

Let Greece his fiery lyric breathe
  Above her hero-urns;
And Scotland, with her holly, wreathe
  The flowers he culled for Burns.

O, stately stand thy palace walls,
  Thy tall ships ride the seas;
To-day thy poet's name recalls
  A prouder thought than these.

Not less thy pulse of trade shall beat,
  Nor less thy tall fleets swim,
That shaded square and dusty street
  Are classic ground through him.

Alive, he loved, like all who sing,
  The echoes of his song;
Too late the tardy meed we bring,
  The praise delayed so long.

Too late, alas!—Of all who knew
  The living man, to-day
Before his unveiled face how few
  Make bare their locks of gray!

Our lips of praise must soon be dumb,
  Our grateful eyes be dim;
O, brothers of the days to come,
  Take tender charge of him!

New hands the wires of song may sweep,
  New voices challenge fame;
But let no moss of years o'ercreep
  The lines of Halleck's name.

JOHN GREENLEAF WHITTIER.

POE'S COTTAGE AT FORDHAM.

HERE lived the soul enchanted
  By melody of song;
Here dwelt the spirit haunted
  By a demoniac throng;
Here sang the lips elated;
Here grief and death were sated;
Here loved and here unmated
  Was he, so frail, so strong.

Here wintry winds and cheerless
  The dying firelight blew,
While he whose song was peerless
  Dreamed the drear midnight through,
And from dull embers chilling

Crept shadows darkly filling
The silent place, and thrilling
　His fancy as they grew.

Here, with brow bared to heaven,
　In starry night he stood,
With the lost star of seven
　Feeling sad brotherhood.
Here in the sobbing showers
Of dark autumnal hours
He heard suspected powers
　Shriek through the stormy wood.

From visions of Apollo
　And of Astarte's bliss,
He gazed into the hollow
　And hopeless vale of Dis,
And though earth were surrounded
By heaven, it still was mounded
With graves. His soul had sounded
　The dolorous abyss.

Proud, mad, but not defiant,
　He touched at heaven and hell,
Fate found a rare soul pliant
　And wrung her changes well.
Alternately his lyre,
Stranded with strings of fire,
Led earth's most happy choir,
　Or flashed with Israfel.

No singer of old story
　Luting accustomed lays,
No harper for new glory,
　No mendicant for praise,

He struck high chords and splendid,
Wherein were fiercely blended
Tones that unfinished ended
    With his unfinished days.

Here through this lowly portal,
    Made sacred by his name,
Unheralded immortal
    The mortal went and came.
And fate that then denied him,
And envy that decried him,
And malice that belied him,
    Have cenotaphed his fame.

JOHN HENRY BONER.

ON THE DEATH OF THOMAS CARLYLE AND GEORGE ELIOT.

Two souls diverse out of our human sight
Pass, followed one with love and each with won-
    der:
The stormy sophist with his mouth of thunder,
Clothed with loud words and mantled in the
    might
Of darkness and magnificence of night;
And one whose eye could smite the night in sun-
    der,
Searching if light or no light were thereunder,
And found in love of loving-kindness light.
Duty Divine and Thought with eyes of fire
Still following Righteousness with deep desire

Shone sole and stern before her and above,
Sure stars and sole to steer by; but more sweet
Shone lower the loveliest lamp for earthly feet,
The light of little children, and their love.

ALGERNON CHARLES SWINBURNE.

CARLYLE AND EMERSON.

A BALE-FIRE kindled in the night,
  By night a blaze, by day a cloud,
With flame and smoke all England woke,—
  It climbed so high, it roared so loud:

While over Massachusetts' pines
  Uprose a white and steadfast star;
And many a night it hung unwatched,—
  It shone so still, it seemed so far.

But Light is Fire, and Fire is Light;
  And mariners are glad for these,—
The torch that flares along the coast,
  The star that beams above the seas.

MONTGOMERY SCHUYLER.

EMERSON.

CONCORD.

"FARTHER horizons every year."
O tossing pines, which surge and wave
Above the poet's just made grave,
And waken for his sleeping ear
The music that he loved to hear,

Through summer's sun and winter's chill,
With purpose staunch and dauntless will,
Sped by a noble discontent
You climb toward the blue firmament:
Climb as the winds climb, mounting high
The viewless ladders of the sky;
Spurning our lower atmosphere,
Heavy with sighs and dense with night,
And urging upward, year by year,
To ampler air, diviner light.

" Farther horizons every year."
Beneath you pass the tribes of men;
Your gracious boughs o'ershadow them.
You hear but do not seem to heed
Their jarring speech, their faulty creed.
Your roots are firmly set in soil
Won from their humming paths of toil;
Content their lives to watch and share,
To serve them, shelter, and upbear,
Yet but to win an upward way
And larger gift of heaven than they,
Benignant view and attitude,
Close knowledge of celestial sign;
Still working for all earthly good,
While pressing on to the Divine.

" Farther horizons every year."
So he, by reverent hands just laid
Beneath your layers of waving shade,
Climbed as you climb the upward way,
Knowing not boundary nor stay.
His eyes surcharged with heavenly lights,

His senses steeped in heavenly sights,
His soul attuned to heavenly keys,
How should he pause for rest or ease,
Or turn his wingèd feet again
To share the common feasts of men?
He blessed them with his word and smile
But, still above their fickle moods,
Wooing, constraining him, the while
Beckoned the shining altitudes.

" Farther horizons every year."
To what immeasurable height,
What clear irradiance of light,
What far and all-transcendent goal,
Hast thou now risen, O steadfast soul!
We may not follow with our eyes
To where the further pathway lies;
Nor guess what vision, vast and free,
God keeps in store for souls like thee.
But still the sentry pines, which wave
Their boughs above thy honored grave,
Shall be thy emblems brave and fit,
Firm rooted in the stalwart sod;
Blessing the earth, while spurning it,
Content with nothing short of God.

SARAH CHAUNCEY WOOLSEY (*Susan Coolidge*).

LOWELL ON HIMSELF.

FROM " A FABLE FOR CRITICS."

THERE is Lowell, who 's striving Parnassus to
climb
With a whole bale of *isms* tied together with
rhyme.
He might get on alone, spite of brambles and
boulders,
But he can't with that bundle he has on his
shoulders.
The top of the hill he will ne'er come nigh reaching
Till he learns the distinction 'twixt singing and
preaching;
His lyre has some chords that would ring pretty
well,
But he 'd rather by half make a drum of the
shell,
And rattle away till he 's old as Methusalem,
At the head of a march to the last new Jerusa-
lem.

JAMES RUSSELL LOWELL.

OUT FROM BEHIND THIS MASK.

TO CONFRONT HIS OWN PORTRAIT FOR " THE WOUND DRESSER " IN " LEAVES OF GRASS."

OUT from behind this bending, rough-cut mask,
These lights and shades, this drama of the whole,
This common curtain of the face, contained in me
for me, in you for you, in each for each.

(Tragedies, sorrows, laughter, tears—O heaven!
The passionate teeming plays this curtain hid!)
This glaze of God's serenest, purest sky,
This film of Satan's seething pit,
This heart's geography's map, this limitless small
    continent, this soundless sea;
Out from the convolutions of this globe,
This subtler astronomic orb than sun or moon,
    than Jupiter, Venus, Mars,
This condensation of the universe (nay, here the
    only universe,
Here the idea, all in this mystic handful wrapt);
These burned eyes, flashing to you, to pass to
    future time,
To launch and spin through space, revolving,
    sideling, from these to emanate
To you—whoe'er you are—a look.

A traveller of thoughts and years, of peace and
    war,
Of youth long sped and middling age declining
(As the first volume of a tale perused and laid
    away, and this the second,
Songs, ventures, speculations, presently to close),
Lingering a moment here and now, to you I op-
    posite turn,
As on the road, or at some crevice door by chance,
    or opened window,
Pausing, inclining, baring my head, you specially
    I greet,
To draw and clinch your soul for once insepara-
    bly with mine,
Then travel, travel on.

                    WALT WHITMAN.

MYSELF.

FROM " THE SONG OF MYSELF."

I CELEBRATE myself, and sing myself,
And what I assume you shall assume,
For every atom belonging to me as good belongs
　　　to you.
I loaf and invite my soul,
I lean and loaf at my ease observing a spear of
　　　summer grass.

My tongue, every atom of my blood, formed from
　　　this soil, this air,
Born here of parents born here from parents the
　　　same, and their parents the same,
I, now thirty-seven years old in perfect health
　　　begin,
Hoping to cease not till death.

Creeds and schools in abeyance,
Retiring back awhile sufficed at what they are, but
　　　never forgotten,
I harbor for good or bad, I permit to speak at
　　　every hazard,
Nature without check with original energy.

WALT WHITMAN.

HAWTHORNE.

HARP of New England Song,
That even in slumber trembled with the touch
Of poets who like the four winds from thee
    waken
All harmonies that to thy strings belong,—
Say, wilt thou blame the younger hands too much
Which from thy laurelled resting place have
    taken
Thee crowned one in their hold? There is a name
Should quicken thee! No carol Hawthorne
    sang,
Yet his articulate spirit, like thine own,
    Made answer, quick as flame,
To each breath of the shore from which he sprang,
And prose like his was poesy's high tone.

   .   .   .   .   .   °

    But he whose quickened eye
Saw through New England's life her inmost
    spirit,—
Her heart, and all the stays on which it leant,—
Returns not, since he laid the pencil by
Whose mystic touch none other shall inherit!
What though its work unfinished lies? Half-
    bent
The rainbow's arch fades out in upper air;
The shining cataract half-way down the height
Breaks into mist; the haunting strain, that fell
    On listeners unaware,
Ends incomplete, but through the starry night
The ear still waits for what it did not tell.

        EDMUND CLARENCE STEDMAN.

HAWTHORNE.

How beautiful it was, that one bright day
    In the long week of rain!
Though all its splendor could not chase away
    The omnipresent pain.

The lovely town was white with apple-blooms,
    And the great elms o'erhead
Dark shadows wove on their aerial looms
    Shot through with golden thread.

Across the meadows, by the gray old manse,
    The historic river flowed:
I was as one who wanders in a trance,
    Unconscious of his road.

The faces of familiar friends seemed strange;
    Their voices I could hear,
And yet the words they uttered seemed to change
    Their meaning to my ear.

For the one face I looked for was not there,
    The one low voice was mute;
Only an unseen presence filled the air,
    And baffled my pursuit.

Now I look back, and meadow, manse, and stream
    Dimly my thought defines;
I only see—a dream within a dream—
    The hill-top hearsed with pines.

I only hear above his place of rest
    Their tender undertone,
The infinite longings of a troubled breast,
    The voice so like his own.

There in seclusion, and remote from men,
    The wizard hand lies cold,
Which at its topmost speed let fall the pen
    And left the tale half told.

Ah! who shall lift that wand of magic power,
    And the lost clew regain?
The unfinished window in Aladdin's tower
    Unfinished must remain!
           HENRY WADSWORTH LONGFELLOW.

HARRIET BEECHER STOWE.

She told the story, and the whole world wept
At wrongs and cruelties it had not known
But for this fearless woman's voice alone.
She spoke to consciences that long had slept:
Her message, Freedom's clear reveille, swept
From heedless hovel to complacent throne.
Command and prophecy were in the tone,
And from its sheath the sword of justice leapt.
Around two peoples swelled a fiery wave,
But both came forth transfigured from the flame.
Blest be the hand that dared be strong to save,
And blest be she who in our weakness came—
Prophet and priestess! At one stroke she gave
A race to freedom and herself to fame.
           PAUL LAWRENCE DUNBAR.

TO HENRY WADSWORTH LONGFELLOW.

ON HIS BIRTHDAY, 27TH FEBRUARY, 1867.

I NEED not praise the sweetness of his song,
  Where limpid verse to limpid verse succeeds
Smooth as our Charles, when, fearing lest he
      wrong
The new moon's mirrored skiff, he slides along,
  Full without noise, and whispers in his reeds.

With loving breath of all the winds his name
  Is blown about the world, but to his friends
A sweeter secret hides behind his fame,
And Love steals shyly through the loud acclaim
  To murmur a *God bless you!* and there ends.

As I muse backward up the checkered years,
  Wherein so much was given, so much was lost,
Blessings in both kinds, such as cheapen tears—
But hush! this is not for profaner ears;
  Let them drink molten pearls nor dream the
      cost.

Some suck up poison from a sorrow's core,
  As naught but nightshade grew upon earth's
      ground;
Love turned all his to heart's-ease, and the more
Fate tried his bastions, she but forced a door,
  Leading to sweeter manhood and more sound.

Even as a wind-waved fountain's swaying shade
   Seems of mixed race, a gray wraith shot with
      sun,
So through his trial faith translucent rayed,
Till darkness, half disnatured so, betrayed
   A heart of sunshine that would fain o'errun.

Surely if skill in song the shears may stay,
   And of its purpose cheat the charmed abyss,
If our poor life be lengthened by a lay,
He shall not go, although his presence may,
   And the next age in praise shall double this.

Long days be his, and each as lusty-sweet
   As gracious natures find his song to be;
May Age steal on with softly cadenced feet
Falling in music, as for him were meet
   Whose choicest verse is harsher-toned than he.
               JAMES RUSSELL LOWELL.

LONGFELLOW.

IN MEMORIAM.

Nec turpem senectam
Degere, nec cithara carentem.

"NOT to be tuneless in old age!"
Ah! surely blest his pilgrimage,
   Who, in his winter's snow,
Still sings with note as sweet and clear
As in the morning of the year
   When the first violets blow!

Blest!—but more blest, whom summer's heat,
Whom spring's impulsive stir and beat,
　Have taught no feverish lure;
Whose Muse, benignant and serene,
Still keeps his autumn chaplet green
　Because his verse is pure!

Lie calm, O white and laureate head!
Lie calm, O Dead, that art not dead,
　Since from the voiceless grave
Thy voice shall speak to old and young
While song yet speaks our English tongue
　By Charles' or Thamis' wave.

AUSTIN DOBSON.

HOUSE.

Shall I sonnet-sing you about myself?
　Do I live in a house you would like to see?
Is it scant of gear, has it store of pelf?
　" Unlock my heart with a sonnet-key? "

Invite the world, as my betters have done?
　" Take notice: this building remains on view,
Its suites of reception every one,
　Its private apartment and bedroom too;

" For a ticket, apply to the Publisher."
　No: thanking the public, I must decline.
A peep through my window, if folk prefer;
　But please you, no foot over threshold of mine!

I have mixed with a crowd and heard free talk
　In a foreign land where an earthquake chanced

And a house stood gaping, naught to balk
Man's eye wherever he gazed or glanced.

The whole of the frontage shaven sheer,
    The inside gaped: exposed to day,
Right and wrong and common and queer,
    Bare, as the palm of your hand, it lay.

The owner? Oh, he had been crushed, no doubt!
    " Odd tables and chairs for a man of wealth!
What a parcel of musty old books about!
    He smoked,—no wonder he lost his health!

" I doubt if he bathed before he dressed.
    A braisier?—the pagan, he burned perfumes!
You see it is proved, what the neighbors guessed:
    His wife and himself had separate rooms."

Friends, the goodman of the house at least
    Kept house to himself till an earthquake came:
'T is the fall of its frontage permits you feast
    On the inside arrangement you praise or blame.

Outside should suffice for evidence:
    And whoso desires to penetrate
Deeper, must dive by the spirit sense—
    No optics like yours, at any rate!

" Hoity-toity! A street to explore,
    Your house the exception! ' *With this same
        key*
Shakespeare unlocked his heart,' once more!"
    Did Shakespeare? If so, the less Shakespeare
        he!

                    ROBERT BROWNING.

PERSONAL: MISCELLANEOUS.

ART CRITICISM.

First bring me Raffael, who alone hath seen
In all her purity heaven's virgin queen,
Alone hath felt true beauty; bring me then
Titian, ennobler of the noblest men;
And next the sweet Correggio, nor chastise
His little Cupids for those wicked eyes.
I want not Rubens's pink puffy bloom,
Nor Rembrandt's glimmer in a dusty room.
With those, and Poussin's nymph-frequented
     woods,
His templed heights and long-drawn solitudes,
I am content, yet fain would look abroad
On one warm sunset of Ausonian Claude.

WALTER SAVAGE LANDOR.

ANNE HATHAWAY.

TO THE IDOL OF MY EYE AND DELIGHT OF MY HEART,
ANNE HATHAWAY.

Would ye be taught, ye feathered throng,
With love's sweet notes to grace your song,
To pierce the heart with thrilling lay,
Listen to mine Anne Hathaway!

She hath a way to sing so clear,
Phœbus might wondering stop to hear.
To melt the sad, make blithe the gay,
And nature charm, Anne hath a way;
    She hath a way,
    Anne Hathaway;
To breathe delight Anne hath a way.

When Envy's breath and rancorous tooth
Do soil and bite fair worth and truth,
And merit to distress betray,
To soothe the heart Anne hath a way;
She hath a way to chase despair,
To heal all grief, to cure all care,
Turn foulest night to fairest day.
Thou know'st, fond heart, Anne hath a way;
    She hath a way,
    Anne Hathaway;
To make grief bliss, Anne hath a way.

Talk not of gems, the orient list,
The diamond, topaz, amethyst,
The emerald mild, the ruby gay;
Talk of my gem, Anne Hathaway!
She hath a way, with her bright eye,
Their various lustres to defy,—
The jewels she, and the foil they,
So sweet to look Anne hath a way;
    She hath a way,
    Anne Hathaway;
To shame bright gems, Anne hath a way.

But were it to my fancy given
To rate her charms, I 'd call them heaven;

For, though a mortal made of clay,
Angels must love Anne Hathaway;
She hath a way so to control,
To rapture, the imprisoned soul,
And sweetest heaven on earth display,
That to be heaven Anne hath a way;
   She hath a way,
   Anne Hathaway;
To be heaven's self, Anne hath a way.

ANONYMOUS.*

THE POET'S FRIEND.

[LORD BOLINGBROKE.]

FROM " AN ESSAY ON MAN," EPISTLE IV.

COME then, my friend! my genius! come along;
O master of the poet, and the song!
And while the muse now stoops, or now ascends,
To man's low passions, or their glorious ends,
Teach me, like thee, in various nature wise,
To fall with dignity, with temper rise;
Formed by thy converse happily to steer
From grave to gay, from lively to severe;
Correct with spirit, eloquent with ease,
Intent to reason, or polite to please.
O, while along the stream of time thy name
Expanded flies, and gathers all its fame;
Say, shall my little bark attendant sail,
Pursue the triumph, and partake the gale?
When statesmen, heroes, kings, in dust repose,

* This poem has sometimes, but without much reason, been attributed to Shakespeare.

Whose sons shall blush their fathers were thy
    foes,
Shall then this verse to future age pretend
Thou wert my guide, philosopher, and friend!
That, urged by thee, I turned the tuneful art
From sounds to things, from fancy to the heart:
For wit's false mirror held up Nature's light;
Showed erring pride, WHATEVER IS, IS RIGHT.
                    ALEXANDER POPE.

A BARD'S EPITAPH.

Is there a whim-inspirèd fool,
Owre fast for thought, owre hot for rule,
Owre blate* to seek, owre proud to snool;†
      Let him draw near,
And owre this grassy heap sing dool,
      And drap a tear.

Is there a bard of rustic song,
Who, noteless, steals the crowd among,
That weekly this area throng;
      O, pass not by;
But, with a frater-feeling strong,
      Here heave a sigh!

Is there a man whose judgment clear
Can others teach the course to steer,
Yet runs himself life's mad career,
      Wild as the wave;
Here pause, and, through the starting tear,
      Survey this grave.

    * Bashful.   † Tamely submit.

The poor inhabitant below
Was quick to learn and wise to know,
And keenly felt the friendly glow,
 And sober flame;
But thoughtless follies laid him low,
 And stained his name!

Reader, attend,—whether thy soul
Soars fancy's flights beyond the pole,
Or darkly grubs this earthly hole,
 In low pursuit;
Know, prudent, cautious self-control
 Is wisdom's root.

ROBERT BURNS.

CHOPIN.

I.

A DREAM of interlinking hands, of feet
 Tireless to spin the unseen, fairy woof
Of the entangling waltz. Bright eyebeams meet,
 Gay laughter echoes from the vaulted roof.
Warm perfumes rise; the soft unflickering glow
 Of branching lights sets off the changeful
  charms
Of glancing gems, rich stuffs, the dazzling snow
 Of necks unkerchieft, and bare, clinging arms.
Hark to the music! How beneath the strain
 Of reckless revelry, vibrates and sobs
One fundamental chord of constant pain,
 The pulse-beat of the poet's heart that throbs.
So yearns, though all the dancing waves rejoice,
The troubled sea's disconsolate, deep voice.

II.

Who shall proclaim the golden fable false
  Of Orpheus' miracles? This subtle strain
  Above our prose world's sordid loss and gain
Lightly uplifts us. With the rhythmic waltz,
The lyric prelude, the nocturnal song
  Of love and languor, varied visions rise,
  That melt and blend to our enchanted eyes.
The Polish poet who sleeps silenced long,
  The seraph-souled musician, breathes again
  Eternal eloquence, immortal pain.
Revived the exalted face we know so well,
  The illuminated eyes, the fragile frame,
  Slowly consuming with its inward flame—
We stir not, speak not, lest we break the spell.

III.

A voice was needed, sweet and true and fine
  As the sad spirit of the evening breeze,
Throbbing with human passion, yet divine
  As the wild bird's untutored melodies.
A voice for him 'neath twilight heavens dim,
  Who mourneth for his dead, while round him
      fall
The wan and noiseless leaves. A voice for him
  Who sees the first green sprout, who hears
      the call
Of the first robin on the first spring day.
  A voice for all whom Fate hath set apart,
Who, still misprized, must perish by the way,
  Longing with love, for that they lack the art
Of their own soul's expression. For all these
Sing the unspoken hope, the vague, sad reveries.

IV.

Then Nature shaped a poet's heart,—a lyre
    From out whose chords the slightest breeze
      that blows
Drew trembling music, wakening sweet desire.
    How shall she cherish him? Behold! she
      throws
This precious, fragile treasure in the whirl
    Of seething passions: he is scourged and
      stung;
Must dive in storm-vext seas, if but one pearl
    Of art or beauty therefrom may be wrung.
No pure-browed pensive nymph his Muse shall be:
    An Amazon of thought with sovereign eyes,
    Whose kiss was poison, man-brained, worldly-
      wise,
Inspired that elfin, delicate harmony.
    Rich gain for us! But with him is it well?—
    The poet who must sound earth, heaven, and
      hell!

EMMA LAZARUS.

THE PRAYER OF AGASSIZ.

On the isle of Penikese,
Ringed about by sapphire seas,
Fanned by breezes salt and cool,
Stood the Master with his school.
Over sails that not in vain
Wooed the west-wind's steady strain,
Line of coast that low and far
Stretched its undulating bar,

Wings aslant along the rim
Of the waves they stooped to skim,
Rock and isle and glistening bay,
Fell the beautiful white day.

Said the Master to the youth:
" We have come in search of truth,
Trying with uncertain key
Door by door of mystery;
We are reaching, through His laws,
To the garment-hem of Cause,
Him, the endless, unbegun,
The Unnameable, the One,
Light of all our light the Source,
Life of life, and Force of force.
As with fingers of the blind,
We are groping here to find
What the hieroglyphics mean
Of the Unseen in the seen,
What the Thought which underlies
Nature's masking and disguise,
What it is that hides beneath
Blight and bloom and birth and death.
By past efforts unavailing,
Doubt and error, loss and failing,
Of our weakness made aware,
On the threshold of our task
Let us light and guidance ask,
Let us pause in silent prayer!"

Then the Master in his place
Bowed his head a little space,
And the leaves by soft airs stirred,
Lapse of wave and cry of bird,

Left the solemn hush unbroken
Of that wordless prayer unspoken,
While its wish, on earth unsaid,
Rose to heaven interpreted.
As in life's best hours we hear
By the spirit's finer ear
His low voice within us, thus
The All-Father heareth us;
And his holy ear we pain
With our noisy words and vain.
Not for him our violence,
Storming at the gates of sense;
His the primal language, his
The eternal silences!
Even the careless heart was moved,
And the doubting gave assent,
With a gesture reverent,
To the Master well-beloved.
As thin mists are glorified
By the light they cannot hide,
All who gazed upon him saw,
Through its veil of tender awe,
How his face was still uplit
By the old sweet look of it,
Hopeful, trustful, full of cheer,
And the love that casts out fear.
Who the secret may declare
Of that brief, unuttered prayer?
Did the shade before him come
Of the inevitable doom,
Of the end of earth so near,
And Eternity's new year?

In the lap of sheltering seas
Rests the isle of Penikese;
But the lord of the domain
Comes not to his own again:
Where the eyes that follow fail,
On a vaster sea his sail
Drifts beyond our beck and hail!
Other lips within its bound
Shall the laws of life expound;
Other eyes from rock and shell
Read the world's old riddles well;
But when breezes light and bland
Blow from Summer's blossomed land,
When the air is glad with wings,
And the blithe song-sparrow sings,
Many an eye with his still face
Shall the living ones displace,
Many an ear the word shall seek
He alone could fitly speak.
And one name forevermore
Shall be uttered o'er and o'er
By the waves that kiss the shore,
By the curlew's whistle, sent
Down the cool, sea-scented air;
In all voices known to her
Nature own her worshipper,
Half in triumph, half lament.
Thither love shall tearful turn,
Friendship pause uncovered there,
And the wisest reverence learn
From the Master's silent prayer.

JOHN GREENLEAF WHITTIER.

KANE.

DIED FEBRUARY 16, 1857.

ALOFT upon an old basaltic crag,
　　Which, scalped by keen winds that defend the
　　　　Pole,
　　Gazes with dead face on the seas that roll
Around the secret of the mystic zone,
A mighty nation's star-bespangled flag
　　　　Flutters alone,
And underneath, upon the lifeless front
　　Of that drear cliff, a simple name is traced;
Fit type of him who, famishing and gaunt,
　　But with a rocky purpose in his soul,
　　　　Breasted the gathering snows,
　　　　Clung to the drifting floes,
　　By want beleaguered, and by winter chased,
Seeking the brother lost amid that frozen waste.

Not many months ago we greeted him,
　　Crowned with the icy honors of the North,
　　Across the land his hard-won fame went forth,
And Maine's deep woods were shaken limb by
　　　　limb.
His own mild Keystone State, sedate and prim,
　　Burst from decorous quiet, as he came.
　　Hot Southern lips, with eloquence aflame,
Sounded in triumph. Texas, wild and grim,
Proffered its horny hand. The large-lunged West,
　　　　From out his giant breast,

Yelled its frank welcome. And from main to
    main
    Jubilant to the sky,
    Thundered the mighty cry,
      HONOR TO KANE!

In vain,—in vain beneath his feet we flung
    The reddening roses! All in vain we poured
    The golden wine, and round the shining board
Sent the toast circling, till the rafters rung
    With the thrice-tripled honors of the feast!
Scarce the buds wilted and the voice ceased
Ere the pure light that sparkled in his eyes,
Bright as auroral fires in Southern skies,
    Faded and faded! And the brave young heart
That the relentless Arctic winds had robbed
Of all its vital heat, in that long quest
For the lost captain, now within his breast
    More and more faintly throbbed.
His was the victory; but as his grasp
Closed on the laurel crown with eager clasp,
    Death launched a whistling dart;
And ere the thunders of applause were done
His bright eyes closed forever on the sun!
Too late,—too late the splendid prize he won
In the Olympic race of Science and of Art!
Like to some shattered berg that, pale and lone,
Drifts from the white North to a Tropic zone,
    And in the burning day
    Wastes peak by peak away,
    Till on some rosy even
It dies with sunlight blessing it; so he
Tranquilly floated to a Southern sea,
    And melted into heaven!

He needs no tears who lived a noble life!
 We will not weep for him who died so well;
 But we will gather round the hearth, and tell
     The story of his strife;
     Such homage suits him well,
Better than funeral pomp or passing bell!

What tale of peril and self-sacrifice!
Prisoned amid the fastnesses of ice,
 With hunger howling o'er the wastes of snow!
 Night length'ning into months; the ravenous
     floe
Crunching the massive ships, as the white bear
Crunches his prey. The insufficient share
     Of loathsome food;
The lethargy of famine; the despair
 Urging to labor, nervelessly pursued;
 Toil done with skinny arms, and faces hued
Like pallid masks, while dolefully behind
Glimmered the fading embers of a mind!
That awful hour, when through the prostrate
     band
Delirium stalked, laying his burning hand
 Upon the ghastly foreheads of the crew;
 The whispers of rebellion, faint and few
 At first, but deepening ever till they grew
Into black thoughts of murder,—such the throng
Of horrors bound the hero. High the song
Should be that hymns the noble part he played!
Sinking himself, yet ministering aid
 To all around him. By a mighty will
 Living defiant of the wants that kill,
Because his death would seal his comrades' fate;
 Cheering with ceaseless and inventive skill

Those polar waters, dark and desolate.
Equal to every trial, every fate,
  He stands, until spring, tardy with relief,
    Unlocks the icy gate,
And the pale prisoners thread the world once
    more,
To the steep cliffs of Greenland's pastoral shore
  Bearing their dying chief!

Time was when he should gain his spurs of gold!
  From royal hands, who wooed the knightly
      state;
The knell of old formalities is tolled,
  And the world's knights are now self-conse-
      crate.
No grander episode doth chivalry hold
  In all its annals, back to Charlemagne,
  Than that lone vigil of unceasing pain,
Faithfully kept through hunger and through cold,
  By the good Christian knight, Elisha Kane!

FITZ-JAMES O'BRIEN.

II.

NATURE AND ART.

ADAM AND EVE.

FROM " PARADISE LOST," BOOK IV.

Two of far nobler shape, erect and tall,
Godlike erect, with native honor clad
In naked majesty, seemed lords of all:
And worthy seemed; for in their looks divine
The image of their glorious Maker shone,
Truth, wisdom, sanctitude severe and pure,
(Severe, but in true filial freedom placed,)
Whence true authority in men; though both
Not equal, as their sex not equal, seemed;
For contemplation he and valor formed;
For softness she and sweet attractive grace;
He for God only, she for God in him:
His fair large front and eye sublime declared
Absolute rule; and hyacinthine locks
Round from his parted forelock manly hung
Clustering, but not beneath his shoulders broad;
She, as a veil, down to the slender waist
Her unadornèd golden tresses wore
Dishevelled, but in wanton ringlets waved
As the vine curls her tendrils; which implied
Subjection, but required with gentle sway,

124

And by her yielded, by him best received,
Yielded with coy submission, modest pride,
And sweet, reluctant, amorous delay.

.   .   .   .   .   .

So passed they naked on, nor shunned the sight
Of God or angel; for they thought no ill:
So hand in hand they passed, the loveliest pair,
That ever since in love's embraces met:
Adam the goodliest man of men since born
His sons, the fairest of her daughters Eve.
Under a tuft of shade that on a green
Stood whispering soft, by a fresh fountain side
They sat them down: and, after no more toil
Of their sweet gardening labor than sufficed
To recommend cool Zephyr, and made ease
More easy, wholesome thirst and appetite
More grateful, to their supper-fruits they fell,
Nectarine fruits which the compliant boughs
Yielded them, sidelong as they sat recline
On the soft downy banks damasked with flowers:
The savory pulp they chew, and in the rind,
Still as they thirsted, scoop the brimming stream;
Nor gentle purpose, nor endearing smiles
Wanted, nor youthful dalliance, as beseems
Fair couple, linked in happy nuptial league,
Alone as they. About them frisking played
All beasts of the Earth, since wild, and of all
    chase
In wood or wilderness, forest or den;
Sporting the lion ramped, and in his paw
Dandled the kid; bears, tigers, ounces, pards,
Gambolled before them; the unwieldy elephant,

To make them mirth, used all his might, and
      wreathed
His lithe proboscis; close the serpent sly,
Insinuating, wove with Gordian twine
His braided train, and of his fatal guile
Gave proof unheeded; others on the grass
Couched, and now filled with pasture gazing sat,
Or bedward ruminating; for the Sun,
Declined, was hastening now with prone career
To the ocean isles, and in the ascending scale
Of Heaven the stars that usher evening rose.

MILTON.

SEVEN AGES OF MAN.

FROM " AS YOU LIKE IT," ACT II. SC. 7.

                  ALL the world's a stage,
And all the men and women merely players:
They have their exits and their entrances;
And one man in his time plays many parts,
His Acts being seven ages. At first the Infant,
Mewling and puking in the nurse's arms.
Then the whining School-boy, with his satchel
And shining morning face, creeping like snail
Unwillingly to school. And then the Lover,
Sighing like furnace, with a woful ballad
Made to his mistress' eyebrow. Then a Soldier,
Full of strange oaths, and bearded like the pard;
Jealous in honor, sudden and quick in quarrel,
Seeking the bubble reputation
Even in the cannon's mouth. And then the Jus-
      tice,
In fair round belly with good capon lined,

With eyes severe, and beard of formal cut,
Full of wise saws and modern instances,—
And so he plays his part. The sixth age shifts
Into the lean and slippered Pantaloon,
With spectacles on nose, and pouch on side;
His youthful hose, well saved, a world too wide
For his shrunk shank; and his big manly voice,
Turning again toward childish treble, pipes
And whistles in his sound. Last scene of all,
That ends this strange eventful history,
Is second childishness, and mere oblivion,—
Sans teeth, sans eyes, sans taste, sans everything.

SHAKESPEARE.

CLEOPATRA.

FROM " ANTONY AND CLEOPATRA," ACT II. SC. 2.

ENOBARBUS.—The barge she sat in, like a bur-
nished throne,
Burned on the water: the poop was beaten gold;
Purple the sails, and so perfumèd that
The winds were lovesick with them; the oars were
silver,
Which to the tune of flutes kept stroke, and made
The water, which they beat, to follow faster,
As amorous of their strokes. For her own person,
It beggared all description: she did lie
In her pavilion (cloth-of-gold of tissue),
O'erpicturing that Venus, where we see
The fancy outwork nature; on each side her
Stood pretty dimpled boys, like smiling Cupids,
With divers-colored fans, whose wind did seem

To glow the delicate cheeks which they did cool,
And what they undid, did.

AGRIPPA.—   O, rare for Antony!

ENO.—Her gentlewomen, like the Nereides,
So many mermaids, tended her i' the eyes,
And made their bends adornings: at the helm
A seeming mermaid steers; the silken tackle
Swell with the touches of those flower-soft hands,
That yarely frame the office. From the barge
A strange invisible perfume hits the sense
Of the adjacent wharfs. The city cast
Her people out upon her; and Antony,
Enthronèd in the market-place, did sit alone,
Whistling to the air; which, but for vacancy,
Had gone to gaze on Cleopatra too,
And made a gap in nature.

AGR.—   Rare Egyptian!

ENO.—Upon her landing, Antony sent to her,
Invited her to supper: she replied,
It should be better he became her guest,
Which she entreated. Our courteous Antony,
Whom ne'er the word of " No " woman heard
    speak,
Being barbered ten times o'er, goes to the feast;
And, for his ordinary, pays his heart
For what his eyes eat only.

AGR.—   Royal wench!

        .   .   .   .   .

MECÆNAS.—Now Antony must leave her ut-
    terly.

ENO.—Never; he will not:
Age cannot wither her, nor custom stale
Her infinite variety: other women cloy
The appetites they feed, but she makes hungry

Where most she satisfies. For vilest things
Become themselves in her; that the holy priests
Bless her when she is riggish.

SHAKESPEARE.

TO IANTHE, SLEEPING.

FROM " QUEEN MAB," I.

How wonderful is Death!
Death and his brother Sleep!
One, pale as yonder waning moon,
    With lips of lurid blue;
The other, rosy as the morn
When, throned on ocean's wave,
    It blushes o'er the world:
Yet both so passing wonderful!

Hath then the gloomy Power,
Whose reign is in the tainted sepulchres,
    Seized on her sinless soul?
Must then that peerless form
Which love and admiration cannot view
Without a beating heart, those azure veins
Which steal like streams along a field of snow,
    That lovely outline, which is fair
    As breathing marble, perish?
Must putrefaction's breath
Leave nothing of this heavenly sight
    But loathsomeness and ruin?
Spare nothing but a gloomy theme,
On which the lightest heart might moralize?
    Or is it only a sweet slumber

Stealing o'er sensation,
Which the breath of roseate morning
    Chaseth into darkness?
    Will Ianthe wake again,
And give that faithful bosom joy,
Whose sleepless spirit waits to catch
Light, life, and rapture from her smile?

    Yes! she will wake again,
Although her glowing limbs are motionless,
    And silent those sweet lips,
    Once breathing eloquence
That might have soothed a tiger's rage,
Or thawed the cold heart of a conqueror.
    Her dewy eyes are closed,
    And on their lids, whose texture fine
    Scarce hides the dark blue orbs beneath,
    The baby Sleep is pillowed:
    Her golden tresses shade
    The bosom's stainless pride,
    Curling like tendrils of the parasite
    Around a marble column.
    .   .   .   .   .

A gentle start convulsed Ianthe's frame:
Her veiny eyelids quietly unclosed;
Moveless awhile the dark blue orbs remained.
She looked around in wonder, and beheld
Henry, who kneeled in silence by her couch,
Watching her sleep with looks of speechless love,
    And the bright-beaming stars
    That through the casement shone.

PERCY BYSSHE SHELLEY.

FREEDOM IN DRESS.

FROM "EPICŒNE; OR, THE SILENT WOMAN," ACT I.
SC. 1.

STILL to be neat, still to be drest,
As you were going to a feast;
Still to be powdered, still perfumed,—
Lady, it is to be presumed,
Though art's hid causes are not found,
All is not sweet, all is not sound.

Give me a look, give me a face,
That makes simplicity a grace;
Robes loosely flowing, hair as free,—
Such sweet neglect more taketh me
Than all the adulteries of art:
They strike mine eyes, but not my heart.

BEN JONSON.

COUSIN LUCRECE.

HERE where the curfew
Still, they say, rings,
Time rested long ago,
Folding his wings;
Here, on old Norwich's
Out-along road,
Cousin Lucretia
Had her abode.

Norridge, not Nor-wich
(See Mother Goose),

Good enough English
    For a song's use.
Side and roof shingled,
    All of a piece,
Here was the cottage
    Of Cousin Lucrece.

Living forlornly
    On nothing a year,
How she took comfort
    Does not appear;
How kept her body,
    On what they gave,
Out of the poor-house,
    Out of the grave.

Highly connected?
    Straight as the Nile
Down from " the Gard'ners "
    Of Gardiner's Isle;
(Three bugles, chevron gules,
    Hand upon sword),
Great-great-granddaughter
    Of the third lord.

Bent almost double,
    Deaf as a witch,
Gout her chief trouble—
    Just as if rich;
Vain of her ancestry,
    Mouth all agrin,
Nose half-way meeting her
    Sky-pointed chin.

Ducking her forehead-top,
　　Wrinkled and bare,
With a colonial
　　Furbelowed air
Greeting her next of kin,
　　Nephew and niece,—
Foolish old, prating old
　　Cousin Lucrece.

Once every year she had
　　All she could eat:
Turkey and cranberries,
　　Pudding and sweet;
Every Thanksgiving,
　　Up to the great
House of her kinsman, was
　　Driven in state.

Oh, what a sight to see
　　Rigged in her best!
Wearing the famous gown
　　Drawn from her chest,—
Worn, ere King George's reign
　　Here chanced to cease,
Once by a forbear
　　Of Cousin Lucrece.

Damask brocaded,
　　Cut very low;
Short sleeves and finger-mitts
　　Fit for a show;
Palsied neck shaking her
　　Rust-yellow curls

Rattling its roundabout
    String of mock pearls.

Over her noddle,
    Draggled and stark,
Two ostrich feathers—
    Brought from the ark.
Shoes of frayed satin,
    All heel and toe,
On her poor crippled feet
    Hobbled below.

My! how the Justice's
    Sons and their wives
Laughed; while the little folk
    Ran for their lives,
Asking if beldames
    Out of the past,
Old fairy godmothers,
    Always could last?

No! One Thanksgiving,
    Bitterly cold,
After they took her home
    (Ever so old),
In her great chair she sank,
    There to find peace;
Died in her ancient dress—
    Poor old Lucrece.

        EDMUND CLARENCE STEDMAN.

DELIGHT IN DISORDER.

A SWEET disorder in the dress
Kindles in clothes a wantonness;
A lawn about the shoulders thrown
Into a fine distraction;
An erring lace, which here and there
Inthralls the crimson stomacher;
A cuff neglectful, and thereby
Ribbons to flow confusedly;
A winning wave, deserving note,
In the tempestuous petticoat;
A careless shoestring, in whose tie
I see a wild civility;—
Do more bewitch me than when art
Is too precise in every part.

ROBERT HERRICK.

THE TOILET.

FROM " THE RAPE OF THE LOCK," CANTO I.

AND now, unveiled, the toilet stands displayed,
Each silver vase in mystic order laid.
First, robed in white, the nymph intent adores,
With head uncovered, the cosmetic powers.
A heavenly image in the glass appears,
To that she bends, to that her eyes she rears;
The inferior priestess, at her altar's side,
Trembling begins the sacred rites of pride.
Unnumbered treasures ope at once, and here
The various offerings of the world appear;

For each she nicely culls with curious toil,
And decks the goddess with the glittering spoil.
This casket India's glowing gems unlocks,
And all Arabia breathes from yonder box.
The tortoise here and elephant unite,
Transformed to combs, the speckled and the
  white.
Here files of pins extend their shining rows,
Puffs, powders, patches, bibles, billets-doux.
Now awful beauty puts on all its arms;
The fair each moment rises in her charms,
Repairs her smiles, awakens every grace,
And calls forth all the wonders of her face;
Sees by degrees a purer blush arise,
And keener lightnings quicken in her eyes.
The busy sylphs surround their darling care,
These set the head, and those divide the hair,
Some fold the sleeve, while others plait the gown;
And Betty's praised for labors not her own.

ALEXANDER POPE.

ODE ON A GRECIAN URN.

THOU still unravished bride of quietness!
  Thou foster-child of Silence and slow Time,
Sylvan historian, who canst thus express
  A flowery tale more sweetly than our rhyme:
What leaf-fringed legend haunts about thy shape
  Of deities or mortals, or of both,
    In Tempe or the dales of Arcady?
  What men or gods are these? What maidens
    loath?

What mad pursuit? What struggles to escape?
  What pipes and timbrels? What wild ecstasy?

Heard melodies are sweet, but those unheard
  Are sweeter; therefore, ye soft pipes, play on;
Not to the sensual ear, but, more endeared,
  Pipe to the spirit ditties of no tone.
Fair youth beneath the trees, thou canst not leave
  Thy song, nor ever can those trees be bare.
  Bold lover, never, never canst thou kiss,
Though winning near the goal,—yet do not
      grieve :
    She cannot fade, though thou hast not thy
      bliss;
  Forever wilt thou love, and she be fair!

Ah, happy, happy boughs! that cannot shed
  Your leaves, nor ever bid the spring adieu;
And happy melodist, unwearièd,
  Forever piping songs forever new;
More happy love! more happy, happy love!
  Forever warm and still to be enjoyed,
    Forever panting and forever young;
All breathing human passion far above,
  That leaves a heart high-sorrowful and cloyed,
    A burning forehead, and a parching tongue.

Who are these coming to the sacrifice?
  To what green altar, O mysterious priest,
Lead'st thou that heifer lowing at the skies,
  And all her silken flanks with garlands drest?
What little town by river or sea-shore,
  Or mountain-built with peaceful citadel,
    Is emptied of its folk, this pious morn?

And, little town, thy streets forevermore
　Will silent be, and not a soul to tell
　Why thou art desolate can e'er return.

O Attic shape! Fair attitude! with brede
Of marble men and maidens overwrought,
With forest branches and the trodden weed;
　Thou, silent form! dost tease us out of thought
As doth eternity. Cold Pastoral!
　When old age shall this generation waste,
　　Thou shalt remain, in midst of other woe
　Than ours, a friend to man, to whom thou
　　　say'st,
" Beauty is truth, truth beauty,"—that is all
Ye know on earth, and all ye need to know.

JOHN KEATS.

LAUS VENERIS.

A PICTURE BY BURNE-JONES.

PALLID with too much longing,
　White with passion and prayer,
Goddess of love and beauty,
　She sits in the picture there,—

Sits with her dark eyes seeking
Something more subtle still
Than the old delights of loving
Her measureless days to fill.

She has loved and been loved so often
In her long, immortal years,

That she tires of the worn-out rapture,
  Sickens of hopes and fears.

No joys or sorrows move her,
  Done with her ancient pride;
For her head she found too heavy
  The crown she has cast aside.

Clothed in her scarlet splendor,
  Bright with her glory of hair,
Sad that she is not mortal,—
  Eternally sad and fair,

Longing for joys she knows not,
  Athirst with a vain desire,
There she sits in the picture,
  Daughter of foam and fire.

LOUISE CHANDLER MOULTON.

ON HEARING A LITTLE MUSIC-BOX.

Hallo!—what?—where, what can it be
That strikes up so deliciously?
I never in my life—what? no!
That little tin box playing so?
It really seemed as if a sprite
Had struck among us swift and light,
And come from some minuter star
To treat us with his pearl guitar.

Hark! It scarcely ends the strain,
But it gives it o'er again,
Lovely thing!—and runs along
Just as if it knew the song,

Touching out, smooth, clear and small,
Harmony, and shake, and all;
Now upon the treble lingering,
Dancing now as if 't were fingering,
And at last upon the close
Coming with serene repose.

O full of sweetness, crispness, ease,
Compound of lovely smallnesses,
Accomplished trifle,—tell us what
To call thee, and disgrace thee not!
Worlds of fancies come about us,
Thrill within, and glance without us.
Now we think that there must be
In thee some humanity,
Such a taste composed and fine
Smiles along that touch of thine.
Now we call thee heavenly rain,
For thy fresh continued strain;
Now a hail that on the ground
Splits into light leaps of sound;
Now the concert, neat and nice,
Of a pygmy paradise;
Sprinkles then from singing fountains;
Fairies heard on tops of mountains;
Nightingales endued with art,
Caught in listening to Mozart;
Stars that make a distant tinkling,
While their happy eyes are twinkling;
Sounds for scattered rills to flow to;
Music for the flowers to blow to.

LEIGH HUNT.

THOSE EVENING BELLS.

THOSE evening bells! those evening bells!
How many a tale their music tells
Of youth, and home, and that sweet time
When last I heard their soothing chime!

Those joyous hours are passed away;
And many a heart that then was gay
Within the tomb now darkly dwells,
And hears no more those evening bells.

And so 't will be when I am gone,—
That tuneful peal will still ring on;
While other bards shall walk these dells,
And sing your praise, sweet evening bells.

THOMAS MOORE.

THE BELLS.

HEAR the sledges with the bells—
Silver bells!
What a world of merriment their melody fore-
tells!
How they tinkle, tinkle, tinkle,
In the icy air of night!
While the stars that oversprinkle
All the heavens seem to twinkle
With a crystalline delight,—
Keeping time, time, time,
In a sort of Runic rhyme,

To the tintinnabulation that so musically wells
　　From the bells, bells, bells, bells,
　　　　Bells, bells, bells,—
　From the jingling and the tinkling of the bells.

　　Hear the mellow wedding bells—
　　　　Golden bells!
What a world of happiness their harmony fore-
　　　　tells!
　　Through the balmy air of night
　　How they ring out their delight!
　　　From the molten-golden notes,
　　　　And all in tune,
　　　What a liquid ditty floats
　To the turtle-dove that listens, while she gloats
　　　　On the moon!
　　O, from out the sounding cells,
What a gush of euphony voluminously wells!
　　　　How it swells!
　　　　How it dwells
　　On the Future! how it tells
　　Of the rapture that impels
　　To the swinging and the ringing
　　　Of the bells, bells, bells,
　　Of the bells, bells, bells, bells,
　　　　Bells, bells, bells,—
　To the rhyming and the chiming of the bells.

　　Hear the loud alarum bells—
　　　　Brazen bells!
What a tale of terror, now, their turbulency tells!
　　In the startled ear of night
　　How they scream out their affright!

Too much horrified to speak,
They can only shriek, shriek,
Out of tune,
In the clamorous appealing to the mercy of the
fire,
In a mad expostulation with the deaf and frantic
fire
Leaping higher, higher, higher,
With a desperate desire,
And a resolute endeavor,
Now—now to sit, or never,
By the side of the pale-faced moon.
O the bells, bells, bells,
What a tale their terror tells
Of despair!
How they clang and clash and roar!
What a horror they outpour
On the bosom of the palpitating air!
Yet the ear it fully knows,
By the twanging,
And the clanging,
How the danger ebbs and flows;
Yet the ear distinctly tells,
In the jangling,
And the wrangling,
How the danger sinks and swells,
By the sinking or the swelling in the anger of
the bells,—
Of the bells,—
Of the bells, bells, bells, bells,
Bells, bells, bells,—
In the clamor and the clangor of the bells!

Hear the tolling of the bells—
Iron bells!
What a world of solemn thought their monody
compels!
In the silence of the night,
How we shiver with affright
At the melancholy menace of their tone!
For every sound that floats
From the rust within their throats
Is a groan.
And the people—ah, the people—
They that dwell up in the steeple,
All alone,
And who tolling, tolling, tolling,
In that muffled monotone,
Feel a glory in so rolling
On the human heart a stone,—
They are neither man nor woman,—
They are neither brute nor human,—
They are ghouls:
And their king it is who tolls;
And he rolls, rolls, rolls,
Rolls,
A pæan from the bells!
And his merry bosom swells
With the pæan of the bells!
And he dances and he yells;
Keeping time, time, time,
In a sort of Runic rhyme,
To the pæan of the bells,—
Of the bells:
Keeping time, time, time,
In a sort of Runic rhyme,

To the throbbing of the bells,—
Of the bells, bells, bells,—
To the sobbing of the bells;
Keeping time, time, time,
As he knells, knells, knells,
In a happy Runic rhyme,
To the rolling of the bells,—
Of the bells, bells, bells,—
To the tolling of the bells,
Of the bells, bells, bells, bells—
Bells, bells, bells,—
To the moaning and the groaning of the bells.

EDGAR ALLAN POE.

THE BELLS OF SHANDON.

Sabbata pango ;
Funera plango ;
Solemnia clango.
—*Inscription on an Old Bell.*

WITH deep affection
And recollection
I often think on
Those Shandon bells,
Whose sounds so wild would,
In the days of childhood,
Fling round my cradle
Their magic spells.

On this I ponder
Where'er I wander,
And thus grow fonder,
Sweet Cork, of thee,—

With thy bells of Shandon,
That sound so grand on
The pleasant waters
    Of the river Lee.

I 've heard bells chiming
Full many a clime in,
Tolling sublime in
    Cathedral shrine,
While at a glib rate
Brass tongues would vibrate;
But all their music
    Spoke naught like thine.

For memory, dwelling
On each proud swelling
Of thy belfry, knelling
    Its bold notes free,
Made the bells of Shandon
Sound far more grand on
The pleasant waters
    Of the river Lee.

I 've heard bells tolling
" Old Adrian's Mole " in,
Their thunder rolling
    From the Vatican,—
And cymbals glorious
Swinging uproarious
In the gorgeous turrets
    Of Notre Dame;

But thy sounds were sweeter
Than the dome of Peter

Flings o'er the Tiber,
  Pealing solemnly.
O, the bells of Shandon
Sound far more grand on
The pleasant waters
  Of the river Lee.

There 's a bell in Moscow;
While on tower and kiosko
  In Saint Sophia
    The Turkman gets,
  And loud in air
  Calls men to prayer,
From the tapering summit
  Of tall minarets.

Such empty phantom
I freely grant them;
But there 's an anthem
  More dear to me,—
'T is the bells of Shandon,
That sound so grand on
The pleasant waters
  Of the river Lee.

FRANCIS MAHONY (*Father Prout*).

CITY BELLS.

FROM " THE LAY OF ST. ALOY'S."

LOUD and clear
From the Saint Nicholas tower, on the listening
      ear,
    With solemn swell,

The deep-toned bell
Flings to the gale a funeral knell;
And hark—at its sound,
As a cunning old hound,
When he opens, at once causes all the young
whelps
Of the cry to put in their less dignified yelps,
So the little bells all,
No matter how small,
From the steeples both inside and outside the
wall,
With bell-metal throat
Respond to the note,
And join the lament that a prelate so pious is
Forced thus to leave his disconsolate diocese,
Or, as Blois' Lord May'r
Is heard to declare,
"Should leave this here world for to go to that
there."

RICHARD HARRIS BARHAM.

THE CUCKOO CLOCK.

FROM " THE BIRTHDAY."

But chief—surpassing all—a cuckoo clock!
That crowning wonder! miracle of art!
How have I stood entranced uncounted minutes,
With held-in breath, and eyes intently fixed
On that small magic door, that when complete
The expiring hour—the irreversible—
Flew open with a startling suddenness
That, though expected, sent the rushing blood

In mantling flushes o'er my upturned face;
And as the bird, (that more than mortal fowl!)
With perfect mimicry of natural tone,
Note after note exact Time's message told,
How my heart's pulse kept time with the charmed
    voice !
And when it ceased made simultaneous pause
As the small door clapt to, and all was still.

            CAROLINE BOWLES SOUTHEY.

AN ETRUSCAN RING.

I.

WHERE, girt with orchard and with olive-yard,
The white hill-fortress glimmers on the hill,
Day after day an ancient goldsmith's skill
Guided the copper graver, tempered hard
By some lost secret, while he shaped the sard
Slowly to beauty, and his tiny drill,
Edged with corundum, ground its way until
The gem lay perfect for the ring to guard.
Then seeing the stone complete to his desire,
With mystic imagery carven thus,
And dark Egyptian symbols fabulous,
He drew through it the delicate golden wire,
And bent the fastening ; and the Etrurian sun
Sank behind Ilva, and the work was done.

II.

What dark-haired daughter of a Lucumo
Bore on her slim white finger to the grave
This the first gift her Tyrrhene lover gave,

Those five-and-twenty centuries ago?
What shadowy dreams might haunt it, lying low
So long, while kings and armies, wave on wave,
Above the rock-tomb's buried architrave
Went million-footed trampling to and fro?
Who knows? but well it is so frail a thing,
Unharmed by conquering Time's supremacy,
Still should be fair, though scarce less old than
    Rome.
Now once again at rest from wandering
Across the high Alps and the dreadful sea,
In utmost England let it find a home.

JOHN WILLIAM MACKAIL.

LEONARDO'S "MONNA LISA."

Make thyself known, Sibyl, or let despair
Of knowing thee be absolute : I wait
Hour-long and waste a soul. What word of fate
Hides 'twixt the lips which smile and still for-
    bear?
Secret perfection! Mystery too fair!
Tangle the sense no more, lest I should hate
The delicate tyranny, the inviolate
Poise of thy folded hands, the fallen hair.
Nay, nay,—I wrong thee with rough words; still
    be
Serene, victorious, inaccessible ;
Still smile but speak not ; lightest irony
Lurk ever 'neath thy eyelids' shadow ; still
O'ertop our knowledge ; Sphinx of Italy,
Allure us and reject us at thy will!

EDWARD DOWDEN.

THE HURRICANE.

Lord of the winds! I feel thee nigh,
I know thy breath in the burning sky!
And I wait, with a thrill in every vein,
For the coming of the hurricane!

And lo! on the wing of the heavy gales,
Through the boundless arch of heaven he sails.
Silent and slow, and terribly strong,
The mighty shadow is borne along,
Like the dark eternity to come;
While the world below, dismayed and dumb,
Through the calm of the thick hot atmosphere
Looks up at its gloomy folds with fear.

They darken fast; and the golden blaze
Of the sun is quenched in the lurid haze,
And he sends through the shade a funeral ray—
A glare that is neither night nor day,
A beam that touches, with hues of death,
The cloud above and the earth beneath.
To its covert glides the silent bird,
While the hurricane's distant voice is heard
Uplifted among the mountains round,
And the forests hear and answer the sound.

He is come! he is come! do ye not behold
His ample robes on the wind unrolled?
Giant of air! we bid thee hail!—
How his gray skirts toss in the whirling gale;
How his huge and writhing arms are bent
To clasp the zone of the firmament,

And fold at length, in their dark embrace,
From mountain to mountain the visible space!

Darker,—still darker! the whirlwinds bear
The dust of the plains to the middle air;
And hark to the crashing, long and loud,
Of the chariot of God in the thunder-cloud!
You may trace its path by the flashes that start
From the rapid wheels where'er they dart,
As the fire-bolts leap to the world below,
And flood the skies with a lurid glow.

What roar is that?—'t is the rain that breaks
In torrents away from the airy lakes,
Heavily poured on the shuddering ground,
And shedding a nameless horror round.
Ah! well-known woods, and mountains, and skies,
With the very clouds!—ye are lost to my eyes.
I seek ye vainly, and see in your place
The shadowy tempest that sweeps through space,
A whirling ocean that fills the wall
Of the crystal heaven, and buries all.
And I, cut off from the world, remain
Alone with the terrible hurricane.

WILLIAM CULLEN BRYANT.

MIST.

Low-anchored cloud,
Newfoundland air,
Fountain-head and source of rivers,
Dew-cloth, dream-drapery,
And napkin spread by fays;
Drifting meadow of the air,
Where bloom the daisied banks and violets
And in whose fenny labyrinth
The bittern booms and heron wades;
Spirit of lakes and seas and rivers,—
Bear only perfumes and the scent
Of healing herbs to just men's fields.

HENRY DAVID THOREAU.

THE COASTERS.

Overloaded, undermanned,
Trusting to a lee,
Playing I-spy with the land,
Jockeying the sea—
That's the way the Coaster goes,
Through calm and hurricane:
Everywhere the tide flows,
Everywhere the wind blows,
From Mexico to Maine.

O East and West! O North and South!
We ply along the shore,
From famous Fundy's foggy mouth,
From voes of Labrador;

Through pass and strait, on sound and sea,
  From port to port we stand—
The rocks of Race fade on our lee,
  We hail the Rio Grande.
Our sails are never lost to sight;
  On every gulf and bay
They gleam, in winter wind-cloud white,
  In summer rain-cloud gray.

We hold the coast with slippery grip;
  We dare from cape to cape:
Our leaden fingers feel the dip
  And trace the channel's shape.
We sail or bide as serves the tide;
  Inshore we cheat its flow,
And side by side at anchor ride
  When stormy head-winds blow.
We are the offspring of the shoal,
  The hucksters of the sea;
From custom theft and pilot toll
  Thank God that we are free.

Legging on and off the beach,
  Drifting up the strait,
Fluking down the river reach,
  Towing through the gate—
That 's the way the Coaster goes,
  Flirting with the gale:
Everywhere the tide flows,
Everywhere the wind blows,
  From York to Beavertail.

———

Here and there to get a load,
  Freighting anything;

Running off with spanker stowed,
Loafing wing-a-wing—
That's the way the Coaster goes,
Chumming with the land:
Everywhere the tide flows,
Everywhere the wind blows,
From Ray to Rio Grande.

We split the swell where rings the bell
On many a shallow's edge,
We take our flight past many a light
That guards the deadly ledge;
We greet Montauk across the foam,
We work the Vineyard Sound,
The Diamond sees us running home,
The Georges outward bound;
Absecom hears our canvas beat
When tacked off Brigantine;
We raise the Gulls with lifted sheet,
Pass wing-and-wing between.

Off Monomoy we fight the gale,
We drift off Sandy Key;
The watch of Fenwick sees our sail
Scud for Henlopen's lee.
With decks awash and canvas torn
We wallow up the Stream;
We drag dismasted, cargo borne,
And fright the ships of steam.
Death grips us with his frosty hands
In calm and hurricane;
We spill our bones on fifty sands
From Mexico to Maine.

Cargo reef in main and fore,
Manned by half a crew,
Romping up the weather shore,
Edging down the Blue—
That 's the way the Coaster goes,
Scouting with the lead:
Everywhere the tide flows,
Everywhere the wind blows,
From Cruz to Quoddy Head.
THOMAS FLEMING DAY.

SMOKE.

LIGHT-WINGED Smoke! Icarian bird,
Melting thy pinions in thy upward flight;
Lark without song, and messenger of dawn
Circling above the hamlets as thy nest;
Or else, departing dream, and shadowy form
Of midnight vision, gathering up thy skirts;
By night star-veiling, and by day
Darkening the light and blotting out the sun;
Go thou, my incense, upward from this hearth,
And ask the gods to pardon this clear flame.
HENRY DAVID THOREAU.

THE EVENING CLOUD.

A CLOUD lay cradled near the setting sun,
A gleam of crimson tinged its braided snow;
Long had I watched the glory moving on
O'er the still radiance of the lake below.
Tranquil its spirit seemed, and floated slow!
Even in its very motion there was rest;

While every breath of eve that chanced to blow
  Wafted the traveller to the beauteous west.
Emblem, methought, of the departed soul!
  To whose white robe the gleam of bliss is given,
And by the breath of mercy made to roll
  Right onwards to the golden gates of heaven,
Where to the eye of faith it peaceful lies,
And tells to man his glorious destinies.

JOHN WILSON (Christopher North).

A STILL DAY IN AUTUMN.

I LOVE to wander through the woodlands hoary
  In the soft light of an autumnal day,
When Summer gathers up her robes of glory,.
  And like a dream of beauty glides away.

How through each loved, familiar path she lin-
      gers,
  Serenely smiling through the golden mist,
Tinting the wild grape with her dewy fingers
  Till the cool emerald turns to amethyst;

Kindling the faint stars of the hazel, shining
  To light the gloom of Autumn's mouldering
      halls,
With hoary plumes the clematis entwining
  Where o'er the rock her withered garland falls.

Warm lights are on the sleepy uplands waning
  Beneath soft clouds along the horizon rolled,
Till the slant sunbeams through their fringes
      raining
  Bathe all the hills in melancholy gold.

The moist winds breathe of crispèd leaves and
    flowers
  In the damp hollows of the woodland sown,
Mingling the freshness of autumnal showers
  With spicy airs from cedarn alleys blown.

Beside the brook and on the umbered meadow,
  Where yellow fern-tufts fleck the faded ground,
With folded lids beneath their palmy shadow
  The gentian nods, in dewy slumbers bound.

Upon those soft, fringed lids the bee sits brood-
    ing,
  Like a fond lover loath to say farewell,
Or with shut wings, through silken folds intrud-
    ing,
  Creeps near her heart his drowsy tale to tell.

The little birds upon the hillside lonely
  Flit noiselessly along from spray to spray,
Silent as a sweet wandering thought that only
  Shows its bright wings and softly glides away.
           SARAH HELEN WHITMAN.

THE SUNSET CITY.

There's a city that lies in the Kingdom of
    Clouds,
  In the glorious country on high,
Which an azure and silvery curtain enshrouds,
  To screen it from mortal eye;

A city of temples and turrets of gold,
  That gleam by a sapphire sea,

Like jewels more splendid than earth may behold,
  Or are dreamed of by you and by me.

And about it are highlands of amber that reach
  Far away till they melt in the gloom;
And waters that hem an immaculate beach
  With fringes of luminous foam.

Aerial bridges of pearl there are,
  And belfries of marvellous shapes,
And lighthouses lit by the evening star,
  That sparkle on violet capes;

And hanging gardens that far away
  Enchantedly float aloof;
Rainbow pavilions in avenues gay,
  And banners of glorious woof!

When the Summer sunset's crimsoning fires
  Are aglow in the western sky,
The pilgrim discovers the domes and spires
  Of this wonderful city on high;

And gazing enrapt as the gathering shade
  Creeps over the twilight lea,
Sees palace and pinnacle totter and fade,
  And sink in the sapphire sea;

Till the vision loses by slow degrees
  The magical splendor it wore;
The silvery curtain is drawn, and he sees
  The beautiful city no more!

HENRY SYLVESTER CORNWELL.

III.

PLACES.

THE NILE.

It flows through old, hushed Ægypt and its
    sands,
  Like some grave, mighty thought threading a
    dream;
And times and things, as in that vision, seem
Keeping along it their eternal stands,—
Caves, pillars, pyramids, the shepherd bands
  That roamed through the young world, the
    glory extreme
Of high Sesostris, and that southern beam,
The laughing queen that caught the world's great
    hands.
Then comes a mightier silence, stern and strong,
As of a world left empty of its throng,
  And the void weighs on us; and then we wake,
And hear the fruitful stream lapsing along
  'Twixt villages, and think how we shall take
  Our own calm journey on for human sake.

LEIGH HUNT.

OZYMANDIAS OF EGYPT.

I MET a traveller from an antique land
Who said: Two vast and trunkless legs of stone
Stand in the desert. Near them on the sand,
Half sunk, a shattered visage lies, whose frown
And wrinkled lip and sneer of cold command
Tell that its sculptor well those passions read
Which yet survive, stamped on those lifeless
    things,
The hand that mocked them and the heart that
    fed;
And on the pedestal these words appear:
" My name is Ozymandias, king of kings:
Look on my works, ye Mighty, and despair! "
Nothing beside remains. Round the decay
Of that colossal wreck, boundless and bare,
The lone and level sands stretch far away.

                    PERCY BYSSHE SHELLEY.

CHRISTMAS IN INDIA.

DIM dawn behind the tamarisks—the sky is saf-
    fron-yellow—
As the women in the village grind the corn,
And the parrots seek the river-side, each calling
    to his fellow
That the Day, the staring Eastern Day is born.
    Oh the white dust on the highway!
        Oh the stenches in the byway!
    Oh the clammy fog that hovers over earth!

And at Home they 're making merry 'neath
the white and scarlet berry—
What part have India's exiles in their
mirth?

Full day behind the tamarisks—the sky is blue
and staring—
As the cattle crawl afield beneath the yoke,
And they bear One o'er the field-path, who is past
all hope or caring,
To the ghât below the curling wreaths of
smoke.
Call on Rama, going slowly, as ye bear a
brother lowly—
Call on Rama —he may hear, perhaps, your
voice!
With our hymn-books and our psalters we
appeal to other altars,
And to-day we bid " good Christian men rejoice! "

High noon behind the tamarisks—the sun is hot
above us—
As Home the Christmas Day is breaking wan.
They will drink our health at dinner—those who
tell us how they love us,
And forget us till another year be gone!
Oh the toil that knows no breaking! Oh! the
Heimweh, ceaseless, aching!
Oh the black dividing Sea and alien Plain!
Youth was cheap—wherefore we sold it.
Gold was good—we hoped to hold it,
And to-day we know the fulness of our
gain.

Gray dusk behind the tamarisks—the parrots fly
  together—
As the sun is sinking slowly over Home;
And his last ray seems to mock us shackled in a
  lifelong tether
That drags us back howe'er so far we roam.
Hard her service, poor her payment—she in
  ancient, tattered raiment—
India, she the grim Stepmother of our
  kind.
If a year of life be lent her, if her temple's
  shrine we enter,
The door is shut—we may not look behind.

Black night behind the tamarisks—the owls be-
  gin their chorus—
As the conches from the temple scream and
  bray.
With the fruitless years behind us, and the hope-
  less years before us,
Let us honor, oh my brothers, Christmas Day!
Call a truce, then, to our labors—let us feast
  with friends and neighbors,
And be merry as the custom of our caste;
For if "faint and forced the laughter,"
  and if sadness follow after,
We are richer by one mocking Christmas
  past.

RUDYARD KIPLING.

THE ORIENT.

FROM "THE BRIDE OF ABYDOS."

Know ye the land where the cypress and myrtle
Are emblems of deeds that are done in their
clime;
Where the rage of the vulture, the love of the
turtle,
Now melt into sorrow, now madden to crime?
Know ye the land of the cedar and vine,
Where the flowers ever blossom, and beams ever
shine;
Where the light wings of Zephyr, oppressed with
perfume,
Wax faint o'er the gardens of Gúl in her bloom?
Where the citron and olive are fairest of fruit,
And the voice of the nightingale never is mute;
Where the tints of the earth, and the hues of the
sky,
In color though varied, in beauty may vie,
And the purple of ocean is deepest in dye;
Where the virgins are soft as the roses they twine,
And all, save the spirit of man, is divine?
'T is the clime of the East; 't is the land of the
Sun,—
Can he smile on such deeds as his children have
done?
O, wild as the accents of lover's farewell
Are the hearts which they bear and the tales
which they tell!

LORD BYRON.

THE VALE OF CASHMERE.

FROM "THE LIGHT OF THE HAREM."

WHO has not heard of the Vale of Cashmere,
  With its roses the brightest that earth ever
      gave,
Its temples, and grottoes, and fountains as clear
  As the love-lighted eyes that hang over their
      wave?

O, to see it at sunset,—when warm o'er the lake
  Its splendor at parting a summer eve throws,
Like a bride, full of blushes, when lingering to
      take
  A last look of her mirror at night ere she
      goes!—
When the shrines through the foliage are gleam-
      ing half shown,
And each hallows the hour by some rites of its
      own.
Here the music of prayer from a minaret swells,
  Here the Magian his urn full of perfume is
      swinging,
And here, at the altar, a zone of sweet bells
  Round the waist of some fair Indian dancer is
      ringing.
Or to see it by moonlight,—when mellowly shines
The light o'er its palaces, gardens, and shrines;
When the waterfalls gleam like a quick fall of
      stars,
And the nightingale's hymn from the Isle of
      Chenars

Is broken by laughs and light echoes of feet
From the cool shining walks where the young
    people meet.
Or at morn, when the magic of daylight awakes
A new wonder each minute as slowly it breaks,
Hills, cupolas, fountains, called forth every one
Out of darkness, as they were just born of the
    sun;
When the spirit of fragrance is up with the day,
From his harem of night-flowers stealing away;
And the wind, full of wantonness, wooes like a
    lover
The young aspen-trees till they tremble all over;
When the east is as warm as the light of first
    hopes,
And day, with its banner of radiance unfurled,
Shines in through the mountainous portal that
    opes,
    Sublime, from that valley of bliss to the world!
                   THOMAS MOORE.

CARILLON.

In the ancient town of Bruges,
In the quaint old Flemish city,
As the evening shades descended,
Low and loud and sweetly blended,
Low at times and loud at times,
And changing like a poet's rhymes,
Rang the beautiful wild chimes
From the belfry in the market
Of the ancient town of Bruges.

Then, with deep sonorous clangor
Calmly answering their sweet anger,
When the wrangling bells had ended,
Slowly struck the clock eleven,
And, from out the silent heaven,
Silence on the town descended.
Silence, silence everywhere,
On the earth and in the air,
Save that footsteps here and there
Of some burgher home returning,
By the street lamps faintly burning,
For a moment woke the echoes
Of the ancient town of Bruges.

But amid my broken slumbers
Still I heard those magic numbers,
As they loud proclaimed the flight
And stolen marches of the night;
Till their chimes in sweet collision
Mingled with each wandering vision,
Mingled with the fortune-telling
Gypsy-bands of dreams and fancies,
Which amid the waste expanses
Of the silent land of trances
Have their solitary dwelling.
All else seemed asleep in Bruges,
In the quaint old Flemish city.

And I thought how like these chimes
Are the poet's airy rhymes,
All his rhymes and roundelays,
His conceits, and songs, and ditties,
From the belfry of his brain,
Scattered downward, though in vain,

On the roofs and stones of cities!
For by night the drowsy ear
Under its curtains cannot hear,
And by day men go their ways,
Hearing the music as they pass,
But deeming it no more, alas!
Than the hollow sound of brass.

Yet perchance a sleepless wight,
Lodging at some humble inn
In the narrow lanes of life,
When the dusk and hush of night
Shut out the incessant din
Of daylight and its toil and strife,
May listen with a calm delight
To the poet's melodies,
Till he hears, or dreams he hears,
Intermingled with the song,
Thoughts that he has cherished long;
Hears amid the chime and singing
The bells of his own village ringing,
And wakes, and finds his slumberous eyes
Wet with most delicious tears.

Thus dreamed I, as by night I lay
In Bruges, at the Fleur-de-Blé,
Listening with a wild delight
To the chimes that, through the night,
Rang their changes from the Belfry
Of that quaint old Flemish city.

HENRY WADSWORTH LONGFELLOW.

THE RHINE.

TO HIS SISTER.

" CHILDE HAROLD," CANTO III.

THE castled crag of Drachenfels
  Frowns o'er the wide and winding Rhine,
Whose breast of waters broadly swells
  Between the banks which bear the vine,
And hills all rich with blossomed trees,
  And fields which promise corn and wine,
And scattered cities crowning these,
  Whose far white walls along them shine,
Have strewed a scene, which I should see
With double joy, wert *thou* with me.

And peasant-girls, with deep-blue eyes,
  And hands which offer early flowers,
Walk smiling o'er this paradise;
  Above, the frequent feudal towers
Through green leaves lift their walls of gray,
  And many a rock which steeply lowers,
And noble arch in proud decay,
  Look o'er this vale of vintage-bowers;
But one thing want these banks of Rhine,—
Thy gentle hand to clasp in mine!

I send the lilies given to me,
  Though long before thy hand they touch
I know that they must withered be,—
  But yet reject them not as such;

For I have cherished them as dear,
  Because they yet may meet thine eye,
And guide thy soul to mine e'en here,
  When thou behold'st them drooping nigh,
And know'st them gathered by the Rhine,
And offered from my heart to thine!

The river nobly foams and flows,
  The charm of this enchanted ground,
And all its thousand turns disclose
  Some fresher beauty varying round:
The haughtiest breast its wish might bound
  Through life to dwell delighted here;
Nor could on earth a spot be found
  To nature and to me so dear,
Could thy dear eyes in following mine
Still sweeten more these banks of Rhine!

                              LORD BYRON.

THE CATARACT OF LODORE.

DESCRIBED IN "RHYMES FOR THE NURSERY."

    " How does the water
    Come down at Lodore!"
    My little boy asked me
    Thus, once on a time;
    And moreover he tasked me
    To tell him in rhyme.
    Anon at the word,
    There first came one daughter,
    And then came another,
    To second and third

The request of their brother,
And to hear how the water
Comes down at Lodore,
With its rush and its roar,
As many a time
They had seen it before.
So I told them in rhyme,
For of rhymes I had store;
And 't was in my vocation
For their recreation
That so I should sing;
Because I was Laureate
To them and the King.

From its sources which well
In the tarn on the fell;
From its fountains
In the mountains,
Its rills and its gills;
Through moss and through brake,
It runs and it creeps
For a while, till it sleeps
In its own little lake.
And thence at departing,
Awakening and starting,
It runs through the reeds,
And away it proceeds,
Through meadow and glade,
In sun and in shade,
And through the wood-shelter,
Among crags in its flurry,
Helter-skelter,
Hurry-skurry.

Here it comes sparkling,
And there it lies darkling;
Now smoking and frothing
Its tumult and wrath in,
Till, in this rapid race
On which it is bent,
It reaches the place
Of its steep descent.

The cataract strong
Then plunges along,
Striking and raging
As if a war waging
Its caverns and rocks among;
Rising and leaping,
Sinking and creeping,
Swelling and sweeping,
Showering and springing,
Flying and flinging,
Writhing and ringing,
Eddying and whisking,
Spouting and frisking,
Turning and twisting,
Around and around
With endless rebound:
Smiting and fighting,
A sight to delight in;
Confounding, astounding,
Dizzying and deafening the ear with its sound.

Collecting, projecting,
Receding and speeding,
And shocking and rocking,

And darting and parting,
And threading and spreading,
And whizzing and hissing,
And dripping and skipping,
And hitting and spitting,
And shining and twining,
And rattling and battling,
And shaking and quaking,
And pouring and roaring,
And waving and raving,
And tossing and crossing,
And flowing and going,
And running and stunning,
And foaming and roaming,
And dinning and spinning,
And dropping and hopping,
And working and jerking,
And guggling and struggling,
And heaving and cleaving,
And moaning and groaning;

And glittering and frittering,
And gathering and feathering,
And whitening and brightening,
And quivering and shivering,
And hurrying and skurrying,
And thundering and floundering;

Dividing and gliding and sliding,
And falling and brawling and sprawling,
And driving and riving and striving,
And sprinkling and twinkling and winkling,
And sounding and bounding and rounding,

And bubbling and troubling and doubling,
And grumbling and rumbling and tumbling,
And clattering and battering and shattering;
Retreating and beating and meeting and sheeting,
Delaying and straying and playing and spraying,
Advancing and prancing and glancing and dan-
  cing,
Recoiling, turmoiling and toiling and boiling,
And gleaming and streaming and steaming and
  beaming,
And rushing and flushing and brushing and gush-
  ing,
And flapping and rapping and clapping and
  slapping,
And curling and whirling and purling and twirl-
  ing,
And thumping and plumping and bumping and
  jumping,
And dashing and flashing and splashing and
  clashing;
And so never ending, but always descending,
Sounds and motions for ever and ever are blend-
  ing
All at once and all o'er, with a mighty uproar,—
And this way the water comes down at Lodore.

ROBERT SOUTHEY.

THE OLD BRIDGE AT FLORENCE.

Taddeo Gaddi built me. I am old,
  Five centuries old. I plant my foot of stone
  Upon the Arno, as Saint Michael's own
Was planted on the dragon. Fold by fold

Beneath me as it struggles, I behold
  Its glistening scales. Twice hath it overthrown
My kindred and companions. Me alone
It moveth not, but is by me controlled.
I can remember when the Medici
  Were driven from Florence: longer still ago
    The final wars of Ghibelline and Guelf.
Florence adorns me with her jewelry;
  And when I think that Michael Angelo
Hath leaned on me, I glory in myself.

          HENRY WADSWORTH LONGFELLOW.

THE WHITE PEACOCK.

FROM "SOSPIRI DI ROMA."

HERE where the sunlight
Floodeth the garden,
Where the pomegranate
Reareth its glory
Of gorgeous blossom ;
Where the oleanders
Dream through the noontides;
And, like surf o' the sea
Round cliffs of basalt,
The thick magnolias
In billowy masses
Front the sombre green of the ilexes :
Here where the heat lies
Pale blue in the hollows,
Where blue are the shadows
On the fronds of the cactus,
Where pale blue the gleaming

Of fir and cypress,
With the cones upon them
Amber or glowing
With virgin gold :
Here where the honey-flower
Makes the heat fragrant,
As though from the gardens
Of Gulistân,
Where the bulbul singeth
Through a mist of roses,
A breath were borne :
Here where the dream-flowers,
The cream-white poppies
Silently waver,
And where the Scirocco,
Faint in the hollows,
Foldeth his soft white wings in the sunlight,
And lieth sleeping
Deep in the heart of
A sea of white violets :
Here, as the breath, as the soul of this beauty,
Moveth in silence, and dreamlike, and slowly,
White as a snow-drift in mountain valleys
When softly upon it the gold light lingers :
White as the foam o' the sea that is driven
O'er billows of azure agleam with sun-yellow :
Cream-white and soft as the breasts of a girl
Moves the White Peacock, as though through the
          noon-tide
A dream of the moonlight were real for a moment.
Dim on the beautiful fan that he spreadeth,
Foldeth and spreadeth abroad in the sunlight,
Dim on the cream-white are blue adumbrations,

Shadows so pale in their delicate blueness
That visions they seem as of vanishing violets,
The fragrant white violets veinèd with azure,
Pale, pale as the breath of blue smoke in far woodlands.
Here, as the breath, as the soul of this beauty
White as the cloud through the heats of the noontide
Moves the White Peacock.

WILLIAM SHARP.

TO ROME

BURIED IN ITS RUINS.

STRANGER, 't is vain! midst Rome thou seek'st for Rome
In vain; thy foot is on her throne—her grave :
Her walls are dust; Time's conquering banners wave
O'er all her hills; hills which themselves entomb.
Yes! the proud Aventine is its own womb;
The royal Palatine is ruin's slave;
And medals, moldering trophies of the brave,
Mark but the triumphs of oblivious gloom.
Tiber alone endures, whose ancient tide
Worshipped the Queen of Cities on her throne
And now, as round her sepulchre, complains.
O Rome! the steadfast grandeur of thy pride
And beauty all is fled; and that alone
Which seemed so fleet and fugitive remains.

From the Spanish of
FRANCISCO DE QUEVEDO Y VILLEGAS.
Translation of BENJ. B. WIFFEN.

THE COLISEUM.

FROM " CHILDE HAROLD," CANTO IV.

ARCHES on arches! as it were that Rome,
Collecting the chief trophies of her line,
Would build up all her triumphs in one dome,
Her Coliseum stands; the moonbeams shine
As 't were its natural torches, for divine
Should be the light which streams here, to
    illume
This long-explored, but still exhaustless, mine
Of contemplation; and the azure gloom
Of an Italian night, where the deep skies assume

Hues which have words, and speak to ye of
    heaven,
Floats o'er this vast and wondrous monument,
And shadows forth its glory. There is given
Unto the things of earth, which Time hath bent,
A spirit's feeling, and where he hath leant
His hand, but broke his scythe, there is a power
And magic in the ruined battlement,
For which the palace of the present hour
Must yield its pomp, and wait till ages are its
    dower.

.   .   .   .   .

And here the buzz of eager nations ran,
In murmured pity, or loud-roared applause,
As man was slaughtered by his fellow-man.
And wherefore slaughtered? wherefore, but be-
    cause

Such were the bloody Circus' genial laws,
And the imperial pleasure.—Wherefore not?
What matters where we fall to fill the maws
Of worms,—on battle-plains or listed spot?
Both are but theatres where the chief actors rot.

I see before me the Gladiator lie;
He leans upon his hand,—his manly brow
Consents to death, but conquers agony,
And his drooped head sinks gradually low,—
And through his side the last drops, ebbing
    slow
From the red gash, fall heavy, one by one,
Like the first of a thunder-shower; and now
The arena swims around him,—he is gone,
Ere ceased the inhuman shout which hailed the
    wretch who won.

He heard it, but he heeded not,—his eyes
Were with his heart, and that was far away.
He recked not of the life he lost, nor prize;
But where his rude hut by the Danube lay,
There were his young barbarians all at play,
There was their Dacian mother,—he, their sire,
Butchered to make a Roman holiday!—
All this rushed with his blood.—Shall he ex-
    pire,
And unavenged? Arise, ye Goths, and glut your
    ire!

But here, where Murder breathed her bloody
    steam,
And here, where buzzing nations choked the
    ways,

And roared or murmured like a mountain
    stream
Dashing or winding as its torrent strays;
Here, where the Roman millions' blame or
    praise
Was death or life, the playthings of a crowd,
My voice sounds much,—and fall the stars'
    faint rays
On the arena void, seats crushed, walls bowed,
And galleries, where my steps seem echoes
    strangely loud.

A ruin,—yet what ruin! from its mass
Walls, palaces, half-cities, have been reared;
Yet oft the enormous skeleton ye pass,
And marvel where the spoil could have ap-
    peared.
Hath it indeed been plundered, or but cleared?
Alas! developed, opens the decay,
When the colossal fabric's form is neared;
It will not bear the brightness of the day,
Which streams too much on all years, man, have
    reft away.

But when the rising moon begins to climb
Its topmost arch, and gently pauses there;
When the stars twinkle through the loops of
    time,
And the low night-breeze waves along the air
The garland-forest, which the gray walls wear,
Like laurels on the bald first Cæsar's head;
When the light shines serene, but doth not ·
    glare,—

Then in this magic circle raise the dead;
Heroes have trod this spot,—'t is on their dust
   ye tread.

" While stands the Coliseum, Rome shall stand;
When falls the Coliseum, Rome shall fall;
And when Rome falls—the World." From our
   own land
Thus spake the pilgrims o'er this mighty wall
In Saxon times, which we are wont to call
Ancient; and these three mortal things are still
On their foundations, and unaltered all;
Rome and her Ruin past Redemption's skill,
The World, the same wide den—of thieves, or
   what ye will.

LORD BYRON.

THE PANTHEON.

FROM " CHILDE HAROLD," CANTO IV.

SIMPLE, erect, severe, austere, sublime,—
Shrine of all saints and temple of all gods,
From Jove to Jesus,—spared and blest by time;
Looking tranquillity, while falls or nods
Arch, empire, each thing round thee, and man
   plods
His way through thorns to ashes,—glorious
   dome !
Shalt thou not last ? Time's scythe and tyrants'
   rods
Shiver upon thee,—sanctuary and home
Of art and piety,—Pantheon!—pride of Rome !

Relic of nobler days and noblest arts !
Despoiled yet perfect, with thy circle spreads
A holiness appealing to all hearts.
To art a model; and to him who treads
Rome for the sake of ages, Glory sheds
Her light through thy sole aperture ; to those
Who worship, here are altars for their beads ;
And they who feel for genius may repose
Their eyes on honored forms, whose busts around
them close.

LORD BYRON.

A DAY IN THE PAMFILI DORIA,

NEAR ROME.

THOUGH the hills are cold and snowy,
And the wind drives chill to-day,
My heart goes back to a spring-time,
Far, far in the past away.

And I see a quaint old city,
Weary and worn and brown,
Where the spring and the birds are so early,
And the sun in such light goes down.

I remember that old-time villa
Where our afternoons went by,
Where the suns of March flushed warmly,
And spring was in earth and sky.

Out of the mouldering city,—
Mouldering, old, and gray,—
We sped, with a lightsome heart-thrill,
For a sunny, gladsome day,—

For a revel of fresh spring verdure,
  For a race mid springing flowers,
For a vision of plashing fountains,
  Of birds and blossoming bowers.

There were violet banks in the shadows,
  Violets white and blue ;
And a world of bright anemones,
  That over the terrace grew,—

Blue and orange and purple,
  Rosy and yellow and white,
Rising in rainbow bubbles,
  Streaking the lawns with light.

And down from the old stone-pine trees,
  Those far-off islands of air,
The birds are flinging the tidings
  Of a joyful revel up there.

And now for the grand old fountains,
  Tossing their silvery spray ;
Those fountains, so quaint and so many,
  That are leaping and singing all day ;

Those fountains of strange weird sculpture,
  With lichens and moss o'ergrown,—
Are they marble greening in moss-wreaths,
  Or moss-wreaths whitening to stone ?

Down many a wild, dim pathway
  We ramble from morning till noon ;
We linger, unheeding the hours,
  Till evening comes all too soon.

And from out the ilex alleys,
  Where lengthening shadows play,

We look on the dreamy Campagna,
  All glowing with setting day,—
All melting in bands of purple,
  In swathings and foldings of gold,
In ribbons of azure and lilac,
  Like a princely banner unrolled.

And the smoke of each distant cottage,
  And the flash of each villa white,
Shines out with an opal glimmer,
  Like gems in a casket of light.

And the dome of old Saint Peter's
  With a strange translucence glows,
Like a mighty bubble of amethyst
  Floating in waves of rose

In a trance of dreamy vagueness,
  We, gazing and yearning, behold
That city beheld by the prophet,
  Whose walls were transparent gold.

And, dropping all solemn and slowly,
  To hallow the softening spell,
There falls on the dying twilight
  The Ave Maria bell.

With a mournful, motherly softness,
  With a weird and weary care,
That strange and ancient city
  Seems calling the nations to prayer.

And the words that of old the angel
  To the mother of Jesus brought
Rise like a new evangel,
  To hallow the trance of our thought.

With the smoke of the evening incense
  Our thoughts are ascending then
To Mary, the mother of Jesus,
  To Jesus, the Master of men.

O city of prophets and martyrs!
  O shrines of the sainted dead!
When, when shall the living day-spring
  Once more on your towers be spread?

When He who is meek and lowly
  Shall rule in those lordly halls,
And shall stand and feed as a shepherd
  The flock which his mercy calls,—

O, then to those noble churches,
  To picture and statue and gem,
To the pageant of solemn worship,
  Shall the *meaning* come back again.

And this strange and ancient city,
  In that reign of his truth and love,
Shall *be* what it *seems* in the twilight,
  The type of that City above.

1860.   HARRIET BEECHER STOWE.

- - -

FEBRUARY IN ROME.

WHEN Roman fields are red with cyclamen,
  And in the palace gardens you may find,
  Under great leaves and sheltering briony-bind,
Clusters of cream-white violets, oh then
The ruined city of immortal men
  Must smile, a little to her fate resigned,
  And through her corridors the slow warm wind

Gush harmonies beyond a mortal ken.
Such soft favonian airs upon a flute,
    Such shadowy censers burning live perfume,
    Shall lead the mystic city to her tomb;
Nor flowerless springs, nor autumns without fruit,
Nor summer mornings when the winds are mute,
    Trouble her soul till Rome be no more Rome.

EDMUND GOSSE.

SAINT PETER'S AT ROME.

FROM " CHILDE HAROLD," CANTO IV.

VASTNESS which grows, but grows to harmonize,
All musical in its immensities;
Rich marbles, richer painting, shrines where flame
The lamps of gold, and haughty dome which vies
In air with earth's chief structures, though their
        frame
Sits on the firm-set ground,—and this the cloud
    must claim.
        .   .   .   .   .   .
                    Here condense thy soul
To more immediate objects, and control
Thy thoughts until thy mind hath got by heart
Its eloquent proportions, and unroll
In mighty graduations, part by part,
The glory which at once upon thee did not dart.

LORD BYRON.

A VIEW ACROSS THE ROMAN CAM-PAGNA.

1861.

Over the dumb campagna-sea,
    Out in the offing through mist and rain,
Saint Peter's Church heaves silently
    Like a mighty ship in pain,
    Facing the tempest with struggle and strain.

Motionless waifs of ruined towers,
    Soundless breakers of desolate land!
The sullen surf of the mist devours
    That mountain-range upon either hand,
    Eaten away from its outline grand.

And over the dumb campagna-sea
    Where the ship of the Church heaves on to
        wreck,
Alone and silent as God must be
    The Christ walks!—Ay, but Peter's neck
    Is stiff to turn on the foundering deck.

Peter, Peter, if such be thy name,
    Now leave the ship for another to steer,
And proving thy faith evermore the same
    Come forth, tread out through the dark and
        drear,
    Since He who walks on the sea is here!

Peter, Peter!—he does not speak,—
    He is not as rash as in old Galilee.
Safer a ship, though it toss and leak,
    Then a reeling foot on a rolling sea!
    —And he's got to be round in the girth, thinks he.

Peter, Peter !—he does not stir,—
  His nets are heavy with silver fish :
He reckons his gains, and is keen to infer,
    " The broil on the shore, if the Lord should
      wish,—
    But the sturgeon goes to the Cæsar's dish."

Peter, Peter, thou fisher of men,
  Fisher of fish wouldst thou live instead,—
Haggling for pence with the other Ten,
    Cheating the market at so much a head,
    Griping the bag of the traitor dead ?

At the triple crow of the Gallic cock
  Thou weep'st not, thou, though thine eyes be
    dazed :
What bird comes next in the tempest shock ?
    Vultures ! See,—as when Romulus gazed,
    To inaugurate Rome for a world amazed !
              ELIZABETH BARRETT BROWNING.

VENICE.

VENICE, thou Siren of sea cities, wrought
  By mirage, built on water, stair o'er stair,
  Of sunbeams and cloud shadows, phantom-fair,
With naught of earth to mar thy sea-born thought !
Thou floating film upon the wonder-fraught
  Ocean of dreams ! Thou hast no dream so rare
  As are thy sons and daughters,—they who wear
Foam flakes of charm from thine enchantment
    caught.
    O dark brown eyes ! O tangles of dark hair !

O heaven-blue eyes, blonde tresses where the breeze
    Plays over sunburned cheeks in sea-blown air!
    Firm limbs of moulded bronze! frank debonair
Smiles of deep-bosomed women! Loves that seize
Man's soul, and waft her on storm melodies!
                    JOHN ADDINGTON SYMONDS.

VENICE.

FROM " ITALY."

THERE is a glorious City in the Sea.
The Sea is in the broad, the narrow streets,
Ebbing and flowing; and the salt sea-weed
Clings to the marble of her palaces.
No track of men, no footsteps to and fro,
Lead to her gates. The path lies o'er the Sea,
Invisible; and from the land we went,
As to a floating City,—steering in,
And gliding up her streets as in a dream,
So smoothly, silently,—by many a dome
Mosque-like, and many a stately portico,
The statues ranged along an azure sky;
By many a pile in more than Eastern splendor,
Of old the residence of merchant kings;
The fronts of some, though Time had shattered them,
Still glowing with the richest hues of art,
As though the wealth within them had run o'er.
    .   .   .   .   .   .
                            A few in fear,
Flying away from him whose boast it was
That the grass grew not where his horse had trod,

Gave birth to Venice. Like the waterfowl,
They built their nests among the ocean waves;
And where the sands were shifting, as the wind
Blew from the north, the south; where they that
    came
Had to make sure the ground they stood upon,
Rose, like an exhalation, from the deep,
A vast Metropolis, with glittering spires,
With theatres, basilicas adorned;
A scene of light and glory, a dominion,
That has endured the longest among men.

And whence the talisman by which she rose
Towering? 'T was found there in the barren sea.
Want led to Enterprise; and, far or near,
Who met not the Venetian?—now in Cairo,
Ere yet the Califa came, listening to hear
Its bells approaching from the Red Sea coast;
Now on the Euxine, on the Sea of Azoph,
In converse with the Persian, with the Russ,
The Tartar; on his lowly deck receiving
Pearls from the gulf of Ormus, gems from Bagdad,
Eyes brighter yet, that shed the light of love
From Georgia, from Circassia.

     .   .   .   .   .   .

                         Thus did Venice rise,
Thus flourish, till the unwelcome tidings came,
That in the Tagus had arrived a fleet
From India, from the region of the Sun,
Fragrant with spices,—that a way was found,
A channel opened, and the golden stream
Turned to enrich another. Then she felt
Her strength departing, and at last she fell,
Fell in an instant, blotted out and razed;

She who had stood yet longer than the longest
Of the Four Kingdoms,—who, as in an Ark,
Had floated down amid a thousand wrecks,
Uninjured, from the Old World to the New.

SAMUEL ROGERS.

THE GONDOLA.

AFLOAT ; we move—delicious !   Ah,
What else is like the gondola ?
This level flow of liquid glass
Begins beneath us swift to pass.
It goes as though it went alone
By some impulsion of its own.
(How light it moves, how softly !   Ah,
Were all things like the gondola !)

How light it moves, how softly !   Ah,
Could life, as does our gondola,
Unvexed with quarrels, aims, and cares,
And moral duties and affairs,
Unswaying, noiseless, swift, and strong,
For ever thus—thus glide along !
(How light we move, how softly !   Ah,
Were life but as the gondola !)

With no more motion than should bear
A freshness to the languid air ;
With no more effort than expressed
The need and naturalness of rest,
Which we beneath a grateful shade
Should take on peaceful pillows laid !
(How light we move, how softly !   Ah,
Were life but as the gondola !)

In one unbroken passage borne
To closing night from opening morn,
Uplift at whiles slow eyes to mark
Some palace-front, some passing bark ;
Through windows catch the varying shore,
And hear the soft turns of the oar !
(How light we move, how softly !   Ah,
Were life but as the gondola !)

ARTHUR HUGH CLOUGH.

VENICE.

FROM " VIEW FROM THE EUGANEAN HILLS."

ALL is bright and clear and still.
Round the solitary hill.

Beneath is spread like a green sea
The waveless plain of Lombardy,
Bounded by the vaporous air,
Islanded by cities fair ;
Underneath day's azure eyes,
Ocean's nursling, Venice, lies,—
A peopled labyrinth of walls,
Amphitrite's destined halls,
Which her hoary sire now paves
With his blue and beaming waves.
Lo! the sun upsprings behind,
Broad, red, radiant, half reclined
On the level quivering line
Of the waters crystalline ;
And before that chasm of light,

As within a furnace bright,
Column, tower, and dome, and spire
Shine like obelisks of fire,
Pointing with inconstant motion
From the altar of dark ocean
To the sapphire-tinted skies;
As the flames of sacrifice
From the marble shrines did rise,
As to pierce the dome of gold
Where Apollo spoke of old.

Sun-girt city! thou hast been
Ocean's child, and then his queen;
Now is come a darker day,
And thou soon must be his prey,
If the power that raised thee here
Hallow so thy watery bier.
A less drear ruin then than now,
With thy conquest-branded brow
Stooping to the slave of slaves
From thy throne among the waves,
Wilt thou be when the sea-mew
Flies, as once before it flew,
O'er thine isles depopulate,
And all is in its ancient state,
Save where many a palace-gate
With green sea-flowers overgrown
Like a rock of ocean's own,
Topples o'er the abandoned sea
As the tides change sullenly.
The fisher on his watery way
Wandering at the close of day
Will spread his sail and seize his oar

Till he pass the gloomy shore,
Lest thy dead should, from their sleep
Bursting o'er the starlight deep,
Lead a rapid mask of death
O'er the waters of his path.

PERCY BYSSHE SHELLEY.

NAPLES.

FROM " ITALY."

THIS region, surely, is not of the earth.
Was it not dropt from heaven?   Not a grove,
Citron or pine or cedar, not a grot
Sea-worn and mantled with the gadding vine,
But breathes enchantment.   Not a cliff but flings
On the clear wave some image of delight,
Some cabin-roof glowing with crimson flowers,
Some ruined temple or fallen monument,
To muse on as the bark is gliding by,
And be it mine to muse there, mine to glide,
From daybreak, when the mountain pales his
        fire
Yet more and more, and from the mountain-top,
Till then invisible, a smoke ascends,
Solemn and slow, as erst from Ararat,
When he, the Patriarch, who escaped the Flood,
Was with his household sacrificing there,—
From daybreak to that hour, the last and best,
When, one by one, the fishing-boats come forth,
Each with its glimmering lantern at the prow,
And, when the nets are thrown, the evening hymn

Steals o'er the trembling waters.
　　　　　　　　　Everywhere
Fable and Truth have shed, in rivalry,
Each her peculiar influence.　Fable came,
And laughed and sung, arraying Truth in flowers,
Like a young child her grandam.　Fable came;
Earth, sea, and sky reflecting, as she flew,
A thousand, thousand colors not their own:
And at her bidding, lo! a dark descent
To Tartarus, and those thrice happy fields,
Those fields with ether pure and purple light
Ever invested, scenes by him described
Who here was wont to wander and record
What they revealed, and on the western shore
Sleeps in a silent grove, o'erlooking thee,
Beloved Parthenope.
　　　　　　　　Yet here, methinks,
Truth wants no ornament, in her own shape
Filling the mind by turns with awe and love,
By turns inclining to wild ecstasy
And soberest meditation.

　　　　　　　　　　　SAMUEL ROGERS.

DRIFTING.

　　My soul to-day
　　Is far away,
Sailing the Vesuvian Bay;
　　My wingèd boat,
　　A bird afloat,
Swims round the purple peaks remote:—

　　Round purple peaks
　　It sails, and seeks

Blue inlets and their crystal creeks,
   Where high rocks throw,
   Through deeps below,
A duplicated golden glow.

   Far, vague, and dim
   The mountains swim;
While, on Vesuvius' misty brim,
   With outstretched hands,
   The gray smoke stands
O'erlooking the volcanic lands.

   Here Ischia smiles
   O'er liquid miles;
And yonder, bluest of the isles,
   Calm Capri waits,
   Her sapphire gates
Beguiling to her bright estates.

   I heed not, if
   My rippling skiff
Float swift or slow from cliff to cliff;—
   With dreamful eyes
   My spirit lies
Under the walls of Paradise.

   Under the walls
   Where swells and falls
The Bay's deep breast at intervals,
   At peace I lie,
   Blown softly by,
A cloud upon this liquid sky.

The day, so mild,
Is Heaven's own child,
With Earth and Ocean reconciled;—
The airs I feel
Around me steal
Are murmuring to the murmuring keel.

Over the rail
My hand I trail
Within the shadow of the sail;
A joy intense,
The cooling sense
Glides down my drowsy indolence.

With dreamful eyes
My spirit lies
Where Summer sings and never dies,—
O'erveiled with vines,
She glows and shines
Among her future oil and wines.

Her children, hid
The cliffs amid,
Are gambolling with the gambolling kid;
Or down the walls,
With tipsy calls,
Laugh on the rocks like waterfalls.

The fisher's child,
With tresses wild,
Unto the smooth, bright sand beguiled,
With glowing lips
Sings as she skips,
Or gazes at the far-off ships.

Yon deep bark goes
Where Traffic blows,
From lands of sun to lands of snows;—
This happier one,
Its course is run
From lands of snow to lands of sun.

O happy ship,
To rise and dip,
With the blue crystal at your lip!
O happy crew,
My heart with you
Sails, and sails, and sings anew!

No more, no more
The worldly shore
Upbraids me with its loud uproar!
With dreamful eyes
My spirit lies
Under the walls of Paradise!

In lofty lines,
Mid palms and pines,
And olives, aloes, elms, and vines,
Sorrento swings
On sunset wings,
Where Tasso's spirit soars and sings.

THOMAS BUCHANAN READ.

ENGLAND.

FROM " THE TRAVELLER."

FIRED at the sound, my genius spreads her wing,
And flies where Britain courts the western
    spring;
Where lawns extend that scorn Arcadian pride,
And brighter streams than famed Hydaspes glide.
There all around the gentlest breezes stray,
There gentler music melts on every spray;
Creation's mildest charms are there combined,
Extremes are only in the master's mind.

Stern o'er each bosom reason holds her state,
With daring aims irregularly great,
Pride in their port, defiance in their eye,
I see the lords of human kind pass by:
Intent on high designs, a thoughtful band,
By forms unfashioned, fresh from nature's hand,
Fierce in their native hardiness of soul,
True to imagined right above control,—
While e'en the peasant boasts these rights to
    scan,
And learns to venerate himself as man.

Thine, freedom, thine the blessing pictured
    here,
Thine are those charms that dazzle and endear!
                    OLIVER GOLDSMITH.

THAT ENGLAND.

FROM " AURORA LEIGH."

WHOEVER lives true life, will love true love.
I learned to love that England. Very oft,
Before the day was born, or otherwise
Through secret windings of the afternoons,
I threw my hunters off and plunged myself
Among the deep hills, as a hunted stag
Will take the waters, shivering with the fear
And passion of the course. And when, at last
Escaped,—so many a green slope built on slope
Betwixt me and the enemy's house behind,
I dared to rest, or wander,—like a rest
Made sweeter for the step upon the grass,—
And view the ground's most gentle dimplement,
(As if God's finger touched but did not press
In making England!) such an up and down
Of verdure,—nothing too much up or down,
A ripple of land; such little hills, the sky
Can stoop to tenderly and the wheatfields climb;
Such nooks of valleys, lined with orchises,
Fed full of noises by invisible streams;
And open pastures, where you scarcely tell
White daisies from white dew,—at intervals
The mythic oaks and elm-trees standing out
Self-poised upon their prodigy of shade,—
I thought my father's land was worthy too
Of being my Shakespeare's.

     .   .   .   .   .   .

             The skies, the clouds, the fields,

The happy violets hiding from the roads
The primroses run down to, carrying gold,—
The tangled hedgerows, where the cows push out
Impatient horns and tolerant churning mouths
'Twixt dripping ash-boughs,—hedgerows all alive
With birds and gnats and large white butterflies
Which look as if the May-flower had sought life
And palpitated forth upon the wind,—
Hills, vales, woods, netted in a silver mist,
Farms, granges, doubled up among the hills,
And cattle grazing in the watered vales,
And cottage-chimneys smoking from the woods,
And cottage-gardens smelling everywhere,
Confused with smell of orchards. " See," I said,
" And see! is God not with us on the earth?
And shall we put Him down by aught we do?
Who says there 's nothing for the poor and vile
Save poverty and wickedness? behold!"
And ankle-deep in English grass I leaped,
And clapped my hands, and called all very fair.

ELIZABETH BARRETT BROWNING.

THE KNIGHT.

FROM " MARMION," CANTO I.

DAY set on Norham's castled steep,
And Tweed's fair river, broad and deep,
    And Cheviot's mountains lone:
The battled towers, the donjon keep,
The loophole grates where captives weep,
The flanking walls that round it sweep,
    In yellow lustre shone.

The warriors on the turrets high,
Moving athwart the evening sky,
   Seemed forms of giant height;
Their armor, as it caught the rays,
Flashed back again the western blaze
   In lines of dazzling light.

Saint George's banner, broad and gay,
Now faded, as the fading ray
   Less bright, and less, was flung;
The evening gale had scarce the power
To wave it on the donjon tower,
   So heavily it hung.
The scouts had parted on their search,
   The castle gates were barred;
Above the gloomy portal arch,
Timing his footsteps to a march,
   The warder kept his guard;
Low humming, as he paced along,
Some ancient Border-gathering song.

A distant trampling sound he hears;
He looks abroad, and soon appears,
O'er Horncliff hill, a plump of spears,
   Beneath a pennon gay;
A horseman, darting from the crowd,
Like lightning from a summer cloud,
Spurs on his mettled courser proud
   Before the dark array.
Beneath the sable palisade,
That closed the castle barricade,
   His bugle-horn he blew;
The warder hasted from the wall,

And warned the captain in the hall,
  For well the blast he knew;
And joyfully that knight did call
To sewer, squire, and seneschal.

" Now broach ye a pipe of Malvoisie,
  Bring pasties of the doe,
And quickly make the entrance free,
And bid my heralds ready be,
And every minstrel sound his glee,
  And all our trumpets blow;
And, from the platform, spare ye not
To fire a noble salvo-shot:
  Lord Marmion waits below."
Then to the castle's lower ward
  Sped forty yeomen tall,
The iron-studded gates unbarred,
Raised the portcullis' ponderous guard,
The lofty palisade unsparred,
  And let the drawbridge fall.

Along the bridge Lord Marmion rode,
Proudly his red-roan charger trode,
His helm hung at the saddle-bow;
Well by his visage you might know
He was a stalworth knight, and keen,
And had in many a battle been.
The scar on his brown cheek revealed
A token true of Bosworth field;
His eyebrow dark, and eye of fire,
Showed spirit proud, and prompt to ire;
Yet lines of thought upon his cheek
Did deep design and counsel speak.

His forehead, by his casque worn bare,
His thick mustache, and curly hair,
Coal-black, and grizzled here and there,
    But more through toil than age;
His square-turned joints, and strength of limb,
Showed him no carpet-knight so trim,
But in close fight a champion grim,
    In camps a leader sage.

Well was he armed from head to heel,
In mail and plate of Milan steel;
But his strong helm, of mighty cost,
Was all with burnished gold embossed;
Amid the plumage of the crest,
A falcon hovered on her nest,
With wings outspread, and forward breast;
E'en such a falcon, on his shield,
Soared sable in an azure field:
The golden legion bore aright,
𝔚𝔥𝔬 𝔠𝔥𝔢𝔠𝔨𝔰 𝔞𝔱 𝔪𝔢 𝔱𝔬 𝔡𝔢𝔞𝔱𝔥 𝔦𝔰 𝔡𝔦𝔤𝔥𝔱.
Blue was the charger's broidered rein;
Blue ribbons decked his arching mane;
The knightly housing's ample fold
Was velvet blue, and trapped with gold.

Behind him rode two gallant squires
Of noble name and knightly sires;
They burned the gilded spurs to claim;
For well could each a war-horse tame,
Could draw the bow, the sword could sway,
And lightly bear the ring away;
Nor less with courteous precepts stored,
Could dance in hall, and carve at board,

And frame love-ditties passing rare,
And sing them to a lady fair.

Four men-at-arms came at their backs,
With halbert, bill, and battle-axe;
They bore Lord Marmion's lance so strong,
And led his sumpter-mules along,
And ambling palfrey, when at need
Him listed ease his battle-steed.
The last and trustiest of the four
On high his forky pennon bore;
Like swallow's tail, in shape and hue,
Fluttered the streamer glossy blue,
Where, blazoned sable, as before,
The towering falcon seemed to soar.
Last, twenty yeomen, two and two,
In hosen black, and jerkins blue,
With falcons broidered on each breast,
Attended on their lord's behest:
Each, chosen for an archer good,
Knew hunting-craft by lake or wood;
Each one a six-foot bow could bend,
And far a cloth-yard shaft could send;
Each held a boar-spear tough and strong,
And at their belts their quivers rung.
Their dusty palfreys and array
Showed they had marched a weary way.

SIR WALTER SCOTT.

O, THE PLEASANT DAYS OF OLD!

O, THE pleasant days of old, which so often
    people praise!
True, they wanted all the luxuries that grace our
    modern days:
Bare floors were strewed with rushes, the walls
    let in the cold;
O, how they must have shivered in those pleasant
    days of old!

O, those ancient lords of old, how magnificent
    they were!
They threw down and imprisoned kings,—to
    thwart them who might dare?
They ruled their serfs right sternly; they took
    from Jews their gold,—
Above both law and equity were those great lords
    of old!

O, the gallant knights of old, for their valor so
    renowned!
With sword and lance and armor strong they
    scoured the country round;
And whenever aught to tempt them they met by
    wood or wold,
By right of sword they seized the prize,—those
    gallant knights of old!

O, the gentle dames of old! who, quite free from
    fear or pain,
Could gaze on joust and tournament, and see
    their champion slain;

They lived on good beefsteaks and ale, which
    made them strong and bold,—
O, more like men than women were those gentle
    dames of old!

O, those mighty towers of old! with their turrets,
    moat, and keep,
Their battlements and bastions, their dungeons
    dark and deep.
Full many a baron held his court within the
    castle hold;
And many a captive languished there, in those
    strong towers of old.

O, the troubadours of old! with the gentle min-
    strelsie
Of hope and joy, or deep despair, whiche'er their
    lot might be;
For years they served their ladye-loves ere they
    their passions told,—
O, wondrous patience must have had those trou-
    badours of old!

O, those blessèd times of old, with their chivalry
    and state!
I love to read their chronicles, which such brave
    deeds relate;
I love to sing their ancient rhymes, to hear their
    legends told,—
But, Heaven be thanked! I lived not in those
    blessèd times of old!

FRANCES BROWNE.

MELROSE ABBEY.

FROM "THE LAY OF THE LAST MINSTREL," CANTO II.

If thou wouldst view fair Melrose aright,
Go visit it by the pale moonlight;
For the gay beams of lightsome day
Gild, but to flout, the ruins gray.
When the broken arches are black in night,
And each shafted oriel glimmers white;
When the cold light's uncertain shower
Streams on the ruined central tower;
When buttress and buttress, alternately,
Seem framed of ebon and ivory:
When silver edges the imagery,
And the scrolls that teach thee to live and die;
When distant Tweed is heard to rave,
And the owlet to hoot o'er the dead man's grave,
Then go,—but go alone the while,—
Then view Saint David's ruined pile;
And, home returning, soothly swear,
Was never seen so sad and fair!

   .   .   .   .   .   .

The pillared arches were over their head,
And beneath their feet were the bones of the dead.

Spreading herbs and flowerets bright
Glistened with the dew of night;
Nor herb nor flower glistened there,
But was carved in the cloister-arches as fair.
  The monk gazed long on the lovely moon,
    Then into the night he lookèd forth;

And red and bright the streamers light
  Were dancing in the glowing north.
So had he seen, in fair Castile,
  The youth in glittering squadrons start,
Sudden the flying jennet wheel,
  And hurl the unexpected dart.
He knew, by the streamers that shot so bright,
That spirits were riding the northern light.

By a steel-clenched postern door,
  They entered now the chancel tall;
The darkened roof rose high aloof
  On pillars lofty and light and small;
The keystone, that locked each ribbèd aisle,
Was a fleur-de-lys, or a quatre-feuille:
The corbells were carved grotesque and grim:
And the pillars, with clustered shafts so trim,
With base and with capital flourished around,
Seemed bundles of lances which garlands had
    bound.

Full many a scutcheon and banner, riven,
Shook to the cold night-wind of heaven,
  Around the screenèd altar's pale;
And there the dying lamps did burn,
Before thy low and lonely urn,
O gallant Chief of Otterburne!
  And thine, dark Knight of Liddesdale!
O fading honors of the dead!
O high ambition lowly laid!

The moon on the east oriel shone
Through slender shafts of shapely stone,

By foliaged tracery combined;
Thou wouldst have thought some fairy's hand
'Twixt poplars straight the osier wand
    In many a freakish knot had twined;
Then framed a spell, when the work was done,
And changed the willow wreaths to stone.
The silver light, so pale and faint,
Showed many a prophet, and many a saint,
    Whose image on the glass was dyed;
Full in the midst, his Cross of Red
Triumphant Michael brandishèd,
    And trampled the Apostate's pride.
The moonbeam kissed the holy pane,
And threw on the pavement a bloody stain.

SIR WALTER SCOTT.

AN OLD TIME CHRISTMAS.

FROM " MARMION," INTRODUCTION TO CANTO VI.

HEAP on more wood!—the wind is chill;
But, let it whistle as it will,
We'll keep our Christmas merry still.
Each age has deemed the new-born year
The fittest time for festal cheer:
Even, heathen yet, the savage Dane
At Iol more deep the mead did drain;
High on the beach his galleys drew,
And feasted all his pirate crew;
Then in his low and pine-built hall,
Where shields and axes decked the wall,
They gorged upon the half-dressed steer;
Caroused in seas of sable beer;

While round, in brutal jest, were thrown
The half-gnawed rib and marrow-bone;
Or listened all, in grim delight,
While scalds yelled out the joys of fight.
Then forth in frenzy would they hie,
While wildly loose their red locks fly;
And, dancing round the blazing pile,
They make such barbarous mirth the while,
As best might to the mind recall
The boisterous joys of Odin's hall.
And well our Christian sires of old
Loved when the year its course had rolled
And brought blithe Christmas back again
With all his hospitable train.
Domestic and religious rite
Gave honor to the holy night:
On Christmas eve the bells were rung;
On Christmas eve the mass was sung;
That only night, in all the year,
Saw the stoled priest the chalice rear.
The damsel donned her kirtle sheen;
The hall was dressed with holly green;
Forth to the wood did merry-men go,
To gather in the mistletoe.
Then opened wide the baron's hall
To vassal, tenant, serf, and all;
Power laid his rod of rule aside,
And Ceremony doffed her pride.
The heir, with roses in his shoes,
That night might village partner choose;
The lord, underogating, share
The vulgar game of " post and pair."
All hailed, with uncontrolled delight,

And general voice, the happy night
That to the cottage, as the crown,
Brought tidings of salvation down.
  The fire, with well-dried logs supplied,
Went roaring up the chimney wide;
The huge hall-table's oaken face,
Scrubbed till it shone, the day to grace,
Bore then upon its massive board
No mark to part the squire and lord.
Then was brought in the lusty brawn,
By old blue-coated serving-man;
Then the grim boar's-head frowned on high
Crested with bays and rosemary.
Well can the green-garbed ranger tell
How, when, and where, the monster fell;
What dogs before his death he tore,
And all the baiting of the boar.
The wassail round, in good brown bowls,
Garnished with ribbons, blithely trowls.
There the huge sirloin reeked; hard by
Plum-porridge stood, and Christmas pie;
Nor failed old Scotland to produce,
At such high tide, her savory goose.
Then came the merry maskers in,
And carols roared with blithesome din;
If unmelodious was the song,
It was a hearty note, and strong.
Who lists may in their mumming see
Traces of ancient mystery;
White skirts supplied the masquerade,
And smutted cheeks the visors made:
But, O, what masquers richly dight
Can boast of bosoms half so light!

England was merry England, when
Old Christmas brought his sports again.
'T was Christmas broached the mightiest ale;
'T was Christmas told the merriest tale;
A Christmas gambol oft could cheer
The poor man's heart through half the year.

SIR WALTER SCOTT.

THE CASTLE RUINS.

A HAPPY day at Whitsuntide,
  As soon 's the zun begun to vall,
We all strolled up the steep hill-zide
  To Meldon, gret an' small;
Out where the Castle wall stood high
A-mwoldrèn to the zunny sky.

An' there wi' Jenny took a stroll
  Her youngest sister, Poll, so gaÿ,
Bezide John Hind, ah! merry soul,
  An' mid her wedlock faÿ;
An' at our zides did play an' run
My little maïd an' smaller son.

Above the beäten mwold upsprung
  The driven doust, a-spreadèn light,
An' on the new-leaved thorn, a-hung,
  Wer wool a-quiv'rèn white;
An' corn, a-sheenèn bright, did bow,
On slopèn Meldon's zunny brow.

There, down the roofless wall did glow
  The zun upon the grassy vloor,

An' weakly-wandrèn winds did blow,
　　Unhindered by a door;
An' smokeless now avore the zun
Did stan' the ivy-girded tun.

My bwoy did watch the daws' bright wings
　　A-flappen vrom their ivy bow'rs;
My wife did watch my maïd's light springs,
　　Out here an' there vor flow'rs;
And John did zee noo tow'rs, the pleäce
Vor him had only Polly's feäce.

An' there, of all that pried about
　　The walls, I overlooked em best,
An' what o' that? Why, I meäde out
　　Noo mwore than all the rest:
That there wer woonce the nest of zome
That wer a-gone avore we come.

When woonce above the tun the smoke
　　Did wreathy blue among the trees,
An' down below, the livèn vo'k
　　Did tweil as brisk as bees;
Or zit wi' weary knees, the while
The sky wer lightless to their tweil.

　　　　　　　　　　WILLIAM BARNES.

THE DESERTED VILLAGE.

Sweet Auburn! loveliest village of the plain,
Where health and plenty cheered the laboring
　　swain,
Where smiling spring its earliest visit paid,

And parting summer's lingering blooms delayed:
Dear lovely bowers of innocence and ease,
Seats of my youth, when every sport could please,
How often have I loitered o'er thy green,
Where humble happiness endeared each scene;
How often have I paused on every charm,
The sheltered cot, the cultivated farm,
The never-failing brook, the busy mill,
The decent church that topped the neighboring
hill,
The hawthorn-bush, with seats beneath the shade,
For talking age and whispering lovers made;
How often have I blessed the coming day,
When toil remitting lent its turn to play,
And all the village train, from labor free,
Led up their sports beneath the spreading tree,
While many a pastime circled in the shade,
The young contending as the old surveyed;
And many a gambol frolicked o'er the ground,
And sleights of art and feats of strength went
round;
And still as each repeated pleasure tired,
Succeeding sports the mirthful band inspired;
The dancing pair that simply sought renown,
By holding out to tire each other down;
The swain mistrustless of his smutted face,
While secret laughter tittered round the place;
The bashful virgin's sidelong looks of love,
The matron's glance that would those looks re-
prove:
These were thy charms, sweet village; sports like
these,
With sweet succession, taught even toil to please;

These round thy bowers their cheerful influence
    shed,
These were thy charms, But all these charms are
    fled.

  Sweet smiling village, loveliest of the lawn,
Thy sports are fled, and all thy charms with-
    drawn;
Amidst thy bowers the tyrant's hand is seen,
And desolation saddens all thy green:
One only master grasps the whole domain,
And half a tillage stints thy smiling plain:
No more thy glassy brook reflects the day,
But choked with sedges, works its weedy way.
Along thy glades, a solitary guest,
The hollow-sounding bittern guards its nest;
Amidst thy desert walks the lapwing flies,
And tires their echoes with unvaried cries.
Sunk are thy bowers, in shapeless ruin all,
And the long grass o'ertops the mouldering wall;
And, trembling, shrinking from the spoiler's
    hand,
Far, far away, thy children leave the land.

  Ill fares the land, to hastening ills a prey,
Where wealth accumulates and men decay:
Princes and lords may flourish, or may fade;
A breath can make them, as a breath has made;
But a bold peasantry, their country's pride,
When once destroyed, can never be supplied.

  A time there was, ere England's griefs began,
When every rood of ground maintained its man;

For him light Labor spread her wholesome store,
Just gave what life required, but gave no more:
His best companions, innocence and health;
And his best riches, ignorance of wealth.

But times are altered; trade's unfeeling train
Usurp the land and dispossess the swain;
Along the lawn, where scattered hamlets rose,
Unwieldy wealth and cumbrous pomp repose;
And every want to luxury allied,
And every pang that folly pays to pride.
Those gentle hours that plenty bade to bloom,
Those calm desires that asked but little room,
Those healthful sports that graced the peaceful
    scene,
Lived in each look, and brightened all the
    green;
These, far departing, seek a kinder shore,
And rural mirth and manners are no more.

Sweet AUBURN! parent of the blissful hour,
Thy glades forlorn confess the tyrant's power.
Here as I take my solitary rounds,
Amidst thy tangling walks, and ruined grounds,
And, many a year elapsed, return to view
Where once the cottage stood, the hawthorn grew,
Remembrance wakes with all her busy train,
Swells at my breast, and turns the past to pain.

In all my wanderings round this world of care,
In all my griefs—and God has given my share—
I still had hopes my latest hours to crown,
Amidst these humble bowers to lay me down;

To husband out life's taper at the close,
And keep the flame from wasting by repose.
I still had hopes, for pride attends us still,
Amidst the swains to show my book-learned skill,
Around my fire an evening group to draw,
And tell of all I felt and all I saw;
And, as a hare, whom hounds and horns pursue,
Pants to the place from whence at first she flew,
I still had hopes, my long vexations past,
Here to return—and die at home at last.

O blest retirement, friend to life's decline,
Retreat from care, that never must be mine,
How blest is he who crowns in shades like these,
A youth of labor with an age of ease;
Who quits a world where strong temptations try,
And, since 't is hard to combat, learns to fly!
For him no wretches, born to work and weep,
Explore the mine, or tempt the dangerous deep;
No surly porter stands in guilty state
To spurn imploring famine from the gate;
But on he moves to meet his latter end,
Angels around befriending Virtue's friend;
Sinks to the grave with unperceived decay,
While Resignation gently slopes the way;
And, all his prospects brightening to the last,
His Heaven commences ere the world be past!

Sweet was the sound, when oft at evening's
    close
Up yonder hill the village murmur rose;
There, as I passed with careless steps and slow,
The mingling notes came softened from below;

The swain responsive as the milkmaid sung,
The sober herd that lowed to meet their young,
The noisy geese that gabbled o'er the pool,
The playful children just let loose from school,
The watch-dog's voice that bayed the whispering
    wind,
And the loud laugh that spoke the vacant mind;
These all in sweet confusion sought the shade,
And filled each pause the nightingale had made.
But now the sounds of population fail,
No cheerful murmurs fluctuate in the gale,
No busy steps the grass-grown foot-way tread,
But all the bloomy flush of life is fled.
All but yon widowed, solitary thing,
That feebly bends beside the plashy spring;
She, wretched matron, forced in age, for bread,
To strip the brook with mantling cresses spread,
To pick her wintry fagot from the thorn,
To seek her nightly shed, and weep till morn;
She only left of all the harmless train,
The sad historian of the pensive plain.

Near yonder copse, where once the garden
    smiled,
And still where many a garden-flower grows wild;
There, where a few torn shrubs the place disclose,
The village preacher's modest mansion rose.
A man he was to all the country dear,
And passing rich with forty pounds a year;
Remote from towns he ran his godly race,
Nor e'er had changed, nor wished to change, his
    place;
Unpractised he to fawn, or seek for power,

By doctrines fashioned to the varying hour;
Far other aims his heart had learned to prize,
More skilled to raise the wretched than to rise.
His house was known to all the vagrant train,
He chid their wanderings, but relieved their pain;
The long-remembered beggar was his guest,
Whose beard descending swept his aged breast;
The ruined spendthrift, now no longer proud,
Claimed kindred there, and had his claims al-
    lowed;
The broken soldier, kindly bade to stay,
Sate by his fire, and talked the night away;
Wept o'er his wounds, or tales of sorrow done,
Shouldered his crutch, and showed how fields were
    won.
Pleased with his guests, the good man learned to
    glow,
And quite forgot their vices in their woe;
Careless their merits or their faults to scan,
His pity gave ere charity began.

Thus to relieve the wretched was his pride,
And even his failings leaned to Virtue's side;
But in his duty prompt at every call,
He watched and wept, he prayed and felt for all.
And, as a bird each fond endearment tries
To tempt its new-fledged offspring to the skies,
He tried each art, reproved each dull delay,
Allured to brighter worlds, and led the way.

Beside the bed where parting life was laid,
And sorrow, guilt, and pain, by turns dismayed
The reverend champion stood.   At his. control,

Despair and anguish fled the struggling soul;
Comfort came down the trembling wretch to raise,
And his last faltering accents whispered praise.

At church, with meek and unaffected grace,
His looks adorned the venerable place;
Truth from his lips prevailed with double sway,
And fools, who came to scoff, remained to pray.
The service past, around the pious man,
With steady zeal, each honest rustic ran;
Even children followed with endearing wile,
And plucked his gown, to share the good man's
    smile.
His ready smile a parent's warmth expressed,
Their welfare pleased him, and their cares dis-
    tressed;
To them his heart, his love, his griefs were given,
But all his serious thoughts had rest in Heaven.
As some tall cliff, that lifts its awful form,
Swells from the vale, and midway leaves the
    storm,
Though round its breast the rolling clouds are
    spread,
Eternal sunshine settles on its head.

Beside yon straggling fence that skirts the way,
With blossomed furze unprofitably gay,
There, in his noisy mansion, skilled to rule,
The village master taught his little school;
A man severe he was, and stern to view;
I knew him well, and every truant knew;
Well had the boding tremblers learned to trace
The day's disasters in his morning face;

Full well they laughed with counterfeited glee
At all his jokes, for many a joke had he;
Full well the busy whisper, circling round,
Conveyed the dismal tidings when he frowned;
Yet he was kind, or, if severe in aught,
The love he bore to learning was in fault.
The village all declared how much he knew,
'T was certain he could write, and cipher too;
Lands he could measure, terms and tides presage,
And even the story ran that he could gauge.
In arguing too, the parson owned his skill,
For even though vanquished, he could argue still;
While words of learnèd length and thundering
　　sound,
Amazed the gazing rustics ranged around;
And still they gazed, and still the wonder grew
That one small head could carry all he knew.

But past is all his fame. The very spot
Where many a time he triumphed, is forgot.
Near yonder thorn, that lifts its head on high,
Where once the sign-post caught the passing eye,
Low lies that house where nut-brown draughts
　　inspired,
Where graybeard mirth and smiling toil retired,
Where village statesmen talked with looks pro-
　　found,
And news much older than their ale went round.
Imagination fondly stoops to trace
The parlor splendors of that festive place;
The whitewashed wall, the nicely sanded floor,
The varnished clock that clicked behind the door;
The chest contrived a double debt to pay,
A bed by night, a chest of drawers by day;

The pictures placed for ornament and use,
The twelve good rules, the royal game of goose;
The hearth, except when winter chilled the day,
With aspen boughs, and flowers, and fennel gay;
While broken teacups, wisely kept for show,
Ranged o'er the chimney, glistened in a row.

Vain transitory splendor! could not all
Reprieve the tottering mansion from its fall!
Obscure it sinks, nor shall it more impart
An hour's importance to the poor man's heart;
Thither no more the peasant shall repair
To sweet oblivion of his daily care;
No more the farmer's news, the barber's tale,
No more the woodman's ballad shall prevail;
No more the smith his dusky brow shall clear,
Relax his ponderous strength, and lean to hear;
The host himself no longer shall be found
Careful to see the mantling bliss go round;
Nor the coy maid, half willing to be prest,
Shall kiss the cup to pass it to the rest.

Yes! let the rich deride, the proud disdain,
These simple blessings of the lowly train;
To me more dear, congenial to my heart,
One native charm, than all the gloss of art;
Spontaneous joys, where Nature has its play,
The soul adopts, and owns their first-born sway;
Lightly they frolic o'er the vacant mind,
Unenvied, unmolested, unconfined:
But the long pomp, the midnight masquerade,
With all the freaks of wanton wealth arrayed,
In these, ere triflers half their wish obtain,

The toiling pleasure sickens into pain;
And, even while fashion's brightest arts decoy,
The heart distrusting asks, if this be joy.

Ye friends to truth, ye statesmen, who survey
The rich man's joys increase, the poor's decay,
'T is yours to judge, how wide the limits stand
Between a splendid and a happy land.
Proud swells the tide with loads of freighted ore,
And shouting Folly hails them from her shore;
Hoards, even beyond the miser's wish abound,
And rich men flock from all the world around.
Yet count our gains.   This wealth is but a name
That leaves our useful products still the same.
Not so the loss.   The man of wealth and pride
Takes up a space that many poor supplied;
Space for his lake, his park's extended bounds,
Space for his horses, equipage, and hounds;
The robe that wraps his limbs in silken sloth
Has robbed the neighboring field of half their
    growth;
His seat, where solitary sports are seen,
Indignant spurns the cottage from the green;
Around the world each needful product flies,
For all the luxuries the world supplies:
While thus the land adorned for pleasure all
In barren splendor feebly waits the fall.

As some fair female unadorned and plain,
Secure to please while youth confirms her reign,
Slights every borrowed charm that dress supplies,
Nor shares with art the triumph of her eyes:
But when those charms are past, for charms are
    frail,

When time advances, and when lovers fail,
She then shines forth, solicitous to bless,
In all the glaring impotence of dress.
Thus fares the land, by luxury betrayed,
In nature's simplest charms at first arrayed;
But verging to decline, its splendors rise,
Its vistas strike, its palaces surprise;
While, scourged by famine from the smiling land
The mournful peasant leads his humble band;
And while he sinks, without one arm to save,
The country blooms—a garden, and a grave.

Where then, ah! where shall poverty reside,
To 'scape the pressure of contiguous pride?
If to some common's fenceless limits strayed
He drives his flock to pick the scanty blade,
Those fenceless fields the sons of wealth divide,
And even the bare-worn common is denied.

If to the city sped—What waits him there?
To see profusion that he must not share;
To see ten thousand baneful arts combined
To pamper luxury, and thin mankind;
To see those joys the sons of pleasure know
Extorted from his fellow-creature's woe.
Here, while the courtier glitters in brocade,
There the pale artist plies the sickly trade;
Here, while the proud their long-drawn pomps
    display,
There the black gibbet glooms beside the way.
The dome where Pleasure holds her midnight reign,
Here, richly decked, admits the gorgeous train;
Tumultuous grandeur crowds the blazing square,
The rattling chariots clash, the torches glare.

Sure scenes like these no troubles e'er annoy!
Sure these denote one universal joy!
Are these thy serious thoughts?—Ah, turn thine
    eyes
Where the poor houseless shivering female lies.
She once, perhaps, in village plenty blest,
Has wept at tales of innocence distrest;
Her modest looks the cottage might adorn,
Sweet as the primrose peeps beneath the thorn;
Now lost to all; her friends, her virtue fled,
Near her betrayer's door she lays her head,
And pinched with cold, and shrinking from the
    shower,
With heavy heart deplores that luckless hour,
When idly first, ambitious of the town,
She left her wheel and robes of country brown.

    Do thine, sweet AUBURN, thine, the loveliest
    train,
Do thy fair tribes participate her pain?
Even now, perhaps, by cold and hunger led,
At proud men's doors they ask a little bread!

    Ah, no. To distant climes, a dreary scene,
Where half the convex world intrudes between,
Through torrid tracks with fainting steps they go,
Where wild Altama murmurs to their woe.
Far different there from all that charmed before,
The various terrors of that horrid shore;
Those blazing suns that dart a downward ray,
And fiercely shed intolerable day;
Those matted woods where birds forget to sing,
But silent bats in drowsy clusters cling;
Those poisonous fields with rank luxuriance
    crowned,

Where the dark scorpion gathers death around;
Where at each step the stranger fears to wake
The rattling terrors of the vengeful snake;
Where crouching tigers wait their hapless prey,
And savage men more murderous still than they;
While oft in whirls the mad tornado flies,
Mingling the ravaged landscape with the skies.
Far different these from every former scene,
The cooling brook, the grassy vested green,
The breezy covert of the warbling grove,
That only sheltered thefts of harmless love.

Good Heaven! what sorrows gloomed that part-
    ing day
That called them from their native walks away;
When the poor exiles, every pleasure past,
Hung round their bowers, and fondly looked their
    last,
And took a long farewell, and wished in vain
For seats like these beyond the western main;
And shuddering still to face the distant deep,
Returned and wept, and still returned to weep.
The good old sire the first prepared to go
To new-found worlds, and wept for others' woe;
But for himself, in conscious virtue brave,
He only wished for worlds beyond the grave.
His lovely daughter, lovelier in her tears,
The fond companion of his helpless years,
Silent went next, neglectful of her charms,
And left a lover's for a father's arms.
With louder plaints the mother spoke her woes,
And blessed the cot where every pleasure rose;
And kissed her thoughtless babes with many a tear,
And clasped them close, in sorrow doubly dear;

Whilst her fond husband strove to lend relief
In all the silent manliness of grief.

O Luxury! thou curst by Heaven's decree,
How ill exchanged are things like these for thee!
How do thy potions, with insidious joy,
Diffuse their pleasures only to destroy!
Kingdoms, by thee, to sickly greatness grown,
Boast of a florid vigor not their own;
At every draught more large and large they grow,
A bloated mass of rank unwieldy woe;
Till sapped their strength, and every part unsound,
Down, down they sink, and spread a ruin round.

Even now the devastation is begun,
And half the business of destruction done;
Even now, methinks, as pondering here I stand,
I see the rural virtues leave the land:
Down where yon anchoring vessel spreads the sail,
That idly waiting flaps with every gale,
Downward they move, a melancholy band,
Pass from the shore, and darken all the strand.
Contented toil, and hospitable care,
And kind connubial tenderness, are there;
And piety with wishes placed above,
And steady loyalty, and faithful love.
And thou, sweet Poetry, thou loveliest maid,
Still first to fly where sensual joys invade;
Unfit in these degenerate times of shame,
To catch the heart, or strike for honest fame;
Dear charming nymph, neglected and decried,
My shame in crowds, my solitary pride;
Thou source of all my bliss, and all my woe,
That found'st me poor at first, and keep'st me so;

Thou guide by which the nobler arts excel,
Thou nurse of every virtue, fare thee well!
Farewell, and O! where'er thy voice be tried,
On Torno's cliffs, or Pambamarca's side,
Whether where equinoctial fervors glow,
Or winter wraps the polar world in snow,
Still let thy voice, prevailing over time,
Redress the rigors of the inclement clime;
Aid slighted truth; with thy persuasive strain
Teach erring man to spurn the rage of gain;
Teach him, that states of native strength possest,
Though very poor, may still be very blest;
That trade's proud empire hastes to swift decay,
As ocean sweeps the labored mole away;
While self-dependent power can time defy,
As rocks resist the billows and the sky.

OLIVER GOLDSMITH.

SONNET.

COMPOSED UPON WESTMINSTER BRIDGE, LONDON, 1802.

EARTH has not anything to show more fair;
Dull would he be of soul who could pass by
A sight so touching in its majesty:
This city now doth, like a garment, wear
The beauty of the morning; silent, bare,
Ships, towers, domes, theatres, and temples lie
Open unto the fields, and to the sky,
All bright and glittering in the smokeless air.
Never did sun more beautifully steep
In his first splendor valley, rock, or hill;
Ne'er saw I, never felt, a calm so deep!

The river glideth at his own sweet will :
Dear God! the very houses seem asleep ;
And all that mighty heart is lying still !

WILLIAM WORDSWORTH.

LONDON.

ATHWART the sky a lowly sigh
From west to east the sweet wind carried ;
The sun stood still on Primrose Hill ;
His light in all the city tarried :
The clouds on viewless columns bloomed
Like smouldering lilies unconsumed.

"O sweetheart, see! how shadowy,
Of some occult magician's rearing,
Or swung in space of heaven's grace
Dissolving, dimly reappearing,
Afloat upon ethereal tides,
St. Paul's above the city rides! "

A rumor broke through the thin smoke
Enwreathing abbey, tower, and palace,
The parks, the squares, the thoroughfares,
The million-peopled lanes and alleys,
An ever-muttering prisoned storm,
The heart of London beating warm.

JOHN DAVIDSON.

THE VILLAGE SCHOOLMISTRESS.

FROM " THE SCHOOLMISTRESS."

Ah me! full sorely is my heart forlorn,
　To think how modest worth neglected lies,
While partial Fame doth with her blasts adorn
　Such deeds alone as pride and pomp disguise;
　Deeds of ill sort, and mischievous emprise.
Lend me thy clarion, goddess! let me try
　To sound the praise of merit, ere it dies,
Such as I oft have chauncèd to espy,
Lost in the dreary shades of dull obscurity.

In every village marked with little spire,
　Embowered in trees, and hardly known to fame,
There dwells, in lowly shed and mean attire,
　A matron old, whom we Schoolmistress name;
　Who boasts unruly brats with birch to tame:
They grieven sore, in piteous durance pent,
　Awed by the power of this relentless dame;
And ofttimes, on vagaries idly bent,
For unkempt air, or task unconned, are sorely shent.

And all in sight doth rise a birchen tree,
　Which Learning near her little dome did stow,
Whilom a twig of small regard to see,
　Though now so wide its waving branches flow,
　And work the simple vassals mickle woe;
For not a wind might curl the leaves that blew,
　But their limbs shuddered, and their pulse beat
　　low;

And as they looked, they found their horror grew,
And shaped it into rods, and tingled at the view.

.   .   .   .   .   .

Her cap, far whiter than the driven snow,
    Emblem right meet of decency does yield :
Her apron dyed in grain, as blue, I trowe,
    As is the harebell that adorns the field :
    And in her hand, for sceptre, she does wield
Tway birchen sprays; with anxious fear entwined,
    With dark distrust, and sad repentance filled ;
And steadfast hate, and sharp affliction joined,
And fury uncontrolled, and chastisement unkind.

A russet stole was o'er her shoulders thrown ;
    A russet kirtle fenced the nipping air :
'T was simple russet, but it was her own ;
    'T was her own country bred the flock so fair,
    'T was her own labor did the fleece prepare ;
And, sooth to say, her pupils, ranged around,
    Through pious awe, did term it passing rare ;
For they in gaping wonderment abound,
And think, no doubt, she been the greatest wight on
        ground.

Albeit ne flattery did corrupt her truth,
    Ne pompous title did debauch her ear ;
Goody, good-woman, gossip, n'aunt forsooth,
    Or dame, the sole additions she did hear ;
    Yet these she challenged, these she held right
        dear :
Ne would esteem him act as mought behove,
    Who should not honor eld with these revere ;

For never title yet so mean could prove,
But there was eke a mind which did that title love.

$\cdot \quad \cdot \quad \cdot \quad \cdot \quad \cdot \quad \cdot$

In elbow-chair (like that of Scottish stem,
   By the sharp tooth of cankering eld defaced,
In which, when he receives his diadem,
   Our sovereign prince and liefest liege is placed)
The matron sat; and some with rank she graced,
   (The source of children's and of courtiers' pride!)
Redressed affronts,—for vile affronts there passed;
And warned them not the fretful to deride,
But love each other dear, whatever them betide.

Right well she knew each temper to descry,
   To thwart the proud, and the submiss to raise;
Some with vile copper-prize exalt on high,
   And some entice with pittance small of praise;
   And other some with baleful sprig she 'frays:
Even absent, she the reins of power doth hold,
   While with quaint arts the giddy crowd she
      sways;
Forewarned, if little bird their pranks behold,
'T will whisper in her ear, and all the scene unfold.

Lo! now with state she utters her command;
   Eftsoons the urchins to their tasks repair,
Their books of stature small they take in hand,
   Which with pellucid horn securèd are,
   To save from finger wet the letters fair:
The work so gay, that on their back is seen,
   Saint George's high achievements does declare;
On which thilk wight that has y-gazing been,

Kens the forthcoming rod,—unpleasing sight, I
    ween!

.   .   .   .   .   .

But now Dan Phœbus gains the middle sky,
    And Liberty unbars her prison door;
And like a rushing torrent out they fly;
    And now the grassy cirque han covered o'er
    With boisterous revel rout and wild uproar;
A thousand ways in wanton rings they run.
    Heaven shield their short-lived pastimes, I im-
        plore;
    For well may freedom erst so dearly won
Appear to British elf more gladsome than the sun.

WILLIAM SHENSTONE.

THE FORGING OF THE ANCHOR.

Come, see the Dolphin's anchor forged; 't is at a
    white heat now:
The bellows ceased, the flames decreased; though
    on the forge's brow
The little flames still fitfully play through the sable
    mound:
And fitfully you still may see the grim smiths
    ranking round,
All clad in leathern panoply, their broad hands
    only bare;
Some rest upon their sledges here, some work
    the windlass there.

The windlass strains the tackle-chains, the black
    mound heaves below,
And red and deep a hundred veins burst out at
    every throe;

It rises, roars, rends all outright,—O Vulcan, what a
  glow!
'T is blinding white, 't is blasting bright, the high
  sun shines not so!
The high sun sees not, on the earth, such a fiery,
  fearful show,—
The roof-ribs swarth, the candent hearth, the ruddy,
  lurid row
Of smiths that stand, an ardent band, like men
  before the foe.
As, quivering through his fleece of flame, the
  sailing monster slow
Sinks on the anvil,—all about the faces fiery grow.
" Hurrah!" they shout, " leap out, leap out; "
  bang, bang, the sledges go;
Hurrah! the jetted lightnings are hissing high and
  low;
A hailing fount of fire is struck at every squashing
  blow;
The leathern mail rebounds the hail; the rattling
  cinders strew
The ground around; at every bound the sweltering
  fountains flow;
And thick and loud the swinking crowd, at every
  stroke, pant " Ho!"

Leap out, leap out, my masters; leap out and lay
  on load!
Let 's forge a goodly anchor, a bower, thick and
  broad;
For a heart of oak is hanging on every blow, I
  bode,
And I see the good ship riding, all in a perillous
  road,—

The low reef roaring on her lee, the roll of ocean
    poured
From stem to stern, sea after sea; the mainmast by
    the board;
The bulwarks down, the rudder gone, the boats
    stove at the chains,—
But courage still, brave mariners, the bower still
    remains,
And not an inch to flinch he deigns save when ye
    pitch sky-high,
Then moves his head, as though he said, "Fear
    nothing,—here am I!"   .

Swing in your strokes in order, let foot and hand
    keep time;
Your blows make music sweeter far than any
    steeple's chime.
But while you sling your sledges, sing; and let the
    burden be,
The Anchor is the Anvil King, and royal crafts-
    men we!
Strike in, strike in, the sparks begin to dull their
    rustling red!
Our hammers ring with sharper din, our work will
    soon be sped;
Our anchor soon must change his bed of fiery rich
    array
For a hammock at the roaring bows, or an oozy
    couch of clay;
Our anchor soon must change the lay of merry
    craftsmen here,
For the Yeo-heave-o, and the Heave-away, and the
    sighing seaman's cheer;

When, weighing slow, at eve they go—far, far from
    love and home,
And sobbing sweethearts, in a row, wail o'er the
    ocean foam.

In livid and obdùrate gloom, he darkens down at
    last:
A shapely one he is, and strong as e'er from cat
    was cast.
O trusted and trustworthy guard, if thou hadst life
    like me,
What pleasures would thy toils reward beneath the
    deep green sea!
O deep-sea diver, who might then behold such
    sights as thou?
The hoary monsters' palaces! methinks what joy
    't were now
To go plumb plunging down amid th' assembly of
    the whales,
And feel the churned sea round me boil beneath
    their scourging tails!
Then deep in tangle-woods to fight the fierce sea
    unicorn,
And send him foiled and bellowing back, for all his
    ivory horn;
To leave the subtle sworder-fish of bony blade for-
    lorn;
And for the ghastly-grinning shark, to laugh his
    jaws to scorn;
To leap down on the kraken's back, where mid Nor-
    wegian isles
He lies, a lubber anchorage for sudden shallowed
    miles,

Till snorting, like an under-sea volcano, off he
    rolls ;
Meanwhile to swing, a-buffeting the far-astonished
    shoals
Of his back-browsing ocean calves ; or, haply in a
    cove,
Shell-strewn, and consecrate of old to some Undinè's
    love,
To find the long-haired mermaidens ; or, hard by
    icy lands,
To wrestle with the sea-serpent upon cerulean
    sands.

O broad-armed fisher of the deep, whose sports can
    equal thine ?
The Dolphin weighs a thousand tons that tugs thy
    cable line ;
And night by night 't is thy delight, thy glory day
    by day,
Through sable sea and breaker white, the giant
    game to play ;
But, shamer of our little sports ! forgive the name I
    gave,—
    A fisher's joy is to destroy, thine office is to save.

O lodger in the sea-king's halls, couldst thou but
    understand
Whose be the white bones by thy side, or who that
    dripping band,
Slow swaying in the heaving waves that round about
    thee bend,
With sounds like breakers in a dream, blessing their
    ancient friend :

O, couldst thou know what heroes glide with larger
    steps round thee,
Thine iron side would swell with pride ; thou 'dst
    leap within the sea !
Give honor to their memories who left the pleasant
    strand
To shed their blood so freely for the love of father-
    land,—
Who left their chance of quiet age and grassy
    churchyard grave
So freely for a restless bed amid the tossing wave ;
O, though our anchor may not be all I have fondly
    sung,
Honor him for their memory whose bones he goes
    among!
                            SAMUEL FERGUSON.

NEWPORT-BEACH.

WAVE after wave successively rolls on
And dies along the shore, until more loud
One billow with concentrate force is heard
To swell prophetic, and exultant rears
A lucent form above its pioneers,
And rushes past them to the farthest goal.
Thus our unuttered feelings rise and fall,
And thought will follow thought in equal waves,
Until reflection nerves design to will,
Or sentiment o'er chance emotion reigns,
And all its wayward undulations blend
In one o'erwhelming surge !
                     HENRY THEODORE TUCKERMAN.

THE SETTLER.

His echoing axe the settler swung
  Amid the sea-like solitude,
And, rushing, thundering, down were flung
  The Titans of the wood;
Loud shrieked the eagle, as he dashed
From out his mossy nest, which crashed
  With its supporting bough,
And the first sunlight, leaping, flashed
  On the wolf's haunt below.

Rude was the garb and strong the frame
  Of him who plied his ceaseless toil:
To form that garb the wildwood game
  Contributed their spoil;
The soul that warmed that frame disdained
The tinsel, gaud, and glare that reigned
  Where men their crowds collect;
The simple fur, untrimmed, unstained,
  This forest-tamer decked.

The paths which wound mid gorgeous trees,
  The stream whose bright lips kissed their
    flowers,
The winds that swelled their harmonies
  Through those sun-hiding bowers,
The temple vast, the green arcade,
The nestling vale, the grassy glade,
  Dark cave, and swampy lair;
These scenes and sounds majestic made
  His world, his pleasures, there.

His roof adorned a pleasant spot;
 Mid the black logs green glowed the grain,
And herbs and plants the woods knew not
 Throve in the sun and rain.
The smoke-wreath curling o'er the dell,
The low, the bleat, the tinkling bell,
 All made a landscape strange,
Which was the living chronicle
 Of deeds that wrought the change.

The violet sprung at spring's first tinge
 The rose of summer spread its glow,
The maize hung out its autumn fringe,
 Rude winter brought his snow;
And still the lone one labored there,
His shout and whistle broke the air,
 As cheerily he plied
His garden-spade, or drove his share
 Along the hillock's side.

He marked the fire-storm's blazing flood
 Roaring and crackling on its path,
And scorching earth, and melting wood,
 Beneath its greedy wrath ;
He marked the rapid whirlwind shoot,
Trampling the pine-tree with its foot,
 And darkening thick the day
With streaming bough and severed root,
 Hurled whizzing on its way.

His gaunt hound yelled, his rifle flashed,
 The grim bear hushed his savage growl ;
In blood and foam the panther gnashed
 His fangs, with dying howl ;

The fleet deer ceased its flying bound,
Its snarling wolf-foe bit the ground,
    And, with its moaning cry,
The beaver sank beneath the wound
    Its pond-built Venice by.

Humble the lot, yet his the race,
    When Liberty sent forth her cry,
Who thronged in conflict's deadliest place,
    To fight,—to bleed,—to die!
Who cumbered Bunker's height of red,
By hope through weary years were led,
    And witnessed Yorktown's sun
Blaze on a nation's banner spread,
    A nation's freedom won.

                    ALFRED B. STREET.

SONG OF THE CHATTAHOOCHEE.

Out of the hills of Habersham,
    Down the valleys of Hall,
I hurry amain to reach the plain,
Run the rapid and leap the fall,
Split at the rock and together again,
Accept my bed, or narrow or wide,
And flee from folly on every side
With a lover's pain to attain the plain
    Far from the hills of Habersham,
    Far from the valleys of Hall.

All down the hills of Habersham,
    All through the valleys of Hall,
The rushes cried, " Abide, abide,"
The wilful water-weeds held me thrall,

The loving laurel turned my tide,
The ferns and fondling grass said " Stay,"
The dewberry dipped for to work delay,
And the little reeds sighed, " Abide, abide,"
  Here in the hills of Habersham,
  Here in the valleys of Hall.

High o'er the hills of Habersham,
  Veiling the valleys of Hall,
The hickory told me manifold
Fair tales of shade; the poplar tall
Wrought me her shadowy self to hold;
The chestnut, the oak, the walnut, the pine,
Overleaning, with flickering meaning and sign,
Said, "Pass not, so cold, these manifold
  Deep shades of the hills of Habersham,
  These glades in the valleys of Hall."

And oft in the hills of Habersham,
  And oft in the valleys of Hall,
The white quartz shone, and the smooth brook-
    stone
Did bar me of passage with friendly brawl;
And many a luminous jewel alone—
Crystal clear or a-cloud with mist,
Ruby, or garnet, or amethyst—
Made lures with the lights of streaming stone
  In the clefts of the hills of Habersham,
  In the beds of the valleys of Hall.

But oh! not the hills of Habersham,
  And oh! not the valleys of Hall
Avail; I am fain for to water the plain.
Downward the voices of duty call;

Downward to toil and be mixed with the main;
The dry fields burn, and the mills are to turn,
And a myriad flowers mortally yearn,
And the lordly main from beyond the plain
    Calls o'er the hills of Habersham,
    Calls through the valleys of Hall.

SIDNEY LANIER.

WEEHAWKEN AND THE NEW YORK BAY.

FROM "FANNY."

WEEHAWKEN! In thy mountain scenery yet,
    All we adore of Nature in her wild
And frolic hour of infancy is met;
    And never has a summer's morning smiled
Upon a lovelier scene than the full eye
Of the enthusiast revels on,—when high

Amid thy forest solitudes he climbs
    O'er crags that proudly tower above the deep,
And knows that sense of danger which sublimes
    The breathless moment,—when his daring step
Is on the verge of the cliff, and he can hear
The low dash of the wave with startled ear,

Like the death-music of his coming doom,
    And clings to the green turf with desperate force,
As the heart clings to life; and when resume
    The currents in his veins their wonted course,
There lingers a deep feeling,—like the moan
Of wearied ocean when the storm is gone.

In such an hour he turns, and on his view
    Ocean and earth and heaven burst before him;

Clouds slumbering at his feet, and the clear blue
  Of summer's sky in beauty bending o'er him,—
The city bright below; and far away,
Sparkling in golden light, his own romantic bay.

Tall spire, and glittering roof, and battlement,
  And banners floating in the sunny air ;
And white sails o'er the calm blue waters bent,
  Green isle, and circling shore, are blended there
In wild reality. When life is old,
And many a scene forgot, the heart will hold

Its memory of this; nor lives there one
  Whose infant breath was drawn, or boyhood's days
Of happiness were passed beneath that sun,
  That in his manhood's prime can calmly gaze
Upon that bay, or on that mountain stand,
Nor feel the prouder of his native land.

FITZ-GREENE HALLECK.

MANNAHATTA.

I was asking for something specific and perfect for
    my city,
Whereupon lo ! upsprang the aboriginal name.

Now I see what there is in a name, a word, liquid,
    sane, unruly, musical, self-sufficient,
I see that the word of my city is that word from of
    old,
Because I see that word nested in nests of water-
    bays, superb,
Rich, hemmed thick all around with sail ships and
    steam ships, an island sixteen miles long, solid-
    founded,

Numberless crowded streets, high growths of iron,
    slender, strong, light, splendidly uprising to-
    ward clear skies,
Tides swift and ample, well-loved by me, towards
    sundown,
The flowing sea-currents, the little islands, larger
    adjoining islands, the heights, the villas,
The countless masts, the white shore-steamers, the
    lighters, the ferry-boats, the black sea-steamers
    well-modelled,
The down-town streets, the jobbers' houses of
    business, the houses of business of the ship-
    merchants and money-brokers, the river-streets,
Immigrants arriving, fifteen or twenty thousand in
    a week,
The carts hauling goods, the manly race of drivers
    of horses, the brown-faced sailors,
The summer air, the bright sun shining, and the
    sailing clouds aloft,
The winter snows, the sleigh-bells, the broken ice
    in the river, passing along up or down with
    the flood-tide or ebb-tide,
The mechanics of the city, the masters, well-formed,
    beautiful-faced, looking you straight in the eyes,
Trottoirs thronged, vehicles, Broadway, the women,
    the shops and shows,
A million people—manners free and superb—open
    voices—hospitality—the most courageous and
    friendly young men,
City of hurried and sparkling waters! city of spires
    and masts!
City nested in bays! my city!

                    WALT WHITMAN.

THE BROOKLYN BRIDGE.

A GRANITE cliff on either shore,
   A highway poised in air ;
Above, the wheels of traffic roar,
   Below, the fleets sail fair ;—
And in and out forevermore,
The surging tides of ocean pour,
And past the towers the white gulls soar,
   And winds the sea-clouds bear.

O peerless this majestic street,
   This road that leaps the brine !
Upon its heights twin cities meet,
   And throng its grand incline,—
To east, to west, with swiftest feet,
Though ice may crash and billows beat,
Though blinding fogs the wave may greet
   Or golden summer shine.

Sail up the Bay with morning's beam,
   Or rocky Hellgate by,—
Its columns rise, its cables gleam,
   Great tents athwart the sky !
And lone it looms, august, supreme,
When, with the splendor of a dream,
Its blazing cressets gild the stream
   Till evening shadows fly.

By Nile stand proud the pyramids,
   But they were for the dead ;
The awful gloom that joy forbids,
   The mourners' silent tread,

The crypt, the coffin's stony lids,—
Sad as a soul the maze that thrids
Of dark Amenti, ere it rids
　　Its way of judgment dread.

This glorious arch, these climbing towers,
　　Are all for life and cheer!
Part of the New World's nobler dowers;
　　Hint of millennial year
That comes apace, though evil lowers,—
When loftier aims and larger powers
Will mould and deck this earth of ours,
　　And heaven at length bring near!

Unmoved its cliffs shall crown the shore;
　　Its arch the chasm dare;
Its network hang, the blue before,
　　As gossamer in air;
While in and out forevermore,
The surging tides of ocean pour,
And past its towers the white gulls soar
　　And winds the sea-clouds bear!

EDNA DEAN PROCTOR.

SCYTHE SONG.

MOWERS, weary and brown, and blithe,
　　What is the word methinks ye know,
Endless over-word that the Scythe
　　Sings to the blades of the grass below?
Scythes that swing in the grass and clover,
　　Something, still, they say as they pass;
What is the word that, over and over,
　　Sings the Scythe to the flowers and grass?

Hush, ah hush, the Scythe was saying,
  Hush, and heed not, and fall asleep ;
Hush, they say to the grasses swaying ;
  Hush, they sing to the clover deep !
Hush—'t is the lullaby Time is singing—
  Hush, and heed not, for all things pass ;
Hush, ah hush ! *and the Scythes are swinging*
  Over the clover, over the grass !

ANDREW LANG.

THE MOWERS.

THE sunburnt mowers are in the swath—
    Swing, swing, swing !
  The towering lilies loath
  Tremble and totter and fall ;
    The meadow-rue
Dashes its tassels of golden dew ;
  And the keen blade sweeps o'er all—
    Swing, swing, swing !

The flowers, the berries, the feathered grass,
  Are thrown in a smothered mass ;
Hastens away the butterfly ;
With half their burden the brown bees hie ;
  And the meadow-lark shrieks distrest,
And leaves the poor younglings all in the nest.
  The daisies clasp and fall ;
And totters the Jacob's-ladder tall.
Weaving and winding and curving lithe,
O'er plumy hillocks—through dewy hollows,
    His subtle scythe
  The nodding mower follows—
    Swing, swing, swing !

Anon, the chiming whetstones ring—
Ting-a-ling! ting-a-ling!
And the mower now
Pauses and wipes his beaded brow.
A moment he scans the fleckless sky;
A moment, the fish-hawk soaring high;
And watches the swallows dip and dive
Anear and far.
They whisk and glimmer, and chatter and
strive;
What do they gossip together?
Cunning fellows they are,
Wise prophets to him!
"Higher or lower they circle and skim—
Fair or foul to-morrow's hay-weather!"

Tallest primroses, or loftiest daisies,
Not a steel-blue feather
Of slim wing grazes:
"Fear not! fear not!" cry the swallows.
Each mower tightens his snath-ring's wedge,
And his finger daintily follows
The long blade's tickle-edge;
Softly the whetstone's last touches ring—
Ting-a-ling! ting-a-ling!
Like a leaf-muffled bird in the woodland nigh,
Faintly the fading echoes reply—
Ting-a-ling! ting-a-ling!

"Perchance the swallows, that flit in their glee,
Of to-morrow's hay-weather know little as we!"
Says Farmer Russet. "Be it hidden in shower
Or sunshine, to-morrow we do not own—
To-day is ours alone!—

Not a twinkle we'll waste of the golden hour.
Grasp tightly the nibs—give heel and give
      toe!—
Lay a goodly swath, shaved smooth and low!
    Prime is the day—
    Swing, swing, swing!"

Farmer Russet is aged and gray—
Gray as the frost, but fresh as the spring,
    Straight is he
    As the green fir-tree;
And with heart most blithe, and sinews lithe,
He leads the row with his merry scythe.
  "Come, boys! strike up the old song
    While we circle around—
The song we always in haytime sing—
    And let the woods ring,
    And the echoes prolong
    The merry sound!"

SONG.

July is just in the nick of time!
    (Hay-weather, hay-weather;)
The midsummer month is the golden prime
For haycocks smelling of clover and thyme;—
    (Swing all together!)
July is just in the nick of time!

Chorus.

O, we'll make our hay while the good sun
    shines—
  We'll waste not a golden minute!
No shadow of storm the blue arch lines;

We 'll waste not a minute—not a minute !
    For the west-wind is fair ;
    O, the hay-day is rare !—
The sky is without a brown cloud in it !

June is too early for richest hay ;
    (Fair weather, fair weather ;)
The corn stretches taller the livelong day ;
But grass is ever too sappy to lay ;—
    (Clip all together !)
June is too early for richest hay.

August 's a month that too far goes by ;
    (Late weather, late weather ;)
Grasshoppers are chipper and kick too high !
And grass that 's standing is fodder scorched dry ;—
    (Pull all together !)
August 's a month that too far goes by.

July is just in the nick of time !
    (Best weather, best weather ;)
The midsummer month is the golden prime
For haycocks smelling of clover and thyme ;
    (Strike all together !)
July is just in the nick of time !

———

    Still hiss the scythes !
Shudder the grasses' defenceless blades—
    The lily-throng writhes ;
And, as a phalanx of wild geese streams,
Where the shore of April's cloudland gleams,
On their dizzy way, in serried grades—
    Wing on wing, wing on wing—
The mowers, each a step in advance

Of his fellow, time their stroke with a glance
  Of swerveless force ;
And far through the meadow leads their course—
  Swing, swing, swing !

MYRON B. BENTON.

CHÂTEAU PAPINEAU.

(AFLOAT.)

I.

THE red-tiled towers of the old Château,
  Perched on the cliff above our bark,
Burn in the western evening glow.

The fiery spirit of Papineau
  Consumes them still with its fever spark,
The red-tiled towers of the old Château !

Drift by and mark how bright they show,
  And how the mullioned windows—mark !
Burn in the western evening glow !

Drift down, or up, where'er you go,
  They flame from out the distant park,
The red-tiled towers of the old Château.

So was it once with friend, with foe ;
  Far off they saw the patriot's ark
Burn in the western evening glow.

Think of him now ! One thought bestow,
  As, blazing against the pine trees dark,
The red-tiled towers of the old Château
Burn in the western evening glow !

(ASHORE.)

II.

Within this charmèd cool retreat
  Where bounty dwelt and beauty waits,
The Old World and the New World meet.

Quitting the straggling village street,
  Enter,—passing the great gray gates,
Within this charmèd cool retreat.

Where thrives a garden, ancient, neat,
  Where vulgar noise ne'er penetrates,
The Old World and the New World meet.

For mouldering vault and carven seat
  Tell us that France predominates
Within this charmèd cool retreat,

Though Canada be felt in beat
  Of summer pulse that enervates:
The Old World and the New World meet

In dial, arbor, tropic heat.
  Enter! And note, how clear all states
That, in this charmèd cool retreat,
The Old World and the New World meet.

III.

The garden 's past. 'T is forest now
  Encircling us with leafy tide,
Close clustering in green branch and bough.

So beautiful a wood, we vow,
  Was never seen, so fresh, so wide.
The garden 's past, 't is forest now,

'T is more, 't is Canada, and how
  Should feudal leaven lurk and hide
Close clustering in green branch and bough?

Quaintly the dial on the brow
  Of yonder open glade is spied;
The garden 's past, 't is forest now,

Yet doth the dial straight endow
  The green with glamour undenied,
Close clustering in green branch and bough.

Such relics who would disallow?
  We pause and ponder; turn aside;
The garden 's past, 't is forest now,
Close clustering in green branch and bough.

IV.

The glint of steel, the gleam of brocade,
  "Monseigneur" up in his tarnished frame,
A long low terrace, half sun, half shade;

Tapestry, dusty, dim, and frayed,
  Fauteuil and sofa, a flickering flame,
A glint of steel, a gleam of brocade;

"Mdme." on the wall as a roguish maid,
  Later—some years—as a portly dame,
The long low terrace, half sun, half shade,

Where "Mdme.'s" ghost and "Monsieur's" parade
  And play at *ombre*, their favorite game!
The glint of steel, the gleam of brocade,

Hang over hall and balustrade.
  Paceth a spectral peacock tame
The long low terrace, half sun, half shade.

Waketh a nightly serenade
  Where daylight now we see proclaim
The glint of steel, the gleam of brocade,
The long low terrace, half sun, half shade!

v.

The spell of Age is over all,
  The lichened vault, the massive keep,
The shaded walks, the shadowy hall,

And mediæval mists enthrall
  The senses bathed in beauty sleep,—
The spell of age is over all!

No marvel if a silken shawl
  Be sometimes heard to trail and sweep
The shaded walks, the shadowy hall.

No marvel if a light footfall
  Adown the stair be heard to creep,—
The spell of age is over all.

A foot—we muse—both arched and small,
  Doth often tread this terrace steep,
Those shaded walks, this shadowy hall—

A foot as white as trilliums tall—
  Musing, the wall we lightly leap.
The spell of Age is over all!
The shaded walks—the shadowy hall.

  S. FRANCES HARRISON *(Seranus).*

IN MEXICO.

THE cactus towers, straight and tall,
Through fallow fields of chapparal;
  And here and there, in paths apart,
  A dusky peon guides his cart,
    And yokes of oxen journey slow,
      In Mexico.

And oft some distant tinkling tells
Of muleteers, with wagon bells
  That jangle sweet across the maize,
  And green agave stalks that raise
    Rich spires of blossoms, row on row,
      In Mexico.

Upon the whitened city walls
The golden sunshine softly falls,
  On archways set with orange trees,
  On paven courts and balconies
    Where trailing vines toss to and fro,
      In Mexico.

And patient little donkeys fare
With laden saddle-bags, and bear
  Through narrow ways quaint water-jars
  Wreathed round with waxen lily stars
    And scarlet poppy-buds that blow,
      In Mexico.

When twilight falls, more near and clear
The tender southern skies appear,
  And down green slopes of blooming limes

Come cascades of cathedral chimes;
And prayerful figures worship low,
In Mexico.

A land of lutes and witching tones,
Of silver, onyx, opal stones;
A lazy land, wherein all seems
Enchanted into endless dreams;
And never any need they know,
In Mexico,

Of life's unquiet, swift advance;
But slipped into such gracious trance,
The restless world speeds on, unfelt,
Unheeded, as by those who dwelt
In olden ages, long ago,
In Mexico.

EVALEEN STEIN.

NARRATIVE POEMS.

NARRATIVE POEMS.

THE FALL OF TROY.

FROM THE " ÆNEID."

Æneas, speaking to Dido, Queen of Carthage.—

Forward we fare,
Called to the palace of Priam by war-shouts rend-
    ing the air.

Here of a truth raged battle, as though no combats
    beside
Reigned elsewhere, no thousands about all Ilion
    died.
Here we beheld in his fury the war-god ; foemen
    the roof
Scaling, the threshold blocked with a penthouse,
    javelin-proof.
Ladders rest on the walls, armed warriors climb by
    the door
Stair upon stair, left hands, to the arrows round
    them that pour,
Holding a buckler, the battlement ridge in the right
    held fast.
Trojans in turn wrench loose from the palace turret
    and tower ;
Ready with these, when the end seems visible,—
    death's dark hour

Closing around them now,—to defend their lives to
the last.
Gilded rafters, the glory of Trojan kings of the
past,
Roll on the enemy.   Others, with javelins flashing
fire,
Form at the inner doors, and around them close
in a ring.
Hearts grow bolder within us to succor the
palace, to bring
Aid to the soldier, and valor in vanquished hearts to
inspire.

There was a gate with a secret door, that a pas-
sage adjoined
Thridding the inner palace—a postern planted be-
hind.
Here Andromache, ill-starred queen, oft entered
alone,
Visiting Hector's parents, when yet they sate on
the throne ;
Oft to his grandsire with her the boy Astyanax led.
Passing the covered way to the roof I mount over-
head,
Where Troy's children were hurling an idle jave-
lin shower.
From it a turret rose, on the topmost battle-
ment height
Raised to the stars, whence Troy and the
Danaan ships and the white
Dorian tents were wont to be seen in a happier
hour.
With bright steel we assailed it, and where high
flooring of tower

Offered a joint that yielded, we wrenched it loose,
    and below
Sent it a-drifting. It fell with a thunderous crash
    on the foe,
Carrying ruin afar. But the ranks close round us
    again,
Stones and the myriad weapons of war unceas-
    ingly rain.
Facing the porch, on the threshold itself, stands
    Pyrrhus in bright
Triumph, with glittering weapons, a flashing mirror
    of light.
As to the light some viper, on grasses poisonous
    fed,
Swollen and buried long by the winter's frost in his
    bed,
Shedding his weeds, uprises in shining beauty and
    strength,
Lifts, new-born, his bosom, and wreathes his slip-
    pery length,
High to the sunlight darting a three-forked
    flickering tongue,—
Periphas huge strides near, and the brave Au-
    tomedon, long
Charioteer to Achilles, an armor-bearer to-day.
All of the flower of Scyros beside him, warriors
    young,
    Crowd to the palace too, while flames on the
    battlement play.
Pyrrhus in front of the host, with a two-edged
    axe in his hand,
Breaches the stubborn doors, from the hinges rends
    with his brand

Brass-clamped timbers, a panel cleaves, to the
    heart of the oak
Strikes, and a yawning chasm for the sunlight
    gapes at his stroke.
Bare to the eye is the palace within : long vistas of
    hall
Open ; the inmost dwelling of Priam is seen of
    them all :
Bare the inviolate chambers of kings of an earlier
    day,
And they descry on the threshold the armed men
    standing at bay.

Groaning and wild uproar through the inner palace
    begin ;
Women's wailings are heard from the vaulted
    cloisters within.
Shrieks to the golden stars are rolled. Scared
    mothers in fear
Over the vast courts wander, embracing the
    thresholds dear,
Clasping and kissing the doors. On strides, as
    his father in might,
Pyrrhus: no gate can stay him, nor guard with-
    stand him to-night ;
Portals yield at the thunder of strokes plied ever
    and aye ;
Down from the hinges the gates are flung on their
    faces to lie.
Entry is broken; the enemy's hosts stream in-
    wards and kill
All in the van, each space with a countless soldiery
    fill.
Not so rages the river, that o'er its barriers flows

White with foam, overturning the earth-built
  mounds that oppose,
When on the fields as a mountain it rolls, by
  meadow and wold,
Sweeping to ruin the herd and the stall. These
  eyes did behold
Pyrrhus maddened with slaughter ; and marked on
  the sill of the gate
Both the Atridæ brethren. I saw where Hecuba
  sate,
Round her a hundred brides of her sons,—saw
  Priam with blood
Staining the altar-fires he had hallowed himself to
  his god.
Fifty his bridal chambers within,—each seeming a
  sweet
Promise of children's children,—in dust all lie at
  his feet !
Doors emblazoned with spoils, and with proud bar-
  barian gold,
Lie in the dust ! Where flames yield passage,
  Danaans hold !

From the Latin of VIRGIL.
Translation of SIR CHARLES BOWEN.

HORATIUS AT THE BRIDGE.

Lars Porsena of Clusium,
  By the Nine Gods he swore
That the great house of Tarquin
  Should suffer wrong no more.
By the Nine Gods he swore it,
  And named a trysting-day,

And bade his messengers ride forth,
East and west and south and north,
To summon his array.

East and west and south and north
The messengers ride fast,
And tower and town and cottage
Have heard the trumpet's blast.
Shame on the false Etruscan
Who lingers in his home,
When Porsena of Clusium
Is on the march for Rome!

The horsemen and the footmen
Are pouring in amain
From many a stately market-place,
From many a fruitful plain,
From many a lonely hamlet,
Which, hid by beech and pine,
Like an eagle's nest hangs on the crest
Of purple Apennine:

From lordly Volaterræ,
Where scowls the far-famed hold
Piled by the hands of giants
For godlike kings of old;
From sea-girt Populonia,
Whose sentinels descry
Sardinia's snowy mountain-tops
Fringing the southern sky;

From the proud mart of Pisæ,
Queen of the western waves,
Where ride Massilia's triremes,
Heavy with fair-haired slaves;

From where sweet Clanis wanders
    Through corn and vines and flowers,
From where Cortona lifts to heaven
    Her diadem of towers.

Tall are the oaks whose acorns
    Drop in dark Auser's rill;
Fat are the stags that champ the boughs
    Of the Ciminian hill;
Beyond all streams, Clitumnus
    Is to the herdsman dear;
Best of all pools the fowler loves
    The great Volsinian mere.

But now no stroke of woodman
    Is heard by Auser's rill;
No hunter tracks the stag's green path
    Up the Ciminian hill;
Unwatched along Clitumnus
    Grazes the milk-white steer;
Unharmed the water-fowl may dip
    In the Volsinian mere.

The harvests of Arretium,
    This year, old men shall reap;
This year, young boys in Umbro
    Shall plunge the struggling sheep;
And in the vats of Luna,
    This year, the must shall foam
Round the white feet of laughing girls
    Whose sires have marched to Rome.

There be thirty chosen prophets,
    The wisest of the land,
Who always by Lars Porsena
    Both morn and evening stand.

Evening and morn the Thirty
  Have turned the verses o'er,
Traced from the right on linen white
  By mighty seers of yore;

And with one voice the Thirty
  Have their glad answer given:
" Go forth, go forth, Lars Porsena,—
  Go forth, beloved of Heaven!
Go, and return in glory
  To Clusium's royal dome,
And hang round Nurscia's altars
  The golden shields of Rome!"

And now hath every city
  Sent up her tale of men;
The foot are fourscore thousand,
  The horse are thousands ten.
Before the gates of Sutrium
  Is met the great array;
A proud man was Lars Porsena
  Upon the trysting-day.

For all the Etruscan armies
  Were ranged beneath his eye,
And many a banished Roman,
  And many a stout ally;
And with a mighty following,
  To join the muster, came
The Tusculan Mamilius,
  Prince of the Latian name.

But by the yellow Tiber
  Was tumult and affright;
From all the spacious champaign
  To Rome men took their flight.

A mile around the city
   The throng stopped up the ways;
A fearful sight it was to see
   Through two long nights and days.

For aged folk on crutches,
   And women great with child,
And mothers, sobbing over babes
   That clung to them and smiled,
And sick men borne in litters
   High on the necks of slaves,
And troops of sunburned husbandmen
   With reaping-hooks and staves,

And droves of mules and asses
   Laden with skins of wine,
And endless flocks of goats and sheep,
   And endless herds of kine,
And endless trains of wagons,
   That creaked beneath the weight
Of corn-sacks and of household goods,
   Choked every roaring gate.

Now, from the rock Tarpeian,
   Could the wan burghers spy
The line of blazing villages
   Red in the midnight sky.
The Fathers of the City,
   They sat all night and day,
For every hour some horseman came
   With tidings of dismay.

To eastward and to westward
   Have spread the Tuscan bands,
Nor house, nor fence, nor dovecote
   In Crustumerium stands.

Verbenna down to Ostia
  Hath wasted all the plain;
Astur hath stormed Janiculum,
  And the stout guards are slain.

I wis, in all the Senate
  There was no heart so bold
But sore it ached, and fast it beat,
  When that ill news was told.
Forthwith up rose the Consul,
  Up rose the Fathers all;
In haste they girded up their gowns,
  And hied them to the wall.

They held a council, standing
  Before the River-gate;
Short time was there, ye well may guess,
  For musing or debate.
Out spake the Consul roundly:
  " The bridge must straight go down;
For, since Janiculum is lost,
  Naught else can save the town."

Just then a scout came flying,
  All wild with haste and fear:
"To arms! to arms! Sir Consul,—
  Lars Porsena is here."
On the low hills to westward
  The Consul fixed his eye,
And saw the swarthy storm of dust
  Rise fast along the sky.

And nearer fast and nearer
  Doth the red whirlwind come;
And louder still, and still more loud,
From underneath that rolling cloud,

Is heard the trumpets' war-note proud,
  The trampling and the hum.
And plainly and more plainly
  Now through the gloom appears,
Far to left and far to right,
In broken gleams of dark-blue light,
The long array of helmets bright,
  The long array of spears.

And plainly and more plainly,
  Above that glimmering line,
Now might ye see the banners
  Of twelve fair cities shine ;
But the banner of proud Clusium
  Was highest of them all,—
The terror of the Umbrian,
  The terror of the Gaul.

And plainly and more plainly
  Now might the burghers know,
By port and vest, by horse and crest,
  Each warlike Lucumo :
There Cilnius of Arretium
  On his fleet roan was seen ;
And Astur of the fourfold shield,
Girt with the brand none else may wield ;
Tolumnius with the belt of gold,
And dark Verbenna from the hold
  By reedy Thrasymene.

Fast by the royal standard,
  O'erlooking all the war,
Lars Porsena of Clusium
  Sat in his ivory car.

By the right wheel rode Mamilius,
  Prince of the Latian name ;
And by the left false Sextus,
  That wrought the deed of shame.

But when the face of Sextus
  Was seen among the foes,
A yell that rent the firmament
  From all the town arose.
On the house-tops was no woman
  But spat towards him and hissed,
No child but screamed out curses,
  And shook its little fist.

But the Consul's brow was sad,
  And the Consul's speech was low,
And darkly looked he at the wall,
  And darkly at the foe ;
" Their van will be upon us
  Before the bridge goes down ;
And if they once may win the bridge,
  What hope to save the town ? "

Then out spake brave Horatius,
  The Captain of the gate :
" To every man upon this earth
  Death cometh soon or late.
And how can man die better
  Than facing fearful odds
For the ashes of his fathers
  And the temples of his gods,

" And for the tender mother
  Who dandled him to rest,

And for the wife who nurses
His baby at her breast,
And for the holy maidens
Who feed the eternal flame,—
To save them from false Sextus
That wrought the deed of shame?

" Hew down the bridge, Sir Consul,
With all the speed ye may ;
I, with two more to help me,
Will hold the foe in play.
In yon strait path a thousand
May well be stopped by three:
Now who will stand on either hand,
And keep the bridge with me? "

Then out spake Spurius Lartius,—
A Ramnian proud was he :
" Lo, I will stand at thy right hand,
And keep the bridge with thee."
And out spake strong Herminius,—
Of Titian blood was he:
" I will abide on thy left side,
And keep the bridge with thee."

" Horatius," quoth the Consul,
" As thou sayest so let it be,"
And straight against that great array
Went forth the dauntless three.
For Romans in Rome's quarrel
Spared neither land nor gold,
Nor son nor wife, nor limb nor life,
In the brave days of old.

Then none was for a party —
  Then all were for the state ;
Then the great man helped the poor,
  And the poor man loved the great ;
Then lands were fairly portioned !
  Then spoils were fairly sold :
The Romans were like brothers
  In the brave days of old.

Now Roman is to Roman
  More hateful than a foe,
And the tribunes beard the high,
  And the fathers grind the low.
As we wax hot in faction,
  In battle we wax cold ;
Wherefore men fight not as they fought
  In the brave days of old.

Now while the three were tightening
  Their harness on their backs,
The Consul was the foremost man
  To take in hand an axe ;
And fathers, mixed with commons,
  Seized hatchet, bar, and crow,
And smote upon the planks above,
  And loosed the props below.

Meanwhile the Tuscan army,
  Right glorious to behold,
Came flashing back the noonday light,
Rank behind rank, like surges bright
  Of a broad sea of gold.
Four hundred trumpets sounded
  A peal of warlike glee,

As that great host with measured tread,
And spears advanced, and ensigns spread,
Rolled slowly toward the bridge's head,
    Where stood the dauntless three.

The three stood calm and silent,
    And looked upon the foes,
And a great shout of laughter
    From all the vanguard rose;
And forth three chiefs came spurring
    Before that deep array;
To earth they sprang, their swords they drew,
And lifted high their shields, and flew
    To win the narrow way.

Aunus, from green Tifernum,
    Lord of the Hill of Vines;
And Seius, whose eight hundred slaves
    Sicken in Ilva's mines;
And Picus, long to Clusium
    Vassal in peace and war,
Who led to fight his Umbrian powers
From that gray crag where, girt with towers,
The fortress of Nequinum lowers
    O'er the pale waves of Nar.

Stout Lartius hurled down Aunus
    Into the stream beneath;
Herminius struck at Seius,
    And clove him to the teeth;
At Picus brave Horatius
    Darted one fiery thrust,
And the proud Umbrian's gilded arms
    Clashed in the bloody dust.

Then Ocnus of Falerii
  Rushed on the Roman three;
And Lausulus of Urgo,
  The rover of the sea;
And Aruns of Volsinium,
  Who slew the great wild boar,—
The great wild boar that had his den
Amidst the reeds of Cosa's fen,
And wasted fields, and slaughtered men,
  Along Albinia's shore.

Herminius smote down Aruns;
  Lartius laid Ocnus low;
Right to the heart of Lausulus
  Horatius sent a blow:
"Lie there," he cried, "fell pirate!
  No more, aghast and pale,
From Ostia's walls the crowd shall mark
The track of thy destroying bark;
No more Campania's hinds shall fly
To woods and caverns, when they spy
  Thy thrice-accursèd sail!"

But now no sound of laughter
  Was heard among the foes;
A wild and wrathful clamor
  From all the vanguard rose.
Six spears' length from the entrance,
  Halted that mighty mass,
And for a space no man came forth
  To win the narrow pass.

But, hark! the cry is Astur:
  And lo! the ranks divide;

And the great lord of Luna
  Comes with his stately stride.
Upon his ample shoulders
  Clangs loud the fourfold shield,
And in his hand he shakes the brand
  Which none but he can wield.

He smiled on those bold Romans,
  A smile serene and high;
He eyed the flinching Tuscans,
  And scorn was in his eye.
Quoth he, "The she-wolf's litter
  Stand savagely at bay;
But will ye dare to follow,
  If Astur clears the way?"

Then, whirling up his broadsword
  With both hands to the height,
He rushed against Horatius,
  And smote with all his might.
With shield and blade Horatius
  Right deftly turned the blow.
The blow, though turned, came yet too nigh;
It missed his helm, but gashed his thigh.
The Tuscans raised a joyful cry
  To see the red blood flow.

He reeled, and on Herminius
  He leaned one breathing-space,
Then, like a wild-cat mad with wounds,
  Sprang right at Astur's face.
Through teeth and skull and helmet
  So fierce a thrust he sped,
The good sword stood a handbreadth out
  Behind the Tuscan's head.

And the great lord of Luna
   Fell at that deadly stroke,
As falls on Mount Avernus
   A thunder-smitten oak.
Far o'er the crashing forest
   The giant arms lie spread;
And the pale augurs, muttering low
   Gaze on the blasted head.

On Astur's throat Horatius
   Right firmly pressed his heel,
And thrice and four times tugged amain,
   Ere he wrenched out the steel.
And " See," he cried, " the welcome,
   Fair guests, that waits you here!
What noble Lucumo comes next
   To taste our Roman cheer?"

But at his haughty challenge
   A sullen murmur ran,
Mingled with wrath and shame and dread,
   Along that glittering van.
There lacked not men of prowess,
   Nor men of lordly race,
For all Etruria's noblest
   Were round the fatal place.

But all Etruria's noblest
   Felt their hearts sink to see
On the earth the bloody corpses,
   In the path the dauntless three;
And from the ghastly entrance,
   Where those bold Romans stood,
All shrank,—like boys who, unaware,
Ranging the woods to start a hare,

Come to the mouth of the dark lair
Where, growling low, a fierce old bear
  Lies amidst bones and blood.

Was none who would be foremost
  To lead such dire attack;
But those behind cried " Forward ! "
  And those before cried " Back ! "
And backward now and forward
  Wavers the deep array;
And on the tossing sea of steel
To and fro the standards reel,
And the victorious trumpet-peal
  Dies fitfully away.

Yet one man for one moment
  Strode out before the crowd;
Well known was he to all the three,
  And they gave him greeting loud:
" Now welcome, welcome, Sextus!
  Now welcome to thy home!
Why dost thou stay, and turn away ?
  Here lies the road to Rome."

Thrice looked he at the city;
  Thrice looked he at the dead:
And thrice came on in fury,
  And thrice turned back in dread;
And, white with fear and hatred,
  Scowled at the narrow way
Where, wallowing in a pool of blood,
  The bravest Tuscans lay.

But meanwhile axe and lever
  Have manfully been plied:

And now the bridge hangs tottering
  Above the boiling tide.
" Come back, come back, Horatius ! "
  Loud cried the Fathers all,—
" Back, Lartius ! back, Herminius !
  Back, ere the ruin fall ! "

Back darted Spurius Lartius,—
  Herminius darted back ;
And, as they passed, beneath their feet
  They felt the timbers crack.
But when they turned their faces,
  And on the farther shore
Saw brave Horatius stand alone,
  They would have crossed once more ;

But with a crash like thunder
  Fell every loosened beam,
And, like a dam, the mighty wreck
  Lay right athwart the stream ;
And a long shout of triumph
  Rose from the walls of Rome,
As to the highest turret-tops
  Was splashed the yellow foam.

And like a horse unbroken,
  When first he feels the rein,
The furious river struggled hard,
  And tossed his tawny mane,
And burst the curb, and bounded,
  Rejoicing to be free ;
And whirling down, in fierce career,
Battlement and plank and pier,
  Rushed headlong to the sea.

Alone stood brave Horatius,
　But constant still in mind,—
Thrice thirty thousand foes before,
　And the broad flood behind.
"Down with him!" cried false Sextus,
　With a smile on his pale face;
"Now yield thee," cried Lars Porsena,
　"Now yield thee to our grace!"

Round turned he, as not deigning
　Those craven ranks to see;
Naught spake he to Lars Porsena,
　To Sextus naught spake he;
But he saw on Palatinus
　The white porch of his home;
And he spake to the noble river
　That rolls by the towers of Rome:

"O Tiber! Father Tiber!
　To whom the Romans pray,
A Roman's life, a Roman's arms,
　Take thou in charge this day!"
So he spake, and, speaking, sheathed
　The good sword by his side,
And, with his harness on his back,
　Plunged headlong in the tide.

No sound of joy or sorrow
　Was heard from either bank,
But friends and foes in dumb surprise,
With parted lips and straining eyes,
　Stood gazing where he sank;
And when above the surges
　They saw his crest appear,

All Rome sent forth a rapturous cry,
And even the ranks of Tuscany
    Could scarce forbear to cheer.

But fiercely ran the current,
    Swollen high by months of rain;
And fast his blood was flowing,
    And he was sore in pain,
And heavy with his armor,
    And spent with changing blows;
And oft they thought him sinking,
    But still again he rose.

Never, I ween, did swimmer.
    In such an evil case,
Struggle through such a raging flood
    Safe to the landing-place;
But his limbs were borne up bravely
    By the brave heart within,
And our good Father Tiber
    Bare bravely up his chin.

" Curse on him ! " quoth false Sextus,—
    " Will not the villain drown?
But for this stay, ere close of day
    We should have sacked the town ! "
" Heaven help him ! " quoth Lars Porsena,
    " And bring him safe to shore;
For such a gallant feat of arms
    Was never seen before."

And now he feels the bottom;
    Now on dry earth he stands;
Now round him throng the Fathers
    To press his gory hands;

And now, with shouts and clapping,
   And noise of weeping loud,
He enters through the River-gate,
   Borne by the joyous crowd.

They gave him of the corn-land,
   That was of public right,
As much as two strong oxen
   Could plough from morn till night;
And they made a molten image,
   And set it up on high,—
And there it stands unto this day
   To witness if I lie.

It stands in the Comitium,
   Plain for all folk to see,—
Horatius in his harness,
   Halting upon one knee;
And underneath is written,
   In letters all of gold,
How valiantly he kept the bridge
   In the brave days of old.

And still his name sounds stirring
   Unto the men of Rome,
As the trumpet-blast that cries to them
   To charge the Volscian home;
And wives still pray to Juno
   For boys with hearts as bold
As his who kept the bridge so well
   In the brave days of old.

And in the nights of winter,
   When the cold north-winds blow,

And the long howling of the wolves
Is heard amidst the snow;
When round the lonely cottage
Roars loud the tempest's din,
And the good logs of Algidus
Roar louder yet within;

When the oldest cask is opened,
And the largest lamp is lit;
When the chestnuts glow in the embers,
And the kid turns on the spit;
When young and old in circle
Around the firebrands close;
When the girls are weaving baskets,
And the lads are shaping bows;

When the goodman mends his armor,
And trims his helmet's plume;
When the goodwife's shuttle merrily
Goes flashing through the loom;
With weeping and with laughter
Still is the story told,
How well Horatius kept the bridge
In the brave days of old.

THOMAS BABINGTON, LORD MACAULAY.

THOR RECOVERS HIS HAMMER FROM THRYM.

Wroth waxed Thor, when his sleep was flown,
And he found his trusty hammer gone;
He smote his brow, his beard he shook,
The son of earth 'gan round him look;
And this the first word that he spoke:

" Now listen what I tell thee, Loke ;
Which neither on earth below is known,
Nor in heaven above : my hammer's gone."
Their way to Freyia's bower they took,
And this the first word that he spoke :
" Thou, Freyia, must lend a wingèd robe,
To seek my hammer round the globe."

FREYIA sang.

" That shouldst thou have, though 't were of gold,
And that, though 't were of silver, hold."

Away flew Loke ; the winged robe sounds,
Ere he has left the Asgard grounds,
And ere he has reached the Jötunheim bounds.
High on a mount, in haughty state,
Thrym, the king of the Thursi, sate ;
For his dogs he was twisting collars of gold,
And trimming the manes of his coursers bold.

THRYM sang.

" How fare the Asi ? the Alfi how ?
Why com'st thou alone to Jötunheim now ? "

LOKE sang.

" Ill fare the Asi ; the Alfi mourn ;
Thor's hammer from him thou hast torn."

THRYM sang.

" I have the Thunderer's hammer bound
Fathoms eight beneath the ground ;
With it shall no one homeward tread,
Till he bring me Freyia to share my bed."

Away flew Loke ; the winged robe sounds,
Ere he has left the Jötunheim bounds,

And ere he has reached the Asgard grounds.
At Mitgard Thor met crafty Loke,
And this the first word that he spoke :
" Have you your errand and labor done?
Tell from aloft the course you run:
For, setting oft, the story fails ;
And, lying oft, the lie prevails."

LOKE sang.

" My labor is past, mine errand I bring;
Thrym has thine hammer, the giant king:
With it shall no one homeward tread,
Till he bear him Freyia to share his bed."

Their way to lovely Freyia they took,
And this the first word that he spoke :
" Now, Freyia, busk, as a blooming bride;
Together we must to Jötunheim ride."
Wroth waxed Freyia with ireful look ;
All Asgard's hall with wonder shook ;
Her great bright necklace started wide :
" Well may ye call me a wanton bride,
If I with ye to Jötunheim ride."
The Asi did all to council crowd,
The Asiniæ all talked fast and loud ;
This they debated, and this they sought,
How the hammer of Thor should home be brought.
Up then and spoke Heimdallar free,
Like the Vani, wise was he :
"Now busk we Thor, as a bride so fair ;
Let him that great bright necklace wear ;
Round him let ring the spousal keys,
And a maiden kirtle hang to his knees,
And on his bosom jewels rare ;

And high and quaintly braid his hair."
Wroth waxed Thor with godlike pride :
" Well may the Asi me deride,
If I let me be dight as a blooming bride."
Then up spoke Loke, Laufeyia's son :
" Now hush thee, Thor; this must be done:
The giants will strait in Asgard reign,
If thou thy hammer dost not regain."
Then busked they Thor, as a bride so fair,
And the great bright necklace gave him to wear.
Round him let ring the spousal keys,
And a maiden kirtle hang to his knees,
And on his bosom jewels rare ;
And high and quaintly braided his hair.
Up then arose the crafty Loke,
Laufeyia's son, and thus he spoke :
" A servant I thy steps will tend,
Together we must to Jötunheim wend."
Now home the goats together hie ;
Yoked to the axle they swiftly fly.
The mountains shook, the earth burned red,
As Odin's son to Jötunheim sped.
Then Thrym, the king of the Thursi, said :
" Giants, stand up ; let the seats be spread :
Bring Freyia, Niorder's daughter, down,
To share my bed, from Noatun.
With horns all gilt each coal-black beast
Is led to deck the giants' feast ;
Large wealth and jewels have I stored ;
I lack but Freyia to grace my board."
Betimes at evening they approached,
And the mantling ale the giants broached.
The spouse of Sifia ate alone

Eight salmons, and an ox full-grown,
And all the cates, on which women feed;
And drank three firkins of sparkling mead.
Then Thrym, the king of the Thursi, said:
" Where have ye beheld such a hungry maid?
Ne'er saw I bride so keenly feed,
Nor drink so deep of the sparkling mead."
Then forward leaned the crafty Loke,
And thus the giant he bespoke:
" Naught has she eaten for eight long nights,
So did she long for the nuptial rites."
He stooped beneath her veil to kiss,
But he started the length of the hall, I wiss:
" Why are the looks of Freyia so dire?
It seems as her eyeballs glistened with fire."
Then forward leaned the crafty Loke,
And thus the giant he bespoke:
" Naught has she slept for eight long nights,
So did she long for the nuptial rites."
Then in the giant's sister came,
Who dared a bridal gift to claim:
" Those rings of gold from thee I crave,
If thou wilt all my fondness have,
All my love and fondness have."
Then Thrym, the king of the Thursi, said:
" Bear in the hammer to plight the maid;
Upon her lap the bruiser lay,
And firmly plight our hands and fay."
The Thunderer's soul smiled in his breast,
When the hammer hard on his lap was placed.
Thrym first, the king of the Thursi, he slew
And slaughtered all the giant crew.
He slew that giant's sister old,

Who prayed for bridal gifts so bold;
Instead of money and rings, I wot,
The hammer's bruises were her lot.
Thus Odin's son his hammer got.

From the Icelandic of SÆMUND'S EDDA.
Translation of W. HERBERT.

FRITHIOF AT THE COURT OF ANGANTYR.

FROM THE "FRITHIOF SAGA," CANTO XI.

'T is time to tell how Angantyr,
The earl, was seated then
High in his hall of stately fir,
Carousing with his men.
Thence he surveyed, in merry mood,
The day-car as it rolled ;
Now cleaving through the purple flood,
All like a swan of gold.

The window near, a trusty swain,
Old Halvar, kept good heed ;
One eye upon the foamy main,
One on the frothy mead.
Oft as the veteran's dole came round,
He quaffed till all was drawn ;
Then straight, with gravity profound,
Replaced the exhausted horn.

Now hurled, it bounded on the floor,
Whilst loud the warder cried,
" The billows, laboring toward the shore,
I see a vessel ride.
Wrestling with death, pale rowers strain,
And now they touch the land ;

And ghastly forms, by giants twain,
　　Are strewed along the strand."

The chieftain o'er the glassy vale
　　Looked from his hall on high:
" Yon pennon is Ellida's sail;
　　Frithiof, I ween, is nigh.
That noble port, that lofty brow,
　　Old Thorsten's son declares;
Such cognizance, brave youth, as thou,
　　No gallant Northman bears."

Swift from the bench, with maddening air,
　　The Berserk Atlè flew;
O'er whose gaunt visage, gore-stained hair
　　A sable horror threw.
" I haste," he roared, " intent to brave
　　This sword-subduer's spell,
Who peace or truce ne'er deigned to crave,
　　As vaunting rumors tell."

Then twice six followers from the board
　　Rushed forth with fierce delight;
They whirled the club, they waved the sword,
　　Impatient for the fight.
Thus storming, to the beach they hied,
　　Where Frithiof on the sand
Seated, by spent Ellida's side,
　　Cheered his disheartened band.

" Conquest," he 'gan, with thundering voice,
　　" Were feat of light emprise,
Yet generous Atlè grants a choice,
　　Ere luckless Frithiof dies.

For proffered peace deign once to sue,
  Else all unwont to plead,
Thy steps, myself, as comrade true,
  To yonder keep will lead."

" Though worn with conflict fell and long,"
  In ire, the Bold replied,
" Ere Frithiof wear a suppliant tongue,
  Be the fresh battle tried."
Then from each sunburnt warrior's steel
  The lightning flashes came,
And Angurvadel's runes reveal
  Dark fate, in signs of flame.

Now on their bucklers, showered like hail,
  The clattering death-strokes beat ;
Till, cleft at once, each shield's bossed mail
  Falls clanging at their feet.
Yet, proof alike 'gainst fear and ruth,
  They played the desperate stake ;
But keen was Angurvadel's tooth,
  And Atlè's falchion brake.

Said Frithiof, " Swordless foeman's life
  Ne'er dyed this gallant blade :
So, list thee to prolong the strife,
  Be equal war essayed."
Like billows driven by autumn's blast,
  The champions met and closed ;
In mutual clutch locked firm and fast,
  Their steel-clad breasts opposed.

They hugged like bears, that, wandering free,
  Meet on their cliff of snow ;

Grappled like eagles o'er the sea,
　That frets its waves below.
Such force had well-nigh torn the rock,
　Deep-rooted, from its bed;
And, shaken less, the iron oak
　Had bowed its leafy head.

Big from their brows the heat-drops roll,
　Cold heaves each laboring chest,
Touched by their tread, stone, bush, and knoll
　Start from their ancient rest.
Trembling, their sturdy followers wait
　The issue of the fray;
And oft shall Northern lips relate
　The wrestling of that day.

'T is o'er; for Frithiof's matchless strength
　Has felled his ponderous size;
And 'neath that knee, a giant length,
　Supine the Viking lies.
" But fails my sword, thou Berserk swart! "
　The voice rang far and wide,
" Its point should pierce thy inmost heart,
　Its hilt should drink the tide."

" Be free to lift the weaponed hand,"
　Undaunted Atlè spoke,
" Hence, fearless quest thy distant brand!
　Thus I abide the stroke:
To track Valhalla's path of light,
　In arms immortal shine,—
My destiny, perchance, this night,
　To-morrow may be thine! "

Nor Frithiof long delayed ; intent
   To close the dread debate,
His blade redeemed 'gainst Atlè bent,
   And aimed the expected fate.
But reckless courage holds a charm
   Can kindred wrath surcease ;
This quelled his ire, this checked his arm,
   Outstretched the hand of peace.

The warder growled, and eyed the cheer,
   Waving his staff of white :
" But little boots our banquet here,
   That Hildur's cates invite ;
For you must stand the savory meat
   Untouched in reeking row,
For you these lips be parched with heat,
   Halvar his horn forego."

Now, brothers sworn, the former foes
   Have passed the spacious gate,
Whose valves to Frithiof's view disclose
   Wonders of wealth and state.
For planks, his walls' rude vest, scant aid
   To exclude the piercing cold,
Rich skins with glittering flowers o'erlaid,
   Berries of pendent gold.

No central balefire in the hall
   With stifling splendor shone ;
But glowed within the caverned wall
   A hearth of polished stone.
No sooty clouds the roof defaced,
   The polished plank distained ;
Glass neatly squared the windows graced ;
   The door a lock restrained.

For torch of pine, whose crackling blaze
    Diffused a flickering gleam,
From branching silver shed, bright rays
    Rivalled the solar beam.
He saw the table's ample sweep
    A larded hart adorn,
With gold-hoof raised for menaced leap,
    And leaf in grove of horn.

Behind the seated chief, serene,
    Appeared a virgin-form ;
So locks the star of beauty's queen,
    Soft, o'er a sky of storm.
There nut-brown ringlets circling flowed ;
    There sparkled eyes of blue ;
And, as a flower 'midst runes, there glowed
    Small lips of roseate hue.

High on a throne of ore-clad elm
    Sat Angantyr sedate ;
Bright as the sun his burnished helm,
    As bright his gilded plate.
His mantle, rich with many a gem,
    Strewed the bespangled ground ;
Along whose border's purple hem
    The spotless ermine wound.

He strode three paces from the dais,
    His gallant guest to greet,
And led, with many a gracious phrase,
    To honor's nearest seat.
" What place a comrade's cherished name
    Might ask for Thorsten's son
Is thine, brave youth ; the due of fame,
    By peerless valor won."

Now flagons from Sicilia's store
Their treasured nectar gave ;
Not Etna's fire could sparkle more,
More froth Charybdis' wave.
"Come, pledge the memory of my friend,
Be welcome pledged," he said,
" And let the brimming goblet blend
The living and the dead."

. . . . .

Whilst jest and social joys engage,
Swift the night-watches fled ;
Freighted with mirth, not fraught with rage,
The golden goblet sped ;
A health to Angantyr they shout,
At the close of each regale :
And Frithiof wears the winter out,
Ere swells Ellida's sail.

From the Swedish of ELIAS TEGNER.
Translation of WILLIAM STRONG.

THE SKELETON IN ARMOR.*

" SPEAK ! speak ! thou fearful guest !
Who, with thy hollow breast
Still in rude armor drest,
    Comest to daunt me !
Wrapt not in Eastern balms,
But with thy fleshless palms
Stretched, as if asking alms,
    Why dost thou haunt me ? "

Then from those cavernous eyes
Pale flashes seemed to rise,
As when the Northern skies
    Gleam in December ;

* Suggested by an armor-clad skeleton dug up at Fall
River, and in the ballad connected with the old Roman
Tower at Newport.

And, like the water's flow
Under December's snow,
Came a dull voice of woe
    From the heart's chamber.

" I was a Viking old !
My deeds, though manifold,
No Skald in song has told,
    No Saga taught thee !
Take heed that in thy verse
Thou dost the tale rehearse,
Else dread a dead man's curse;
    For this I sought thee.

" Far in the Northern Land,
By the wild Baltic's strand,
I, with my childish hand,
    Tamed the gerfalcon ;
And, with my skates fast-bound,
Skimmed the half-frozen Sound,
That the poor whimpering hound
    Trembled to walk on.

" Oft to his frozen lair
Tracked I the grisly bear,
While from my path the hare
    Fled like a shadow;
Oft through the forest dark
Followed the were-wolf's bark,
Until the soaring lark
    Sang from the meadow.

" But when I older grew,
Joining a corsair's crew,
O'er the dark sea I flew
    With the marauders.

Wild was the life we led;
Many the souls that sped,
Many the hearts that bled,
 By our stern orders.

" Many a wassail-bout
Wore the long Winter out;
Often our midnight shout
 Set the cocks crowing,
As we the Berserk's tale
Measured in cups of ale,
Draining the oaken pail
 Filled to o'erflowing.

" Once as I told in glee
Tales of the stormy sea,
Soft eyes did gaze on me,
 Burning yet tender ;
And as the white stars shine
On the dark Norway pine,
On that dark heart of mine
 Fell their soft splendor.

" I wooed the blue-eyed maid,
Yielding, yet half afraid,
And in the forest's shade
 Our vows were plighted.
Under its loosened vest
Fluttered her little breast,
Like birds within their nest
 By the hawk frighted.

" Bright in her father's hall
Shields gleamed upon the wall,
Loud sang the minstrels all,
 Chanting his glory ;

When of old Hildebrand
I asked his daughter's hand,
Mute did the minstrels stand
    To hear my story.

" While the brown ale he quaffed,
Loud then the champion laughed,
And as the wind-gusts waft
    The sea-foam brightly,
So the loud laugh of scorn,
Out of those lips unshorn,
From the deep drinking-horn
    Blew the foam lightly.

" She was a Prince's child,
I but a Viking wild,
And though she blushed and smiled,
    I was discarded !
Should not the dove so white
Follow the sea-mew's flight ?
Why did they leave that night
    Her nest unguarded ?

" Scarce had I put to sea,
Bearing the maid with me,—
Fairest of all was she
    Among the Norsemen !—
When on the white sea-strand,
Waving his armèd hand,
Saw we old Hildebrand,
    With twenty horsemen.

" Then launched they to the blast,
Bent like a reed each mast,
Yet we were gaining fast,
    When the wind failed us ;

And with a sudden flaw
Came round the gusty Skaw,
So that our foe we saw
    Laugh as he hailed us.

" And as to catch the gale
Round veered the flapping sail,
'Death!' was the helmsman's hail,
    'Death without quarter!'
Midships with iron keel
Struck we her ribs of steel;
Down her black hulk did reel
    Through the black water!

" As with his wings aslant,
Sails the fierce cormorant,
Seeking some rocky haunt,
    With his prey laden,
So toward the open main,
Beating to sea again,
Through the wind hurricane,
    Bore I the maiden.

" Three weeks we westward bore,
And when the storm was o'er,
Cloud-like we saw the shore
    Stretching to leeward;
There for my lady's bower
Built I the lofty tower,
Which, to this very hour,
    Stands looking seaward.

" There lived we many years;
Time dried the maiden's tears;

She had forgot her fears,
    She was a mother;
Death closed her mild blue eyes;
Under that tower she lies;
Ne'er shall the sun arise
    On such another.

"Still grew my bosom then,
Still as a stagnant fen!
Hateful to me were men,
    The sunlight hateful!
In the vast forest here,
Clad in my warlike gear,
Fell I upon my spear,
    Oh, death was grateful!

"Thus seamed with many scars,
Bursting these prison bars,
Up to its native stars
    My soul ascended!
There from the flowing bowl
Deep drinks the warrior's soul,
Skoal! to the Northland! *skoal!*"
    Thus the tale ended.

                HENRY WADSWORTH LONGFELLOW.

THE BARON'S LAST BANQUET.

O'ER a low couch the setting sun
    Had thrown its latest ray,
Where in his last strong agony
    A dying warrior lay,—
The stern old Baron Rudiger,
    Whose frame had ne'er been bent

By wasting pain, till time and toil
    Its iron strength had spent.

" They come around me here, and say
    My days of life are o'er,
That I shall mount my noble steed
    And lead my band no more ;
They come, and to my beard they dare
    To tell me now, that I,
Their own liege lord and master born,—
    That I—ha ! ha !—must die.

" And what is Death ? I 've dared him oft
    Before the Paynim spear—
Think ye he 's entered at my gate,
    Has come to seek me here ?
I 've met him, faced him, scorned him,
    When the fight was raging hot,—
I 'll try his might—I 'll brave his power ;
    Defy, and fear him not.

" Ho ! sound the tocsin from my tower,—
    And fire the culverin,—
Bid each retainer arm with speed,—
    Call every vassal in ;
Up with my banner on the wall,—
    The banquet-board prepare,—
Throw wide the portal of my hall,
    And bring my armor there ! "

A hundred hands were busy then,—
    The banquet forth was spread,—
And rung the heavy oaken floor
    With many a martial tread,
While from the rich, dark tracery
    Along the vaulted wall,

Lights gleamed on harness, plume, and spear,
    O'er the proud old Gothic hall.

Fast hurrying through the outer gate,
    The mailed retainers poured,
On through the portal's frowning arch,
    And thronged around the board.
While at its head, within his dark,
    Carved oaken chair of state,
Armed cap-a-pie, stern Rudiger,
    With girded falchion, sate.

" Fill every beaker up, my men,
    Pour forth the cheering wine ;
There 's life and strength in every drop,—
    Thanksgiving to the vine !
Are ye all there, my vassals true ?—
    Mine eyes are waxing dim ;—
Fill round, my tried and fearless ones,
    Each goblet to the brim.

" Ye 're there, but yet I see ye not.
    Draw forth each trusty sword,—
And let me hear your faithful steel
    Clash once around my board :
I hear it faintly :—Louder yet !—
    What clogs my heavy breath ?
Up, all,—and shout for Rudiger,
    ' Defiance unto Death ! ' "

Bowl rang to bowl,—steel clanged to steel,
    And rose a deafening cry
That made the torches flare around,
    And shook the flags on high :—
" Ho ! cravens, do ye fear him ?—
    Slaves, traitors ! have ye flown ?

Ho! cowards, have ye left me
    To meet him here alone?

"But *I* defy him :—let him come!"
    Down rang the massy cup,
While from its sheath the ready blade
    Came flashing half-way up;
And, with the black and heavy plumes
    Scarce trembling on his head,
There, in his dark, carved, oaken chair,
    Old Rudiger sat, *dead*.

ALBERT G. GREENE.

THE NOBLEMAN AND THE PENSIONER.

"OLD man, God bless you! does your pipe taste
    sweetly?
    A beauty, by my soul!
A red-clay flower-pot, rimmed with gold so neatly!
    What ask you for the bowl?"

"O sir, that bowl for worlds I would not part
    with;
    A brave man gave it me,
Who won it—now what think you?—of a bashaw
    At Belgrade's victory.

"There, sir, ah! there was booty worth the show-
    ing,—
    Long life to Prince Eugene!
Like after-grass you might have seen us mowing
    The Turkish ranks down clean."

"Another time I'll hear your story;—
    Come, old man, be no fool;

Take these two ducats,—gold for glory,
    And let me have the bowl ! "

" I 'm a poor churl, as you may say, sir;
    My pension 's all I 'm worth :
Yet I 'd not give that bowl away, sir,
    For all the gold on earth.

" Just hear now ! Once, as we hussars, all merry,
    Hard on the foe's rear pressed,
A blundering rascal of a janizary
    Shot through our captain's breast.

" At once across my horse I hove him,—
    The same would he have done,
And from the smoke and tumult drove him
    Safe to a nobleman.

" I nursed him, and, before his end, bequeathing
    His money and this bowl
To me, he pressed my hand, just ceased his breath-
      ing,
    And so he died, brave soul !

" The money thou must give mine host,—so thought
    I,—
    Three plunderings suffered he :
And, in remembrance of my old friend, brought I
    The pipe away with me.

" Henceforth in all campaigns with me I bore it,
    In flight or in pursuit;
It was a holy thing, sir, and I wore it
    Safe-sheltered in my boot.

" This very limb, I lost it by a shot, sir,
    Under the walls of Prague :
First at my precious pipe, be sure, I caught, sir,
    And then picked up my leg."

" You move me even to tears, old sire :
    What was the brave man's name ?
Tell me, that I, too, may admire,
    And venerate his fame."

" They called him only the brave Walter ;
    His farm lay near the Rhine."—
" God bless your old eyes ! 't was my father,
    And that same farm is mine.

" Come, friend, you 've seen some stormy weather,
    With me is now your bed ;
We 'll drink of Walter's grapes together,
    And eat of Walter's bread."

" Now,—done ! I march in, then, to-morrow ;
    You 're his true heir, I see ;
And when I die, your thanks, kind master,
    The Turkish pipe shall be."

From the German of GOTTLIEB CONRAD PFEFFEL.
Translation of CHARLES TIMOTHY BROOKS.

MAHMOUD.

THERE came a man, making his hasty moan
Before the Sultan Mahmoud on his throne,
And crying out, " My sorrow is my right,
And I *will* see the Sultan, and to-night."
" Sorrow," said Mahmoud, " is a reverend thing :

I recognize its right, as king with king ;
Speak on." " A fiend has got into my house,"
Exclaimed the staring man, " and tortures us,—
One of thine officers ; he comes, the abhorred,
And takes possession of my house, my board,
My bed ;—I have two daughters and a wife,
And the wild villain comes and makes me mad with
    life."
" Is he there now ? " said Mahmoud. " No ; he left
The house when I did, of my wits bereft,
And laughed me down the street, because I vowed
I 'd bring the prince himself to lay him in his shroud.
I 'm mad with want, I 'm mad with misery,
And, O thou Sultan Mahmoud, God cries out for
    thee ! "

The Sultan comforted the man, and said,
" Go home, and I will send thee wine and bread "
(For he was poor) " and other comforts. Go ;
And should the wretch return, let Sultan Mahmoud
    know."

In three days' time, with haggard eyes and beard,
And shaken voice, the suitor reappeared,
And said, " He's come."   Mahmoud said not a word,
But rose and took four slaves, each with a sword,
And went with the vexed man. They reach the
    place,
And hear a voice, and see a woman's face,
That to the window fluttered in affright :
" Go in," said Mahmoud, " and put out the light ;
But tell the females first to leave the room ;
And when the drunkard follows them, we come."

The man went in. There was a cry, and hark!
A table falls, the window is struck dark :
Forth rush the breathless women, and behind
With curses comes the fiend in desperate mind.
In vain : the sabres soon cut short the strife,
And chop the shrieking wretch, and drink his bloody
    life.

" Now *light* the light," the Sultan cried aloud :
'T was done : he took it in his hand and bowed
Over the corpse, and looked upon the face ;
Then turned and knelt, and to the throne of grace
Put up a prayer, and from his lips there crept
Some gentle words of pleasure, and he wept.
In reverent silence the beholders wait,
Then bring him at his call both wine and meat ;
And when he had refreshed his noble heart,
He bade his host be blest, and rose up to depart.

The man amazed, all mildness now and tears,
Fell at the Sultan's feet with many prayers,
And begged him to vouchsafe to tell his slave
The reason first of that command he gave
About the light ; then, when he saw the face,
Why he knelt down ; and lastly, how it was
That fare so poor as his detained him in the place.

The Sultan said, with a benignant eye,
" Since first I saw thee come, and heard thy cry,
I could not rid me of a dread, that one
By whom such daring villanies were done,
Must be some lord of mine,—ay, e'en perhaps a *son.*
For this I had the light put out : but when
I saw the face, and found a stranger slain,
I knelt and thanked the sovereign Arbiter,

Whose work I had performed through pain and fear;
And then I rose and was refreshed with food,
The first time since thy voice had marred my soli-
　　tude."

LEIGH HUNT.

PRINCE ADEB.

In Sana, O, in Sana, God, the Lord,
Was very kind and merciful to me!
Forth from the Desert in my rags I came,
Weary and sore of foot. I saw the spires
And swelling bubbles of the golden domes
Rise through the trees of Sana, and my heart
Grew great within me with the strength of God
And I cried out, "Now shall I right myself,—
I, Adeb the despised,—for God is just!"
There he who wronged my father dwelt in peace,—
My warlike father, who, when gray hairs crept
Around his forehead, as on Lebanon
The whitening snows of winter, was betrayed
To the sly Imam, and his tented wealth
Swept from him, 'twixt the roosting of the cock
And his first crowing,—in a single night:
And I, poor Adeb, sole of all my race,
Smeared with my father's and my kinsmen's blood,
Fled through the Desert, till one day a tribe
Of hungry Bedouins found me in the sand,
Half mad with famine, and they took me up,
And made a slave of me,—of me, a prince!
All was fulfilled at last. I fled from them,
In rags and sorrow. Nothing but my heart,
Like a strong swimmer, bore me up against

The howling sea of my adversity.
At length o'er Sana, in the act of swoop,
I stood like a young eagle on a crag.
The traveller passed me with suspicious fear:
I asked for nothing; I was not a thief.
The lean dogs snuffed around me: my lank bones,
Fed on the berries and the crusted pools,
Were a scant morsel. Once a brown-skinned girl
Called me a little from the common path,
And gave me figs and barley in a bag.
I paid her with a kiss, with nothing more,
And she looked glad; for I was beautiful,
And virgin as a fountain, and as cold.
I stretched her bounty, pecking like a bird
Her figs and barley, till my strength returned.
So when rich Sana lay beneath my eyes,
My foot was as the leopard's, and my hand
As heavy as the lion's brandished paw;
And underneath my burnished skin the veins
And stretching muscles played, at every step,
In wondrous motion. I was very strong.
I looked upon my body, as a bird
That bills his feathers ere he takes to flight,—
I, watching over Sana. Then I prayed;
And on a soft stone, wetted in the brook,
Ground my long knife; and then I prayed again.
God heard my voice, preparing all for me,
As, softly stepping down the hills, I saw
The Imam's summer-palace all ablaze
In the last flash of sunset. Every fount
Was spouting fire, and all the orange-trees
Bore blazing coals, and from the marble walls
And gilded spires and columns, strangely wrought,

Glared the red light, until my eyes were pained
With the fierce splendor. Till the night grew
    thick,
I lay within the bushes, next the door,
Still as a serpent, as invisible.
The guard hung round the portal. Man by man
They dropped away, save one lone sentinel,
And on his eyes God's finger lightly fell;
He slept half standing. Like a summer wind
That threads the grove, yet never turns a leaf,
I stole from shadow unto shadow forth ;
Crossed all the marble courtyard, swung the door
Like a soft gust, a little way ajar,—
My body's narrow width, no more,—and stood
Beneath the cresset in the painted hall.
I marvelled at the riches of my foe ;
I marvelled at God's ways with wicked men.
Then I reached forth, and took God's waiting hand :
And so he led me over mossy floors,
Flowered with the silken summer of Shiraz,
Straight to the Imam's chamber. At the door
Stretched a brawn eunuch, blacker than my eyes :
His woolly head lay like the Kaba-stone
In Mecca's mosque, as silent and as huge.
I stepped across it, with my pointed knife
Just missing a full vein along his neck,
And, pushing by the curtains, there I was,—
I, Adeb the despised,—upon the spot
That, next to heaven, I longed for most of all.
I could have shouted for the joy in me.
Fierce pangs and flashes of bewildering light
Leaped through my brain and danced before my
    eyes

So loud my heart beat, that I feared its sound
Would wake the sleeper ; and the bubbling blood
Choked in my throat till, weaker than a child,
I reeled against a column, and there hung
In a blind stupor. Then I prayed again :
And, sense by sense, I was made whole once more.
I touched myself ; I was the same ; I knew
Myself to be lone Adeb, young and strong,
With nothing but a stride of empty air
Between me and God's justice. In a sleep,
Thick with the fumes of the accursèd grape,
Sprawled the false Imam. On his shaggy breast,
Like a white lily heaving on the tide
Of some foul stream, the fairest woman slept
These roving eyes have ever looked upon.
Almost a child, her bosom barely showed
The change beyond her girlhood. All her charms
Were budding, but half opened ; for I saw
Not only beauty wondrous in itself,
But possibility of more to be
In the full process of her blooming days.
I gazed upon her, and my heart grew soft,
As a parched pasture with the dew of heaven.
While thus I gazed she smiled, and slowly raised
The long curve of her lashes ; and we looked
Each upon each in wonder, not alarm,—
Not eye to eye, but soul to soul, we held
Each other for a moment. All her life
Seemed centred in the circle of her eyes.
She stirred no limb ; her long-drawn, equal breath
Swelled out and ebbed away beneath her breast,
In calm unbroken. Not a sign of fear
Touched the faint color on her oval cheek,

Or pinched the arches of her tender mouth.
She took me for a vision, and she lay
With her sleep's smile unaltered, as in doubt
Whether real life had stolen into her dreams,
Or dreaming stretched into her outer life.
I was not graceless to a woman's eyes.
The girls of Damar paused to see me pass,
I walking in my rags, yet beautiful.
One maiden said, " He has a prince's air ! "
I am a prince ; the air was all my own.
So thought the lily on the Imam's breast ;
And lightly as a summer mist, that lifts
Before the morning, so she floated up,
Without a sound or rustle of a robe,
From her coarse pillow, and before me stood
With asking eyes.   The Imam never moved.
A stride and blow were all my need, and they
Were wholly in my power.   I took her hand,
I held a warning finger to my lips,
And whispered in her small, expectant ear,
" Adeb, the son of Akem ! "   She replied
In a low murmur whose bewildering sound
Almost lulled wakeful me to sleep, and sealed
The sleeper's lids in tenfold slumber, " Prince,
Lord of the Imam's life and of my heart,
Take all thou seest,—it is thy right, I know,—
But spare the Imam for thy own soul's sake ! "
Then I arrayed me in a robe of state,
Shining with gold and jewels ; and I bound
In my long turban gems that might have bought
The lands 'twixt Babelmandeb and Sahan.
I girt about me, with a blazing belt,
A scimitar o'er which the sweating smiths

In far Damascus hammered for long years,
Whose hilt and scabbard shot a trembling light
From diamonds and rubies. And she smiled,
As piece by piece I put the treasures on,
To see me look so fair,—in pride she smiled.
I hung long purses at my side. I scooped,
From off a table, figs and dates and rice,
And bound them to my girdle in a sack.
Then over all I flung a snowy cloak,
And beckoned to the maiden. So she stole
Forth like my shadow, past the sleeping wolf
Who wronged my father, o'er the woolly head
Of the swart eunuch, down the painted court,
And by the sentinel who standing slept.
Strongly against the portal, through my rags,—
My old base rags,—and through the maiden's veil,
I pressed my knife,—upon the wooden hilt
Was " Adeb, son of Akem," carved by me
In my long slavehood,—as a passing sign
To wait the Imam's waking. Shadows cast
From two high-sailing clouds upon the sand
Passed not more noiseless than we two, as one,
Glided beneath the moonlight, till I smelt
The fragrance of the stables. As I slid
The wide doors open, with a sudden bound
Uprose the startled horses : but they stood
Still as the man who in a foreign land
Hears his strange language, when my Desert call,
As low and plaintive as the nested dove's,
Fell on their listening ears. From stall to stall,
Feeling the horses with my groping hands,
I crept in darkness ; and at length I came
Upon two sister mares whose rounded sides,

Fine muzzles, and small heads, and pointed ears,
And foreheads spreading 'twixt their eyelids wide,
Long slender tails, thin manes, and coats of silk,
Told me, that, of the hundred steeds there stalled,
My hand was on the treasures.   O'er and o'er
I felt their bony joints, and down their legs
To the cool hoofs ;—no blemish anywhere :
These I led forth and saddled.   Upon one
I set the lily, gathered now for me,—
My own, henceforth, forever.   So we rode
Across the grass, beside the stony path,
Until we gained the highway that is lost,
Leading from Sana, in the eastern sands :
When, with a cry that both the desert-born
Knew without hint from whip or goading spur,
We dashed into a gallop.   Far behind
In sparks and smoke the dusty highway rose ;
And ever on the maiden's face I saw,
When the moon flashed upon it, the strange smile
It wore on waking.   Once I kissed her mouth
When she grew weary, and her strength returned.
All through the night we scoured between the hills :
The moon went down behind us, and the stars
Dropped after her ; but long before I saw
A planet blazing straight against our eyes,
The road had softened, and the shadowy hills
Had flattened out, and I could hear the hiss
Of sand spurned backward by the flying mares.
Glory to God !   I was at home again !
The sun rose on us ; far and near I saw
The level Desert ; sky met sand all round.
We paused at midday by a palm-crowned well,
And ate and slumbered.   Somewhat, too, was said :

The words have slipped my memory. That same eve
We rode sedately through a Hamoum camp,—
I, Adeb, prince amongst them, and my bride.
And ever since amongst them I have ridden,
A head and shoulders taller than the best;
And ever since my days have been of gold,
My nights have been of silver,—God is just!

GEORGE HENRY BOKER.

THE LEPER.

"Room for the leper! room!" And as he came
The cry passed on,—"Room for the leper!
room!"

 . . . .

     And aside they stood,
Matron, and child, and pitiless manhood,—all
Who met him on his way,—and let him pass.
And onward through the open gate he came,
A leper with the ashes on his brow,
Sackcloth about his loins, and on his lip
A covering, stepping painfully and slow,
And with a difficult utterance, like one
Whose heart is with an iron nerve put down,
Crying, " Unclean! unclean!"

 . . . . .

     Day was breaking
When at the altar of the temple stood
The holy priest of God. The incense-lamp
Burned with a struggling light, and a low chant
Swelled through the hollow arches of the roof,
Like an articulate wail, and there, alone,
Wasted to ghastly thinness, Helon knelt.

The echoes of the melancholy strain
Died in the distant aisles, and he rose up,
Struggling with weakness, and bowed down his
    head
Unto the sprinkled ashes, and put off
His costly raiment for the leper's garb,
And with the sackcloth round him, and his lip
Hid in a loathsome covering, stood still,
Waiting to hear his doom :—

    " Depart ! depart, O child
Of Israel, from the temple of thy God,
For he has smote thee with his chastening rod,
    And to the desert wild
From all thou lov'st away thy feet must flee,
That from thy plague his people may be free.

    " Depart ! and come not near
The busy mart, the crowded city, more ;
Nor set thy foot a human threshold o'er ;
    And stay thou not to hear
Voices that call thee in the way ; and fly
From all who in the wilderness pass by.

    " Wet not thy burning lip
In streams that to a human dwelling glide ;
Nor rest thee where the covert fountains hide,
    Nor kneel thee down to dip
The water where the pilgrim bends to drink,
By desert well, or river's grassy brink.

    " And pass not thou between
The weary traveller and the cooling breeze,
And lie not down to sleep beneath the trees
    Where human tracks are seen ;

Nor milk the goat that browseth on the plain
Nor pluck the standing corn or yellow grain.

"And now depart! and when
Thy heart is heavy, and thine eyes are dim,
Lift up thy prayer beseechingly to Him
Who, from the tribes of men,
Selected thee to feel his chastening rod.
Depart! O leper! and forget not God!"

And he went forth—alone! not one of all
The many whom he loved, nor she whose name
Was woven in the fibres of the heart
Breaking within him now, to come and speak
Comfort unto him. Yea, he went his way,
Sick and heart-broken and alone,—to die!
For God had cursed the leper!

           It was noon,
And Helon knelt beside a stagnant pool
In the lone wilderness, and bathed his brow,
Hot with the burning leprosy, and touched
The loathsome water to his fevered lips,
Praying that he might be so blest,—to die!
Footsteps approached, and, with no strength to
    flee,
He drew the covering closer on his lip,
Crying, "Unclean! unclean!" and in the folds
Of the coarse sackcloth shrouding up his face,
He fell upon the earth till they should pass.
Nearer the stranger came, and, bending o'er
The leper's prostrate form, pronounced his name.
—"Helon!"—the voice was like the master-tone
Of a rich instrument,—most strangely sweet;
And the dull pulses of disease awoke,

And for a moment beat beneath the hot
And leprous scales with a restoring thrill.
"Helon! arise!" and he forgot his curse,
And rose and stood before him.

      Love and awe
Mingled in the regard of Helon's eye
As he beheld the stranger. He was not
In costly raiment clad, nor on his brow
The symbol of a princely lineage wore;
No followers at his back, nor in his hand
Buckler or sword or spear,—yet in his mien
Command sat throned serene, and if he smiled,
A kingly condescension graced his lips
The lion would have crouched to in his lair.
His garb was simple, and his sandals worn;
His stature modelled with a perfect grace;
His countenance, the impress of a God,
Touched with the open innocence of a child;
His eye was blue and calm, as is the sky
In the serenest noon; his hair unshorn
Fell to his shoulders; and his curling beard
The fulness of perfected manhood bore.
He looked on Helon earnestly awhile,
As if his heart was moved, and, stooping down,
He took a little water in his hand
And laid it on his brow, and said, "Be clean!"
And lo! the scales fell from him, and his blood
Coursed with delicious coolness through his veins,
And his dry palms grew moist, and on his brow
The dewy softness of an infant's stole.
His leprosy was cleansed, and he fell down
Prostrate at Jesus' feet, and worshipped him.

       NATHANIEL PARKER WILLIS.

ERMINIA AND THE WOUNDED TANCRED.

"Though gone, though dead, I love thee still; be-
    hold
  Death wounds but kills not love: yet if thou live,
Sweet soul, still in his breast, my follies bold
  Ah pardon, love's desires and stealth forgive:
Grant me from his pale mouth some kisses cold,
  Since death doth love of just reward deprive,
And of thy spoils, sad death, afford me this,—
Let me his mouth, pale, cold, and bloodless, kiss.

"O gentle mouth! with speeches kind and sweet
  Thou didst relieve my grief, my woe, and pain;
Ere my weak soul from this frail body fleet,
  Ah, comfort me with one dear kiss or twain;
Perchance, if we alive had happed to meet,
  They had been given which now are stolen: oh
    vain,
O feeble life, betwixt his lips out fly!
Oh, let me kiss thee first, then let me die!

"Receive my yielded spirit, and with thine
  Guide it to heaven, where all true love hath
    place."
This said, she sighed and tore her tresses fine,
  And from her eyes two streams poured on his
    face.
The man, revivèd with those showers divine,
  Awaked, and openèd his lips a space;
His lips were opened, but fast shut his eyes,
And with her sighs one sigh from him upflies.

The dame perceived that Tancred breathed and
    sight,
  Which calmed her grief some deal and eased her
    fears :
" Unclose thine eyes " (she says), " my lord and
    knight,
  See my last services, my plaints, and tears ;
See her that dies to see thy woful plight,
    That of thy pain her part and portion bears ;
Once look on me : small is the gift I crave,—
The last which thou canst give, or I can have."

Tancred looked up, and closed his eyes again,
  Heavy and dim ; and she renewed her woe.
Quoth Vafrine, " Cure him first and then complain :
  Medicine is life's chief friend, plaint her worst
    foe."
They plucked his armor off, and she each vein,
  Each joint, and sinew felt and handled so,
And searched so well each thrust, each cut ; and
    wound,
That hope of life her love and skill soon found.

From weariness and loss of blood she spied
  His greatest pains and anguish most proceed.
Naught but her veil amid those deserts wide
  She had to bind his wounds in so great need :
But love could other bands (though strange) pro-
    vide,
  And pity wept for joy to see that deed ;
For with her amber locks, cut off, each wound
She tied—O happy man, so cured, so bound !

For why ? her veil was short and thin, those deep
  And cruel hurts to fasten, roll, and bind :

Nor salve nor simple had she ; yet to keep
   Her knight alive, strong charms of wondrous kind
She said, and from him drove that deadly sleep,
   That now his eyes he lifted, turned, and twined,
And saw his squire, and saw that courteous dame
In habits strange, and wondered whence she came.

He said, "O Vafrine, tell me whence com'st thou,
   And who this gentle surgeon is, disclose."
She smiled, she sighed, she looked she wist not how,
   She wept, rejoiced, she blushed as red as rose :
" You shall know all " (she says) ; " your surgeon
     now
Commands your silence, rest, and soft repose ;
You shall be sound, prepare my guerdon meet."
His head then laid she in her bosom sweet.
From the Italian of TORQUATO TASSO.

Translation of EDWARD FAIRFAX.

ALONZO THE BRAVE AND THE FAIR IMOGINE.

A WARRIOR so bold, and a virgin so bright,
   Conversed as they sat on the green ;
They gazed on each other with tender delight :
Alonzo the Brave was the name of the knight,—
   The maiden's, the Fair Imogine.

" And O," said the youth, " since to-morrow I go
   To fight in a far distant land,
Your tears for my absence soon ceasing to flow,
Some other will court you, and you will bestow
   On a wealthier suitor your hand ! "

" O, hush these suspicions," Fair Imogine said,
    " Offensive to love and to me;
For, if you be living, or if you be dead,
I swear by the Virgin that none in your stead
    Shall husband of Imogine be.

" If e'er I, by lust or by wealth led aside,
    Forget my Alonzo the Brave,
God grant that, to punish my falsehood and pride,
Your ghost at the marriage may sit by my side,
May tax me with perjury, claim me as bride,
    And bear me away to the grave! "

To Palestine hastened the hero so bold,
    His love she lamented him sore ;
But scarce had a twelvemonth elapsed when, be-
        hold !
A baron, all covered with jewels and gold,
    Arrived at Fair Imogine's door.

His treasures, his presents, his spacious domain,
    Soon made her untrue to her vows ;
He dazzled her eyes, he bewildered her brain;
He caught her affections, so light and so vain,
    And carried her home as his spouse.

And now had the marriage been blest by the
        priest ;
    The revelry now was begun ;
The tables they groaned with the weight of the
        feast,
Nor yet had the laughter and merriment ceased,
    When the bell at the castle tolled—one.

Then first with amazement Fair Imogine found
  A stranger was placed by her side :
His air was terrific ; he uttered no sound,—
He spake not, he moved not, he looked not
      around,—
  But earnestly gazed on the bride.

His visor was closed, and gigantic his height,
  His armor was sable to view ;
All pleasure and laughter were hushed at his
      sight ;
The dogs, as they eyed him, drew back in affright ;
  The lights in the chamber burned blue !

His presence all bosoms appeared to dismay ;
  The guests sat in silence and fear ;
At length spake the bride,—while she trembled,
      —" I pray,
Sir knight, that your helmet aside you would lay
  And deign to partake of our cheer."

The lady is silent ; the stranger complies—
  His visor he slowly unclosed ;
O God ! what a sight met Fair Imogine's eyes !
What words can express her dismay and surprise,
  When a skeleton's head was exposed !

All present then uttered a terrified shout,
  All turned with disgust from the scene ;
The worms they crept in, and the worms they
      crept out,
And sported his eyes and his temples about,
  While the spectre addressed Imogine :

"Behold me, thou false one, behold me!" he
    cried,
    "Remember Alonzo the Brave!
God grants that, to punish thy falsehood and pride,
My ghost at thy marriage should sit by thy side;
Should tax thee with perjury, claim thee as bride,
    And bear thee away to the grave!"

Thus saying his arms round the lady he wound,
    While loudly she shrieked in dismay;
Then sunk with his prey through the wide-
    yawning ground,
Nor ever again was Fair Imogine found,
    Or the spectre that bore her away.

Not long lived the baron; and none, since that
    time,
    To inhabit the castle presume;
For chronicles tell that, by order sublime,
There Imogine suffers the pain of her crime,
    And mourns her deplorable doom.

At midnight, four times in each year, does her
    sprite,
    When mortals in slumber are bound,
Arrayed in her bridal apparel of white,
Appear in the hall with the skeleton knight,
    And shriek as he whirls her around!

While they drink out of skulls newly torn from
    the grave,
    Dancing round them the spectres are seen;
Their liquor is blood, and this horrible stave
They howl: "To the health of Alonzo the Brave,
    And his consort, the Fair Imogine!"

MATTHEW GREGORY LEWIS.

THE BROKEN PITCHER.

It was a Moorish maiden was sitting by a well,
And what that maiden thought of, I cannot, cannot
    tell,
When by there rode a valiant knight, from the town
    of Oviedo—
Alphonso Guzman was he hight, the Count of
    Desparedo.

" O maiden, Moorish maiden ! why sitt'st thou by
    the spring ?
Say, dost thou seek a lover, or any other thing ?
Why gazest thou upon me, with eyes so large and
    wide,
And wherefore doth the pitcher lie broken by thy
    side ? "

" I do not seek a lover, thou Christian knight so gay,
Because an article like that hath never come my
    way ;
But why I gaze upon you, I cannot, cannot tell,
Except that in your iron hose you look uncommon
    swell.

" My pitcher it is broken, and this the reason is—
A shepherd came behind me, and tried to snatch a
    kiss ;
I would not stand his nonsense, so ne'er a word I
    spoke,
But scored him on the costard, and so the jug was
    broke.

" My uncle, the Alcaydè, he waits for me at home,
And will not take his tumbler until Zorayda come.

I cannot bring him water,—the pitcher is in pieces;
And so I'm sure to catch it, 'cos he wallops all his
    nieces."

" O maiden, Moorish maiden! wilt thou be ruled by
    me ?
So wipe thine eyes and rosy lips, and give me
    kisses three;
And I'll give thee my helmet, thou kind and cour-
    teous lady,
To carry home the water to thine uncle, the
    Alcaydè."

He lighted down from off his steed—he tied him to
    a tree—
He bowed him to the maiden, and took his kisses
    three :
" To wrong thee, sweet Zorayda, I swear would be
    a sin !"
He knelt him at the fountain, and dipped his hel-
    met in.

Up rose the Moorish maiden—behind the knight
    she steals,
And caught Alphonso Guzman up tightly by the
    heels;
She tipped him in, and held him down beneath the
    bubbling water,—
" Now, take thou that for venturing to kiss Al
    Hamet's daughter!"

A Christian maid is weeping in the town of Oviedo;
She waits the coming of her love, the Count of
    Desperedo.

I pray you all in charity, that you will never tell
How he met Moorish maiden beside the lonely well.

WILLIAM EDMONSTOUNE AYTOUN.

THE BALLAD OF GUIBOUR.

FROM "CALENDAU."

At Arles in the Carlovingian days,
    By the swift Rhone water,
A hundred thousand on either side,
Christian and Saracen, fought till the tide
    Ran red with the slaughter.

May God forefend such another flood
    Of direful war!
The Count of Orange on that black morn
By seven great kings was overborne,
    And fled afar,

Whenas he would avenge the death
    Of his nephew slain.
Now are the kings upon his trail;
He slays as he flies: like fiery hail
    His sword-strokes rain.

He hies him into the Aliscamp,—
    No shelter there!
A Moorish hive is the home of the dead,
And hard he spurs his goodly steed
    In his despair.

Over the mountain and over the moor
    Flies Count Guillaume;
By sun and by moon he ever sees

The coming cloud of his enemies;
    Thus gains his home.

Halts and lifts at the castle gate;
    A mighty cry,
Calling his haughty wife by name;
"Guibour, Guibour, my gentle dame,
    Open! 'T is I!

"Open the gate to thy Guillaume!
    Ta'en is the city
By thirty thousand Saracen,
Lo, they are hunting me to my den:
    Guibour, have pity!"

But the countess from the rampart cried,
    "Nay, chevalier,
I will not open my gates to thee;
For, save the women and babes," said she,
    "Whom I shelter here,

"And the priest who keeps the lamps alight,
    Alone am I.
My brave Guillaume and his barons all
Are fighting the Moor by the Aliscamp wall,
    And scorn to fly!"

"Guibour, Guibour, it is I myself!
    And those men of mine
(God rest their souls!) they are dead," he cried,
"Or rowing with slaves on the salt sea-tide.
    I have seen the shine

"Of Arles on fire in the dying day;
    I have heard one shriek
Go up from all the arenas where

The nuns disfigure their bodies fair
    Lest the Marran wreak

" His brutal will. Avignon's self
        Will fall to-day !
Sweetheart, I faint ; oh, let me in
Before the savage Mograbin
        Fall on his prey ! "

" I swear thou liest," cried Guibour,
        " Thou base deceiver !
Thou art perchance thyself a Moor
Who whinest thus outside my door ;—
        My Guillaume, never !

" Guillaume to look on burning towns
        And fired by—*thee !*
Guillaume to see his comrades die,
Or borne to sore captivity,
        And then to *flee !*

" He knows not flight !   He is a tower
        Where others fly !
The heathen spoiler's doom is sure,
The virgin's honor aye secure,
        When he is by ! "

Guillaume leapt up, his bridle set
        Between his teeth,
While tears of love and tears of shame
Under his burning eyelids came,
        And hard drew breath,

And seized his sword and plunged his spurs
  Right deep, and so
A storm, a demon, did descend
To roar and smite, to rout and rend
  The Moorish foe.

As when one shakes an almond-tree,
  The heathen slain
Upon the tender grass fall thick,
Until the flying remnant seek
  Their ships again.

Four kings with his own hand he slew,
  And when once more
He turned him homeward from the fight,
Upon the drawbridge long in sight
  Stood brave Guibour.

" By the great gateway enter in,
  My lord ! " she cried ;
And might no further welcome speak,
But loosed his helm, and kissed his cheek,
  With tears of pride.

From the Provençal of FREDERIC MISTRAL.
Translation of HARRIET WATERS PRESTON.

THE GLOVE AND THE LIONS.

KING FRANCIS was a hearty king, and loved a royal
    sport,
And one day, as his lions fought, sat looking on
    the court.

The nobles filled the benches, with the ladies in
their pride,
And 'mongst them sat the Count de Lorge, with
one for whom he sighed:
And truly 't was a gallant thing to see that crowning show,
Valor and love, and a king above, and the royal
beasts below.

Ramped and roared the lions, with horrid laughing jaws;
They bit, they glared, gave blows like beams, a
wind went with their paws;
With wallowing might and stifled roar they rolled
on one another,
Till all the pit with sand and mane was in a
thunderous smother;
The bloody foam above the bars came whisking
through the air;
Said Francis then, " Faith, gentlemen, we're
better here than there."

De Lorge's love o'erheard the King, a beauteous
lively dame,
With smiling lips and sharp bright eyes, which
always seemed the same;
She thought, the Count, my lover, is brave as
brave can be;
He surely would do wondrous things to show his
love of me;
King, ladies, lovers, all look on; the occasion is
divine;

I'll drop my glove, to prove his love; great glory
 will be mine.

She dropped her glove, to prove his love, then
 looked at him and smiled;
He bowed, and in a moment leaped among the
 lions wild;
The leap was quick, return was quick, he has re-
 gained his place,
Then threw the glove, but not with love, right in
 the lady's face.
" By Heaven," said Francis, " rightly done! " and
 he rose from where he sat;
" No love," quoth he, " but vanity, sets love a task
 like that."

LEIGH HUNT.

THE GLOVE.

(PETER RONSARD loquitur.)

" HEIGHO," yawned one day King Francis,
" Distance all value enhances !
When a man's busy, why, leisure
Strikes him as wonderful pleasure—
'Faith, and at leisure once is he?
Straightway he wants to be busy.
Here we 've got peace; and aghast I 'm
Caught thinking war the true pastime !
Is there a reason in metre?
Give us your speech, Master Peter ! "
I who, if mortal dare say so,
Ne'er am at loss with my Naso,

"Sire," I replied, "joys prove cloudlets :
Men are the merest Ixions "—
Here the King whistled aloud, "Let 's
. . Heigho . . go look at our lions!"
Such are the sorrowful chances
If you talk fine to King Francis.

And so, to the court-yard proceeding,
Our company, Francis was leading,
Increased by new followers tenfold
Before he arrived at the penfold;
Lords, ladies, like clouds which bedizen
At sunset the western horizon.
And Sir De Lorge pressed 'mid the foremost
With the dame he professed to adore most—
Oh, what a face ! One by fits eyed
Her, and the horrible pitside ;
For the penfold surrounded a hollow
Which led where the eye scarce dared follow,
And shelved to the chamber secluded
Where Bluebeard, the great lion, brooded.
The King hailed his keeper, an Arab
As glossy and black as a scarab,
And bade him make sport and at once stir
Up and out of his den the old monster.
They opened a hole in the wire-work
Across it, and dropped there a firework,
And fled ; one's heart's beating redoubled ;
A pause, while the pit's mouth was troubled,
The blackness and silence so utter,
By the firework's slow sparkling and sputter,
Then earth in a sudden contortion
Gave out to our gaze her abortion!

Such a brute ! Were I friend Clement Marot
(Whose experience of Nature 's but narrow,
And whose faculties move in no small mist
When he versifies David the Psalmist)
I should study that brute to describe you
Illum Juda Leonem de Tribu !

One's whole blood grew curdling and creepy
To see the black mane, vast and heapy,
The tail in the air stiff and straining,
The wide eyes, nor waxing nor waning,
As over the barrier which bounded
His platform, and us who surrounded
The barrier, they reached and they rested
On the space that might stand him in best stead ;
For, who knew, he thought, what the amazement,
The eruption of clatter and blaze meant,
And if, in this minute of wonder,
No outlet 'mid lightning and thunder,
Lay broad, and, his shackles all shivered,
The lion at last was delivered ?
Ay, that was the open sky o'erhead !
And you saw by the flash on his forehead,
By the hope in those eyes wide and steady,
He was leagues in the desert already,
Driving the flocks up the mountain,
Or catlike couched hard by the fountain,
To waylay the date-gathering negress :
So guarded he entrance or egress.
" How he stands ! " quoth the King ; " we may well
        swear,
No novice, we 've won our spurs elsewhere,
And so can afford the confession,

We exercise wholesome discretion
In keeping aloof from his threshold ;
Once hold you, those jaws want no fresh hold,
Their first would too pleasantly purloin
The visitor's brisket or surloin :
But who 's he would prove so foolhardy ?
Not the best man of Marignam, pardie ! "

The sentence no sooner was uttered,
Than over the rails a glove fluttered,
Fell close to the lion, and rested :
The dame 't was, who flung it and jested
With life so, De Lorge had been wooing
For months past ; he sate there pursuing
His suit, weighing out with nonchalance
Fine speeches like gold from a balance.

Sound the trumpet, no true knight 's a tarrier !
De Lorge made one leap at the barrier,
Walked straight to the glove—while the lion
Ne'er moved, kept his far-reaching eye on
The palm-tree-edged desert spring's sapphire,
And the musky oiled skin of the Kaffir—
Picked it up, and as calmly retreated,
Leaped back where the lady was seated,
And full in the face of its owner
Flung the glove—

          " Your heart's queen, you dethrone her ?
So should I "—cried the King—" 't was mere van-
          ity,
Not love, set that task to humanity ! "
Lords and ladies alike turned with loathing
From such a proved wolf in sheep's clothing.

Not so I ; for I caught an expression
In her brow's undisturbed self-possession
Amid the Court's scoffing and merriment—
As if from no pleasing experiment
She rose, yet of pain not much heedful
So long as the process was needful—
As if she had tried in a crucible,
To what " speeches like gold " were reducible,
And, finding the finest prove copper,
Felt the smoke in her face was but proper;
To know what she had *not* to trust to,
Was worth all the ashes, and dust too.
She went out 'mid hooting and laughter;
Clement Marot stayed; I followed after,
And asked, as a grace, what it all meant—
If she wished not the rash deed's recallment?
" For I "— so I spoke—" am a poet:
Human nature behooves that I know it ! "

She told me, " Too long had I heard
Of the deed proved alone by the word :
For my love—what De Lorge would not dare !
With my scorn—what De Lorge could compare!
And the endless descriptions of death
He would brave when my lip formed a breath,
I must reckon as braved, or, of course,
Doubt his word—and moreover, perforce,
For such gifts as no lady could spurn,
Must offer my love in return.
When I looked on your lion, it brought
All the dangers at once to my thought,
Encountered by all sorts of men,
Before he was lodged in his den—

From the poor slave whose club or bare hands
Dug the trap, set the snare on the sands,
With no King and no Court to applaud,
By no shame, should he shrink, overawed,
Yet to capture the creature made shift,
That his rude boys might laugh at the gift,
To the page who last leaped o'er the fence
Of the pit, on no greater pretence
Than to get back the bonnet he dropped,
Lest his pay for a week should be stopped—
So, wiser I judged it to make
One trial what 'death for my sake'
Really meant, while the power was yet mine,
Than to wait until time should define
Such a phrase not so simply as I,
Who took it to mean just 'to die.'
The blow a glove gives is but weak—
Does the mark yet discolor my cheek?
But when the heart suffers a blow,
Will the pain pass so soon, do you know?"

I looked, as away she was sweeping,
And saw a youth eagerly keeping
As close as he dared to the doorway:
No doubt that a noble should more weigh
His life than befits a plebeian;
And yet, had our brute been Nemean—
(I judge by a certain calm fervor
The youth stepped with, forward to serve her)
—He 'd have scarce thought you did him the worst
    turn
If you whispered, " Friend, what you 'd get, first
    earn ! "

And when, shortly after, she carried
Her shame from the Court, and they married,
To that marriage some happiness, maugre
The voice of the court I dared augur.

For De Lorge, he made women with men vie,
Those in wonder and praise, these in envy ;
And in short stood so plain a head taller
That he wooed and won . . . How do you call her ?
The beauty, that rose in the sequel
To the King's love, who loved her a week well ;
And 't was noticed he never would honor
De Lorge (who looked daggers upon her)
With the easy commission of stretching
His legs in the service, and fetching
His wife, from her chamber, those straying
Sad gloves she was always mislaying,
While the King took the closet to chat in—
But of course this adventure came pat in ;
And never the King told the story,
How bringing a glove brought such glory,
But the wife smiled—" His nerves are grown
     firmer—
Mine he brings now and utters no murmur ! "

Venienti occurrite morbo !
With which moral I drop my theorbo.

                              ROBERT BROWNING.

LOUIS XV.

The King with all his kingly train
Had left his Pompadour behind,
And forth he rode in Senart's wood
The royal beasts of chase to find.
That day by chance the Monarch mused,
And turning suddenly away,
He struck alone into a path
That far from crowds and courtiers lay.

He saw the pale green shadows play
Upon the brown untrodden earth ;
He saw the birds around him flit
As if he were of peasant birth ;
He saw the trees that know no king
But him who bears a woodland axe ;
He thought not, but he looked about
Like one who skill in thinking lacks.

Then close to him a footstep fell,
And glad of human sound was he,
For truth to say he found himself
A weight from which he fain would flee.
But that which he would ne'er have guessed
Before him now most plainly came ;
The man upon his weary back
A coffin bore of rudest frame.

" Why, who art thou ? " exclaimed the King,
" And what is that I see thee bear ? "
" I am a laborer in the wood,
And 't is a coffin for Pierre.

Close by the royal hunting-lodge
You may have often seen him toil;
But he will never work again,
And I for him must dig the soil."

The laborer ne'er had seen the King,
And this he thought was but a man,
Who made at first a moment's pause,
And then anew his talk began :
" I think I do remember now,—
He had a dark and glancing eye,
And I have seen his slender arm
With wondrous blows the pick-axe ply.

" Pray tell me, friend, what accident
Can thus have killed our good Pierre ? "
" Oh! nothing more than usual, sir,
He died of living upon air.
'T was hunger killed the poor good man,
Who long on empty hopes relied ;
He could not pay gabell and tax,
And feed his children, so he died."

The man stopped short, and then went on,—
" It is, you know, a common thing ;
Our children's bread is eaten up
By Courtiers, Mistresses, and King."
The King looked hard upon the man,
And afterwards the coffin eyed,
Then spurred to ask of Pompadour,
How came it that the peasants died.

JOHN STERLING.

HERVÉ RIEL.

ON the sea and at the Hogue, sixteen hundred
   ninety-two,
Did the English fight the French—woe to France!
And the thirty-first of May, helter-skelter through
   the blue,
Like a crowd of frightened porpoises a shoal of
   sharks pursue,
Came crowding ship on ship to St. Malo on the
   Rance,
With the English fleet in view.

'T was the squadron that escaped, with the victor
   in full chase;
First and foremost of the drove, in his great ship,
   Damfreville;
Close on him fled, great and small,
   Twenty-two good ships in all;
And they signalled to the place,
" Help the winners of a race!
Get us guidance, give us harbor, take us quick;
   or, quicker still,
Here 's the English can and will ! "

Then the pilots of the place put out brisk, and
   leaped on board ;
" Why, what hope or chance have ships like
   these to pass ? " laughed they :
Rocks to starboard, rocks to port, all the passage
   scarred and scored,
Shall the ' Formidable,' here with her twelve-and-
   eighty guns,

Think to make the river-mouth by the single
        narrow way,
Trust to enter where 't is ticklish for a craft of
        twenty tons,
    And with flow at full beside ?
    Now 't is slackest ebb of tide.
Reach the mooring ?   Rather say,
While rock stands, or water runs,
    Not a ship will leave the bay ! "

Then was called a council straight :
Brief and bitter the debate.
" Here 's the English at our heels : would you have
        them take in tow
All that 's left us of the fleet, linked together stern
        and bow ;
For a prize to Plymouth Sound ?
Better run the ships aground ! "
    (Ended Damfreville his speech.)
" Not a minute more to wait !
    Let the captains all and each
    Shove ashore, then blow up, burn the vessels on
        the beach !
France must undergo her fate ! "
" Give the word ! "   But no such word
Was ever spoke or heard :
    For up stood, for out stepped, for in struck, amid
        all these,
A captain ? a lieutenant ? a mate,—first, second,
        third ?
    No such man of mark, and meet
    With his betters to compete !
    But a simple Breton sailor, pressed by Tour-
        ville for the fleet,

A poor coasting-pilot, he,—Hervé Riel, the Croi-
sickese.

And "What mockery or malice have we here?"
cried Hervé Riel.
"Are you mad, you Malouins? Are you cowards,
fools, or rogues?
Talk to me of rocks and shoals?—me, who took the
soundings, tell
On my fingers every bank, every shallow, every
swell,
'Twixt the offering here and Grève, where the
river disembogues?
Are you bought for English gold? Is it love the
lying 's for?
Morn and eve, night and day,
Have I piloted your bay,
Entered free and anchored fast at the foot of Soli-
dor.
Burn the fleet, and ruin France? That were
worse than fifty Hogues!
Sirs, then know I speak the truth! Sirs, be-
lieve me, there 's a way!
Only let me lead the line,
Have the biggest ship to steer,
Get this ' Formidable' clear,
Make the others follow mine,
And I lead them, most and least, by a passage I
know well,
Right to Solidor past Grève,
And there lay them safe and sound;
And if one ship misbehave,
—Keel so much as grate the ground,

Why, I've nothing but my life ; here's my head! "
cries Hervé Riel.

Not a minute more to wait.
" Steer us in, then, small and great!
    Take the helm, lead the line, save the squad-
    ron! " cried its chief.
    Captains, give the sailor place !
    He is admiral, in brief.
    Still the north wind, by God's grace.
    See the noble fellow's face,
    As the big ship, with a bound,
    Clears the entry like a hound,
Keeps the passage, as its inch of way were the wide
    sea's profound !
    See, safe through shoal and rock,
    How they follow in a flock ;
Not a ship that misbehaves, not a keel that grates
    the ground,
    Not a spar that comes to grief!
    The peril, see, is past !
    All are harbored to the last !
And, just as Hervé Riel hollas " Anchor! " sure as
    fate,
Up the English come,—too late !

So the storm subsides to calm ;
    They see the green trees wave
    On the heights o'erlooking Grève ;
Hearts that bled are stanched with balm.
    " Just our rupture to enhance,
      Let the English rake the bay,
    Gnash their teeth, and glare askance
      As they cannonade away !

'Neath rampired Solidor pleasant riding on her
   Rance ! ”
How hope succeeds despair on each captain's coun-
   tenance !
    Out burst all with one accord,
      “ This is paradise for hell !
    Let France, let France's king,
    Thank the man that did the thing ! ”
    What a shout, and all one word,
      “ Hervê Riel ! ”
As he stepped in front once more ;
    Not a symptom of surprise
    In the frank blue Breton eyes,—
Just the same man as before.

    Then said Damfreville, “ My friend,
    I must speak out at the end,
      Though I find the speaking hard ;
    Praise is deeper than the lips :
    You have saved the king his ships ;
      You must name your own reward.
    Faith, our sun was near eclipse!
    Demand whate'er you will,
    France remains your debtor still.
    Ask to heart's content, and have ! or my
      name 's not Damfreville.”

    Then a beam of fun outbroke
    On the bearded mouth that spoke,
      As the honest heart laughed through
    Those frank eyes of Breton blue :
    “ Since I needs must say my say,
    Since on board the duty's done,

And from Malo Roads to Croisic Point, what is it
    but a run?—
Since 't is ask and have, I may;
  Since the others go ashore,—
Come! A good whole holiday!
    Leave to go and see my wife, whom I call the
    Belle Aurore!"
  That he asked, and that he got,—nothing more.

Name and deed alike are lost;
Not a pillar nor a post
  In his Croisic keeps alive the feat as it befell;
Not a head in white and black
On a single fishing-smack
In memory of the man but for whom had gone to
    wrack
    All that France saved from the fight whence
    England bore the bell.
Go to Paris; rank on rank
  Search the heroes flung pell-mell
On the Louvre, face and flank;
    You shall look long enough ere you come to
    Hervé Riel.
So, for better and for worse,
Hervé Riel, accept my verse!
In my verse, Hervé Riel, do thou once more
Save the squadron, honor France, love thy wife
    the Belle Aurore!

ROBERT BROWNING.

NAPOLEON AND THE BRITISH SAILOR.

I LOVE contemplating—apart
From all his homicidal glory—
The traits that soften to our heart
    Napoleon's glory!

'T was when his banners at Boulogne
Armed in our island every freeman,
His navy chanced to capture one
    Poor British seaman.

They suffered him—I know not how—
Unprisoned on the shore to roam;
And aye was bent his longing brow
    On England's home.

His eye, methinks! pursued the flight
Of birds to Britain half-way over;
With envy *they* could reach the white
    Dear cliffs of Dover.

A stormy midnight watch, he thought,
Than this sojourn would have been dearer,
If but the storm his vessel brought
    To England nearer.

At last, when care had banished sleep,
He saw one morning, dreaming, doting,
An empty hogshead from the deep
    Come shoreward floating;

He hid it in a cave, and wrought
The livelong day laborious; lurking

Until he launched a tiny boat
　　By mighty working.

Heaven help us ! 't was a thing beyond
　　Description wretched ; such a wherry
Perhaps ne'er ventured on a pond,
　　Or crossed a ferry.

For, ploughing in the salt-sea field,
　　It would have made the boldest shudder ;
Untarred, uncompassed, and unkeeled,—
　　No sail, no rudder.

From neighboring woods he interlaced
　　His sorry skiff with wattled willows ;
And thus equipped he would have passed
　　The foaming billows,—

But Frenchmen caught him on the beach,
　　His little Argo sorely jeering ;
Till tidings of him chanced to reach
　　Napoleon's hearing.

With folded arms Napoleon stood,
　　Serene alike in peace and danger ;
And, in his wonted attitude,
　　Addressed the stranger :—

" Rash man, that wouldst yon Channel pass
　　On twigs and staves so rudely fashioned,
Thy heart with some sweet British lass
　　Must be impassioned."

" I have no sweetheart," said the lad ;
　　" But—absent long from one another—
Great was the longing that I had
　　To see my mother."

" And so thou shalt," Napoleon said,
  " Ye 've both my favor fairly won ;
A noble mother must have bred
  So brave a son."

He gave the tar a piece of gold,
  And, with a flag of truce, commanded
He should be shipped to England Old,
  And safely landed.

Our sailor oft could scarcely shift
  To find a dinner, plain and hearty,
But *never* changed the coin and gift
  Of Bonapartè.

THOMAS CAMPBELL.

HOW THEY BROUGHT THE GOOD NEWS FROM GHENT TO AIX.

I SPRANG to the stirrup, and Joris and he ;
I galloped, Dirck galloped, we galloped all three ;
" Good speed ! " cried the watch as the gatebolts
  undrew,
" Speed ! " echoed the wall to us galloping through.
Behind shut the postern, the lights sank to rest ;
And into the midnight we galloped abreast.

Not a word to each other ; we kept the great pace,—
Neck by neck, stride by stride, never changing our
  place ;
I turned in my saddle and made its girths tight,
Then shortened each stirrup and set the pique right,
Rebuckled the check-strap, chained slacker the bit,
Nor galloped less steadily Roland a whit.

'T was a moonset at starting; but while we drew
    near
Lokeren, the cocks crew and twilight dawned clear;
At Boom a great yellow star came out to see;
At Düffeld 't was morning as plain as could be;
And from Mecheln church-steeple we heard the
    half-chime,—
So Joris broke silence with " Yet there is time!"

At Aerschot up leaped of a sudden the sun,
And against him the cattle stood black every one,
To stare through the mist at us galloping past;
And I saw my stout galloper Roland at last,
With resolute shoulders, each butting away
The haze, as some bluff river headland its spray;

And his low head and crest, just one sharp ear
    bent back
For my voice, and the other pricked out on his
    track;
And one eye's black intelligence,—ever that glance
O'er its white edge at me, his own master, askance;
And the thick heavy spume-flakes, which aye and
    anon
His fierce lips shook upward in galloping on.

By Hasselt, Dirck groaned; and cried Joris, " Stay
    spur!
Your Roos galloped bravely, the fault 's not in her;
We 'll remember at Aix,"—for one heard the quick
    wheeze
Of her chest, saw the stretched neck, and stagger-
    ing knees,
And sunk tail, and horrible heave of the flank,
As down on her haunches she shuddered and sank.

So we were left galloping, Joris and I,
Past Looz and past Tongres, no cloud in the sky;
The broad sun above laughed a pitiless laugh;
'Neath our feet broke the brittle, bright stubble like
    chaff;
Till over by Dalhem a dome-spire sprang white,
And " Gallop," gasped Joris, " for Aix is in sight! "

" How they 'll greet us ! "—and all in a moment his
    roan
Rolled neck and croup over, lay dead as a stone;
And there was my Roland to bear the whole weight
Of the news which alone could save Aix from her
    fate,
With his nostrils like pits full of blood to the brim,
And with circles of red for his eye-sockets' rim.

Then I cast loose my buff-coat, each holster let fall,
Shook off both my jack-boots, let go belt and all,
Stood up in the stirrup, leaned, patted his ear,
Called my Roland his pet name, my horse without
    peer,—
Clapped my hands, laughed and sung, any noise, bad
    or good,
Till at length into Aix Roland galloped and stood.

And all I remember is, friends flocking round,
As I sate with his head 'twixt my knees on the
    ground;
And no voice but was praising this Roland of mine,
As I poured down his throat our last measure of
    wine,
Which (the burgesses voted by common consent)
Was no more than his due who brought good news
    from Ghent.

ROBERT BROWNING

MORT D'ARTHUR.

So all day long the noise of battle rolled
Among the mountains by the winter sea;
Until King Arthur's Table, man by man,
Had fallen in Lyoness about their lord,
King Arthur: then, because his wound was deep,
The bold Sir Bedivere uplifted him,
Sir Bedivere, the last of all his Knights,
And bore him to a chapel nigh the field,
A broken chancel with a broken cross,
That stood on a dark strait of barren land.
On one side lay the Ocean, and on one
Lay a great water, and the moon was full.

Then spake King Arthur to Sir Bedivere:
"The sequel of to-day unsolders all
The goodliest fellowship of famous knights
Whereof this world holds record. Such a sleep
They sleep—the men I loved. I think that we
Shall nevermore, at any future time,
Delight our souls with talk of knightly deeds,
Walking about the gardens and the halls
Of Camelot, as in the days that were.
I perish by this people which I made,—
Though Merlin sware that I should come again
To rule once more; but let what will be, be.
I am so deeply smitten through the helm
That without help I cannot last till morn.
Thou therefore take my brand Excalibur,
Which was my pride: for thou rememberest how
In those old days, one summer noon, an arm

Rose up from out the bosom of the lake,
Clothed in white samite, mystic, wonderful,
Holding the sword—and how I rowed across
And took it, and have worn it, like a king;
And, wheresoever I am sung or told
In after-time, this also shall be known:
But now delay not: take Excalibur,
And fling him far into the middle mere:
Watch what thou seest, and lightly bring me word."

To him replied the bold Sir Bedivere:
" It is not meet, Sir King, to leave thee thus,
Aidless, alone, and smitten through the helm.
A little thing may harm a wounded man;
Yet I thy hest will all perform at full,
Watch what I see, and lightly bring thee word."

So saying, from the ruined shrine he stept
And in the moon athwart the place of tombs,
Where lay the mighty bones of ancient men,
Old knights, and over them the sea-wind sang
Shrill, chill, with flakes of foam. He, stepping
        down
By zigzag paths, and juts of pointed rock,
Came on the shining levels of the lake.

There drew he forth the brand Excalibur,
And o'er him, drawing it, the winter moon,
Brightening the skirts of a long cloud, ran forth
And sparkled keen with frost against the hilt:
For all the haft twinkled with diamond studs,
Myriads of topaz-lights, and jacinth-work
Of subtlest jewelry.   He gazed so long
That both his eyes were dazzled as he stood,

This way and that dividing the swift mind,
In act to throw : but at the last it seemed
Better to leave Excalibur concealed
There in the many-knotted water-flags,
That whistled stiff and dry about the marge.
So strode he back slow to the wounded King.

Then spake King Arthur to Sir Bedivere :
"Hast thou performed my mission which I gave?
What is it thou hast seen? or what hast heard?"

And answer made the bold Sir Bedivere :
"I heard the ripple washing in the reeds,
And the wild water lapping on the crag."

To whom replied King Arthur, faint and pale :
"Thou hast betrayed thy nature and thy name,
Not rendering true answer, as beseemed
Thy fealty, nor like a noble knight :
For surer sign had followed, either hand,
Or voice, or else a motion of the mere.
This is a shameful thing for men to lie.
Yet now, I charge thee, quickly go again,
As thou art lief and dear, and do the thing
I bade thee, watch, and lightly bring me word."

Then went Sir Bedivere the second time
Across the ridge, and paced beside the mere,
Counting the dewy pebbles, fixed in thought;
But when he saw the wonder of the hilt,
How curiously and strangely chased, he smote
His palms together, and he cried aloud :—

"And if indeed I cast the brand away,
Surely a precious thing, one worthy note,

Should thus be lost forever from the earth,
Which might have pleased the eyes of many men.
What good should follow this, if this were done?
What harm, undone? deep harm to disobey,
Seeing obedience is the bond of rule.
Were it well to obey then, if a king demand
An act unprofitable, against himself?
The King is sick, and knows not what he does.
What record, or what relic of my lord
Should be to after-time, but empty breath
And rumors of a doubt? but were this kept,
Stored in some treasure-house of mighty kings,
Some one might show it at a joust of arms,
Saying, 'King Arthur's sword, Excalibur,
Wrought by the lonely maiden of the Lake.
Nine years she wrought it, sitting in the deeps
Upon the hidden bases of the hills.'
So might some old man speak in the after-time
To all the people, winning reverence.
But now much honor and much fame were lost."

    So spake he, clouded with his own conceit,
And hid Excalibur the second time,
And so strode back slow to the wounded King.

    Then spoke King Arthur, breathing heavily:
" What is it thou hast seen? or what hast heard? "

    And answer made the bold Sir Bedivere:
" I heard the water lapping on the crag,
And the long ripple washing in the reeds."

    To whom replied King Arthur, much in wrath:
" Ah, miserable and unkind, untrue,
Unknightly, traitor-hearted! Woe is me!
Authority forgets a dying king,

Laid widowed of the power in his eye
That bowed the will. I see thee what thou art,
For thou, the latest-left of all my knights
In whom should meet the offices of all,
Thou wouldst betray me for the precious hilt;
Either from lust of gold, or like a girl
Valuing the giddy pleasure of the eyes.
Yet, for a man may fail in duty twice,
And the third time may prosper, get thee hence:
But, if thou spare to fling Excalibur,
I will arise and slay thee with my hands."

Then quickly rose Sir Bedivere, and ran,
And, leaping down the ridges lightly, plunged
Among the bulrush-beds, and clutched the sword,
And strongly wheeled and threw it. The great
    brand
Made lightnings in the splendor of the moon,
And flashing round and round, and whirlèd in an
    arch,
Shot like a streamer of the northern morn,
Seen where the moving isles of winter shock
By night, with noises of the northern sea.
So flashed and fell the brand Excalibur:
But ere he dipt the surface, rose an arm
Clothed in white samite, mystic, wonderful,
And caught him by the hilt, and brandished him
Three times, and drew him under in the mere.
And lightly went the other to the King.

Then spoke King Arthur, drawing thicker breath:
" Now see I by thine eyes that this is done.
Speak out: what is it thou hast heard, or seen?"

And answer made the bold Sir Bedivere:
" Sir King, I closed mine eyelids, lest the gem
Should blind my purpose, for I never saw,
Nor shall see, here or elsewhere, till I die,
Not though I live three lives of mortal men,
So great a miracle as yonder hilt.
Then with both hands I flung him, wheeling him;
But when I looked again, behold an arm,
Clothed in white samite, mystic, wonderful,
That caught him by the hilt, and brandished him
Three times, and drew him under in the mere."

And answer made King Arthur, breathing hard:
" My end draws nigh; 't is time that I were gone.
Make broad thy shoulders to receive my weight,
And bear me to the margin; yet I fear
My wound hath taken cold, and I shall die."

So saying, from the pavement he half rose,
Slowly, with pain, reclining on his arm,
And looking wistfully with wide blue eyes
As in a picture. Him Sir Bedivere
Remorsefully regarded through his tears,
And would have spoken, but he found not words ;
Then took with care, and kneeling on one knee,
O'er both his shoulders drew the languid hands,
And rising bore him through the place of tombs.

But, as he walked, King Arthur panted hard,
Like one that feels a nightmare on his bed
When all the house is mute. So sighed the King,
Muttering and murmuring at his ear " Quick, quick !
I fear it is too late, and I shall die."
But the other swiftly strode from ridge to ridge,

Clothed with his breath, and looking, as he walked,
Larger than human on the frozen hills.
He heard the deep behind him, and a cry
Before.   His own thought drove him like a goad.
Dry clashed his harness in the icy caves
And barren chasms, and all to left and right
The bare black cliff clangèd round him, as he based
His feet on juts of slippery crag that rang
Sharp-smitten with the dint of armèd heels—
And on a sudden, lo! the level lake,
And the long glories of the winter moon.

Then saw they how there hove a dusky barge,
Dark as a funeral scarf from stem to stern,
Beneath them; and descending they were ware
That all the decks were dense with stately forms,
Black-stoled, black-hooded, like a dream,—by these
Three Queens with crowns of gold,—and from them
　　rose
A cry that shivered to the tingling stars,
And, as it were one voice, an agony
Of lamentation, like a wind that shrills
All night in a waste land, where no one comes,
Or hath come, since the making of the world.

Then murmured Arthur, " Place me in the barge ; "
So to the barge they came.   There those three
　　Queens
Put forth their hands, and took the King, and wept.
But she that rose the tallest of them all,
And fairest, laid his head upon her lap,
And loosed the shattered casque, and chafed his
　　hands,
And called him by his name, complaining loud,

And dropping bitter tears against his brow
Striped with dark blood: for all his face was white
And colorless, and like the withered moon
Smote by the fresh beam of the springing east;
And all his greaves and cuisses dashed with drops
Of onset; and the light and lustrous curls—
That made his forehead like a rising sun
High from the daïs-throne—were parched with
        dust;
Or, clotted into points and hanging loose,
Mixed with the knightly growth that fringed his
        lips.
So like a shattered column lay the King;
Not like that Arthur, who, with lance in rest,
From spur to plume a star of tournament,
Shot through the lists at Camelot, and charged
Before the eyes of ladies and of kings.

  Then loudly cried the bold Sir Bedivere:
" Ah! my Lord Arthur, whither shall I go?
Where shall I hide my forehead and my eyes?
For now I see the true old times are dead,
When every morning brought a noble chance,
And every chance brought out a noble knight.
Such times have been not since the light that led
The holy Elders with the gift of myrrh.
But now the whole Round Table is dissolved
Which was an image of the mighty world;
And I, the last, go forth companionless,
And the days darken round me, and the years,
Among new men, strange faces, other minds."

  And slowly answered Arthur from the barge:
" The old order changeth, yielding place to new,

And God fulfils himself in many ways,
Lest one good custom should corrupt the world.
Comfort thyself : what comfort is in me ?
I have lived my life, and that which I have done
May He within himself make pure ! but thou,
If thou shouldst never see my face again,
Pray for my soul. More things are wrought by
        prayer
Than this world dreams of. Wherefore, let thy
        voice
Rise like a fountain for me night and day.
For what are men better than sheep or goats
That nourish a blind life within the brain,
If, knowing God, they lift not hands of prayer
Both for themselves and those who call them
        friend ?
For so the whole round earth is every way
Bound by gold chains about the feet of God.
But now farewell. I am going a long way
With these thou seest,—if indeed I go
(For all my mind is clouded with a doubt)—
To the island-valley of Avilion ;
Where falls not hail, or rain, or any snow,
Nor ever wind blows loudly ; but it lies
Deep-meadowed, happy, fair with orchard-lawns
And bowery hollows crowned with summer sea,
Where I will heal me of my grievous wound."

    So said he, and the barge with oar and sail
Moved from the brink, like some full-breasted
        swan,
That, fluting a wild carol ere her death,
Ruffles her pure cold plume, and takes the flood

With swarthy webs. Long stood Sir Bedivere
Revolving many memories, till the hull
Looked one black dot against the verge of dawn,
And on the mere the wailing died away.

ALFRED, LORD TENNYSON.

GODIVA.

I waited for the train at Coventry ;
I hung with grooms and porters on the bridge,
To watch the three tall spires : and there I shaped
The city's ancient legend into this :

Not only we, the latest seed of Time,
New men, that in the flying of a wheel
Cry down the past ; not only we, that prate
Of rights and wrongs, have loved the people well,
And loathed to see them overtaxed ; but she
Did more, and underwent, and overcame,
The woman of a thousand summers back,
Godiva, wife to that grim Earl who ruled
In Coventry : for when he laid a tax
Upon his town, and all the mothers brought
Their children, clamoring, " If we pay, we starve ! "
She sought her lord, and found him, where he
    strode
About the hall, among his dogs, alone,
His beard a foot before him, and his hair
A yard behind. She told him of their tears,
And prayed him, " If they pay this tax they starve."
Whereat he stared, replying, half amazed,
" You would not let your little finger ache
For such as *these ?* " " But I would die," said she.

He laughed, and swore by Peter and by Paul:
Then filliped at the diamond in her ear;
" O, ay, ay, ay, you talk ! "   " Alas ! " she said,
" But prove me what it is I would not do."
And from a heart as rough as Esau's hand,
He answered, " Ride you naked through the town,
And I repeal it ; " and nodding, as in scorn,
He parted, with great strides among his dogs.

So left alone, the passions of her mind,
As winds from all the compass shift and blow,
Made war upon each other for an hour,
Till pity won. She sent a herald forth,
And bade him cry, with sound of trumpet, all
The hard condition; but that she would loose
The people : therefore, as they loved her well,
From then till noon no foot should pace the street,
No eye look down, she passing ; but that all
Should keep within, door shut and window barred.

Then fled she to her inmost bower, and there
Unclasped the wedded eagles of her belt,
The grim Earl's gift ; but ever at a breath
She lingered, looking like a summer moon
Half dipt in cloud : anon she shook her head,
And showered the rippled ringlets to her knee ;
Unclad herself in haste ; adown the stair
Stole on ; and, like a creeping sunbeam, slid
From pillar unto pillar, until she reached
The gateway ; there she found her palfrey trapt
In purple blazoned with armorial gold.

Then she rode forth, clothed on with chastity :
The deep air listened round her as she rode,
And all the low wind hardly breathed for fear.
The little wide-mouthed heads upon the spout

Had cunning eyes to see: the barking cur
Made her cheek flame : her palfrey's footfall shot
Light horrors through her pulses : the blind walls
Were full of chinks and holes; and overhead
Fantastic gables, crowding, stared : but she
Not less through all bore up, till, last, she saw
The white-flowered elder-thicket from the field
Gleam through the Gothic archways in the wall.

Then she rode back, clothed on with chastity :
And one low churl, compact of thankless earth,
The fatal byword of all years to come,
Boring a little auger hole in fear,
Peeped—but his eyes, before they had their will,
Were shrivelled into darkness in his head,
And dropt before him. So the Powers, who wait
On noble deeds, cancelled a sense misused ;
And she, that knew not, passed : and all at once,
With twelve great shocks of sound, the shameless
    noon
Was clashed and hammered from a hundred towers,
One after one : but even then she gained
Her bower ; whence reissuing, robed and crowned,
To meet her lord, she took the tax away,
And built herself an everlasting name.

ALFRED, LORD TENNYSON.

THE CANTERBURY PILGRIMS.

FROM " THE CANTERBURY TALES : PROLOGUE."

WHAN that Aprille with hise shourès soote [1]
The droghte of March hath percèd to the roote,
And bathèd every veyne in swich [2] licour,

---

[1] sweet.   [2] such.

Of which vertue engendred is the flour;
Whan Zephirus eek with his swete breeth
Inspirèd hath in every holt [1] and heeth
The tendre croppès, and the yongè sonne
Hath in the Ram his halfè cours y-ronne,
And smalè fowelès maken melodye
That slepen al the nyght with open eye,—
So priketh hem nature in hir corages,[2]—
Thanne longen folk to goon on pilgrimages,
And palmeres for to seken straungè strondes,
To ferne halwes,[3] kowthe [4] in sondry londes;
And specially, from every shirès ende
Of Engelond, to Caunterbury they wende
The hooly blisful martir [5] for to seke,
That hem hath holpen whan that they were seeke.

   Bifil that, in that seson on a day,
In Southwerk at the Tabard as I lay,
Redy to wenden on my pilgrymage
To Caunterbury with ful devout corage,
At nyght were come in-to that hostelrye
Wel nyne-and-twenty in a compaignye,
Of sondry folk, by aventure y-falle
In felaweshipe, and pilgrimes were thei alle,
That toward Caunterbury wolden ryde.

         .   .   .   .   .

   A Knyght ther was, and that a worthy man,
That fro the tymè that he first bigan
To riden out, he lovèd chivalrie,
Trouthe and honour, fredom and curteisie,
Ful worthy was he in his lordès werre,
And therto hadde he riden, noman ferre,[6]
As wel in cristendom as in hethenesse,

---

[1] wood.   [2] their hearts.   [3] ancient saints.
[4] renowned.   [5] Thomas-à-Becket.   [6] farther.

And evere honoured for his worthynesse.

And though that he were worthy, he was wys,
And of his port as meeke as is a mayde.
He nevere yet no vileynye [1] ne sayde
In al his lyf unto no maner wight.
He was a verray parfit, gentil knyght.

With hym ther was his sone, a young Squier,
A lovyere and a lusty bacheler,
With lokkès crulle [2] as they were leyd in presse.
Of twenty yeer of age he was I gesse.
Of his stature he was of evene lengthe,
And wonderly delyvere,[3] and of greet strengthe.
And he hadde ben somtyme in chyvachie,[4]
In Flaundres, in Artoys, and Pycardie,
And born hym weel, as of so litel space,
In hope to stonden in his lady grace.
Embrouded [5] was he, as it were a meede
Al ful of fresshè flourès whyte and reede.
Syngynge he was, or floytynge,[6] al the day;
He was as fressh as is the monthe of May.
Short was his gowne, with slevès longe and wyde.
Wel cowde he sitte on hors, and fairè ryde.
He koudè songès make and wel endite,
Juste and eek daunce, and weel purtreye [7] and
    write.
So hoote he lovedè, that by nyghtertale [8]
He sleep no more than dooth a nyghtyngale;
Curteis he was, lovely and servysable,
And carf [9] biforn his fader at the table.

[1] nothing unmannerly.   [2] curled.
[3] active.   [4] a military expedition.
[5] embroidered.   [6] playing on a flute.
[7] portray—draw.   [8] night-time.   [9] carved.

Ther was also a Nonne, a Prioresse,
That of hire smylyng was ful symple and coy;
Hire gretteste ooth ne was but by seint Loy;[1]
And she was clepèd madame Eglentyne.
Ful weel she soonge the servicè dyvyne,
Entunèd in hir nose ful semeely;
And Frenssh she spak ful faire and fetisly,[2]
After the scole of Stratford-attè-Bowe,
For Frenssh of Parys was to hire unknowe.
At metè[3] wel ytaught was she with alle,
She leet no morsel from hir lippès falle,
Ne wett hire fyngres in hire saucè deepe.
Wel koude she carie a morsel and wel kepe,
That no dropè ne fille up-on hire breste;
In curteisie was set ful muchel hir leste.[4]
Hire over-lippè wypèd she so clene,
That in hir coppe ther was no ferthyng[5] sene
Of grecè, whan she dronken hadde hir draughte.
Ful semèly after hir mete she raughte,[6]
And sikerly[7] she was of greet disport,
And ful plesaunt, and amyable of port,
And peynèd hir[8] to countrefetè cheere
Of Court, and to ben estatlich of manere,
And to ben holden digne of reverence;
But for to speken of hire conscience,
She was so charitable and so pitous,
She woldè wepe if that she saugh a mous
Kaught in a trappe, if it were deed or bledde.
Of smalè houndès hadde she, that she fedde
With rosted flessh, or mylk and wastel-breed;[9]
But soore wepte she if any of hem were deed,

---

[1] probably St. Louis.   [2] featly—neatly.   [3] meat—table.
[4] pleasure.   [5] morsel.   [6] reached.
[7] surely.   [8] took pains.   [9] cake (gasteau) bread.

Or if men smoot it with a yerdè[1] smerte:
And al was conscience and tendre herte.
Ful semlèy hire wympul pynchèd was;
Hir nose tretys,[2] hire eyèn greye as glas,
Hir mouth ful smal, and ther to softe and reed,
But sikerly she hadde a fair forheed;
It was almoost a spannè brood, I trowe,
For hardily she was nat undergrowe.
Ful fetys was hir cloke, as I was war;
Of smal coral aboute hire arm she bar
A peire of bedès gauded[3] al with grene;
And ther-on heng a broch of gold ful schene,
On which ther was first write a crownèd A,
And after, *Amor vincit omnia.*
Another Nonnè with hire haddè she,
That was hire Chapeleyne, and Preestès thre.

.   .   .   .   .

A Clerk ther was of Oxenford also
That un-to logyk haddè longe ygo.
And leenè was his hors as is a rake,
And he was nat right fat, I undertake,
But lookèd holwe, and ther to sobrely;
Full thredbare was his overeste courtepy,[4]
For he hadde geten hym yet no benefice,
Ne was so worldly to have office;
For hym was levere have at his beddes heed
Twenty bookès, clad in blak or reed,
Of Aristotle and his philosophie,
Than robès riche, or fithele,[5] or gay sautrie.[6]
But al be that he was a philosophre,
Yet haddè he but litel gold in cofre;

---

[1] rod.   [2] straight.   [3] The *gaudies* were the larger beads.
[4] uppermost short cloak.   [5] fiddle.   [6] psaltery.

But al that he mighte of his freendès hente [1]
On bookès and his lernynge he it spente,
And bisily gan for the soulès preye
Of hem that gaf him wher with to scoleye,[2]
Of studie took he moost cure and moost heede,
Noght o word spak he moorè than was neede,
And that was seyd in forme and reverence
And short and quyk and ful of hy sentence.
Sownynge in [3] moral vertu was his speche
And gladly wolde he lerne, and gladly teche.

A Sergeant of the Lawe, war [4] and wys,
That often haddè ben at the Parvys,[5]
Ther was also ful riche of excellence.
Discreet he was and of greet reverence;
He semèd swich, hise wordès weren so wise.
Justice he was ful often in Assise,
By patente, and by pleyn commissioun,
For his science and for his heigh renoun.
Of fees and robès hadde he many oon;
So gret a purchasour [6] was nowher noon.
Al was fee symple to hym in effect,
His purchasyng myghte nat ben infect.[7]
Nowhere so bisy a man as he ther nas,[8]
And yet he semèd bisier than he was.

.   .   .   .   .

And good man was ther of religioun,
And was Povre Persoun [9] of a Toun;
But riche he was of hooly thoght and werk;
He was also a lernèd man, a clerk

[1] get.
[2] study.
[3] tending towards.
[4] wary—prudent.
[5] portico of St. Paul's, where lawyers met.
[6] prosecutor.
[7] tainted.
[8] he was—was not.
[9] Poor parson.

That Cristès Gospel trewèly wolde preche,
Hise parisshens devoutly wolde he teche.
Benygne he was, and wonder diligent,
And in adversitee ful pacient ;
And such he was y-prevèd oftè sithes.[1]
Ful looth were hym to cursè for his tythes,
But rather wolde he geven,[2] out of doute,
Un-to his povrè parisshens aboute,
Of his offryng and eek of his substaunce.
He koude in litel thyng have suffisaunce.
Wyd was his parisshe, and houses fer a-sonder
But he ne laftè[3] nat for reyn ne thonder,
In siknesse nor in meschief to visite
The ferreste[4] in his parisshe muche and lite[5]
Up-on his feet, and in his hand a staf.
This noble ensample to his sheepe he gaf,[6]
That firste he wroghte, and afterward he taughte.

. . . . .

A bettre preest, I throwe, that nowher noon is:
He waiteth after no pompe and reverence,
Ne makèd him a spicèd conscience,
But Cristès loore, and his Apostles twelve,
He taughte, but first he folwed it hym selve.

. . . . .

Now have I toold you shortly in a clause
The staat, tharray, the nombre, and eek the cause
Why that assembled was this compaignye
In Southwerk at this gentil hostelrye,
That highte the Tabard, fastè by the Belle.
But now is tymè to yow for to telle
How that we baren us that ilke[7] nyght,
When we were in that hostelrie alyght,

---

[1] times. [2] give. [3] ceased.
[4] farthest. [5] great and small. [6] gave. [7] same.

And after wol I telle of our viage,
And al the remenaunt of oure pilgrimage.
  But first, I pray yow of your curteisye,
That ye narette it nat my vileinye,[1]
Thogh that I pleynly speke in this mateere,
To tellè yow hir wordès and hir cheere;
Ne thogh I speke hir wordès proprely.
For this ye knowen al so wel as I,
Whoso shal telle a tale after a man,
He moote reherce, as ny as evere he kan
Everich a word, if it be in his charge,
Al spekc he never so rudèliche[2] or large;[3]
Or ellis he moot telle his tale untrewe,
Or feynè thyng, or fyndè wordès newe.
He may nat spare al thogh he were his brother,
He moot as wel seye o word as another.
Crist spak hym self ful brode in hooly writ
And wel ye woot no vileynye is it.
Eek Plato seith, who so can hym rede,
" The wordès moote be cosyn[4] to the dede."
  Also I prey yow to forgeve it me,
Al have I nat set folk in hir degree
Heere in this tale, as that they scholdè stonde;
My wit is short ye may wel understonde.
  Greet chierè made oure host us everichon,
And to the soper sette he us anon
And servèd us with vitaille at the beste.
Strong was the wyn and wel to drynke us leste.[5]
  A semely man Oure Hoost he was withalle
For to han been a marchal in an halle;
A largè man he was with eyen stepe,

---

[1] that ye ascribe it not to my ill-breeding.   [2] rudely.
[3] free.   [4] germane.   [5] pleased.

A fairer burgeys was ther noon in Chepe :
Boold of his speche, and wys and wel ytaught,
And of manhod hym lakkedè right naught.

Eek therto he was right a myrie [1] man,
And after soper pleyen he bygan,
And spak of myrthè amonges othere thinges,
Whan that we haddè maad our rekenynges ;
And seydè thus : " Lo, lordynges, trewèly
Ye ben to me right welcome hertèly :
For by my trouthe, if that I shal nat lye,
I saugh nat this yeer so myrie a compaignye
Atones in this herberwe [2] as is now.
Fayn wolde I doon [3] yow myrthè, wiste I how.
And of a myrthe I am right now bythoght,
To doon you ese, and it shal costè noght.

Ye goon to Caunterbury, God you speede,
The blisful martir quitè yow youre meede! [4]
And wel I woot as ye goon by the weye
Ye shapen yow [5] to talen [6] and to pleye ;
For trewèly confort ne myrthe is noon
To ridè by the weye doumb as the stoon ;
And therefore wol I maken you disport,
As I seyde erst, and doon you som confort.

. . . . .

That ech of yow to shortè with oure weye,
In this viage shall tellè talès tweye,[7]—
To Caunterburyward, I mean it so,
And homward he shal tellen othere two,—
Of aventures that whilom han bifalle.
And which of yow that bereth hym best of alle,
That is to seyn, that telleth in this caas

---

[1] merry.   [2] harborage—inn.   [3] make.   [4] reward.
[5] purpose.   [6] tell tales.   [7] two.

Talès of best sentence [1] and most solaas,[2]
Shall have soper at oure aller cost,
Heere in this place, syttynge by this post,
Whan that we come agayn fro Caunterbury.
And for to make you the moore mury,
I wol my-selfè gladly with yow ryde,
Right at myn owenè cost, and be youre gyde.
And who so wole my juggèment withseye [3]
Shal paye al that we spenden by the weye.
And if ye vouchè-sauf that it be so,
Tel me anon, with-outen wordès mo,
And I wol erly shapè [4] me therfore."
This thyng was graunted, and oure othès swore
With ful glad herte, and preyden hym also
That he would vouchè-sauf for to do so,
And that he woldè been our governour,
And of oure talès juge and reportour,
And sette a soper at a certeyn pris
And we wol reulèd been [5] at his devys
In heigh and lough; and thus by oon assent
We been acorded to his juggèment.
And ther-up-on the wyn was fet anon;
We dronken and to reste wente echon
With-outen any lenger taryÿnge.

GEOFFREY CHAUCER.

---

[1] sense.   [2] solace—mirth.   [3] gainsay.
[4] shape my affairs—prepare.   [5] be ruled.

LORD LOVEL.

LORD LOVEL he stood at his castle gate,
 Combing his milk-white steed;
When up came Lady Nancy Belle,
 To wish her lover good speed, speed,
 To wish her lover good speed.

" Where are you going, Lord Lovel? " she said,
 " Oh! where are you going? " said she;
" I'm going, my Lady Nancy Belle,
 Strange countries for to see, to see,
 Strange countries for to see."

" When will you be back, Lord Lovel? " said she:
 " O! when will you come back? " said she;
" In a year or two—or three, at the most,
 I'll return to my fair Nancy-cy,
 I'll return to my fair Nancy."

But he had not been gone a year and a day,
 Strange countries for to see,
When languishing thoughts came into his head,
 Lady Nancy Belle he would go see, see,
 Lady Nancy Belle he would go see.

So he rode, and he rode, on his milk-white steed,
 Till he came to London town,
And there he heard St. Pancras' bells,
 And the people all mourning, round, round,
 And the people all mourning round.

" Oh, what is the matter," Lord Lovel he said,
  " Oh! what is the matter? " said he;
" A lord's lady is dead," a woman replied,
  " And some call her Lady Nancy-cy,
  And some call her Lady Nancy."

So he ordered the grave to be opened wide,
  And the shroud he turnèd down,
And there he kissed her clay-cold lips,
  Till the tears came trickling down, down,
  Till the tears came trickling down.

Lady Nancy she died as it might be to-day,
  Lord Lovel he died as to-morrow;
Lady Nancy she died out of pure, pure grief,
  Lord Lovel he died out of sorrow, sorrow,
  Lord Lovel he died out of sorrow.

Lady Nancy was laid in St. Pancras' church,
  Lord Lovel was laid in the choir;
And out of her bosom there grew a red rose,
  And out of her lover's a brier, brier,
  And out of her lover's a brier.

They grew, and they grew, to the church steeple
    top,
  And then they could grow no higher:
So there they entwined in a true lover's knot,
  For all lovers true to admire-mire,
  For all lovers true to admire.

ANONYMOUS.

ROBIN HOOD AND ALLAN-A-DALE.

COME, listen to me, you gallants so free,
  All you that love mirth for to hear,
And I will tell you of a bold outlaw,
  That lived in Nottinghamshire.

As Robin Hood in the forest stood,
  All under the greenwood tree,
There he was aware of a brave young man,
  As fine as fine might be,

The youngster was clad in scarlet-red,
  In scarlet fine and gay;
And he did frisk it over the plain,
  And chanted a roundelay.

As Robin Hood next morning stood
  Amongst the leaves so gay,
There did he espy the same young man
  Come drooping along the way.

The scarlet he wore the day before
  It was clean cast away;
And at every step he fetched a sigh,
  "Alack and well-a-day!"

Then stepped forth brave Little John,
  And Midge, the miller's son;
Which made the young man bend his bow,
  Whenas he see them come.

"Stand off! stand off!" the young man said,
  "What is your will with me?"
"You must come before our master straight,
  Under yon greenwood tree."

And when he came bold Robin before,
  Robin asked him courteously,
"O, hast thou any money to spare,
  For my merry men and me?"

"I have no money," the young man said,
  "But five shillings and a ring;
And that I have kept these seven long years,
  To have at my wedding.

"Yesterday I should have married a maid,
  But she was from me ta'en,
And chosen to be an old knight's delight,
  Whereby my poor heart is slain."

"What is thy name?" then said Robin Hood,
  "Come tell me without any fail."
"By the faith of my body," then said the young
      man,
  "My name it is Allan-a-Dale."

"What wilt thou give me," said Robin Hood,
  "In ready gold or fee,
To help thee to thy true-love again,
  And deliver her unto thee?"

"I have no money," then quoth the young man,
  "No ready gold or fee,

But I will swear upon a book
Thy true servant for to be."

" How many miles is it to thy true-love?
Come tell me without guile."
" By the faith of my body," then said the young
man,
" It is but five little mile."

Then Robin he hasted over the plain,
He did neither stint nor lin,*
Until he came unto the church
Where Allan should keep his wedding.

" What hast thou here? " the bishop then said,
" I prithee now tell unto me."
" I am a bold harper," quoth Robin Hood,
" And the best in the north country."

" O, welcome, O, welcome," the bishop he said,
" That music best pleaseth me."
" You shall have no music," quoth Robin Hood,
" Till the bride and bridegroom I see."

With that came in a wealthy knight,
Which was both grave and old;
And after him a finikin lass,
Did shine like the glistering gold.

" This is not a fit match," quoth Robin Hood,
" That you do seem to make here;

* Stop nor stay.

For since we are come into the church,
　　The bride shall chuse her own dear."

Then Robin Hood put his horn to his mouth,
　　And blew blasts two and three;
When four-and-twenty yeomen bold
　　Came leaping over the lea.

And when they came into the churchyard,
　　Marching all in a row,
The very first man was Allan-a-Dale,
　　To give bold Robin his bow.

" This is thy true-love," Robin he said,
　　" Young Allan, as I hear say;
And you shall be married at this same time,
　　Before we depart away."

" That shall not be," the bishop he cried,
　　" For thy word shall not stand;
They shall be three times asked in the church,
　　As the law is of our land."

Robin Hood pulled off the bishop's coat,
　　And put it upon Little John;
" By the faith of my body," then Robin said,
　　" This cloth doth make thee a man."

When Little John went into the quire,
　　The people began to laugh;
He asked them seven times in the church
　　Lest three times should not be enough.

"Who gives me this maid?" said Little John,
  Quoth Robin Hood, "That do I;
And he that takes her from Allan-a-Dale,
  Full dearly he shall her buy."

And then, having ended this merry wedding,
  The bride looked like a queen;
And so they returned to the merry greenwood,
  Amongst the leaves so green.

ANONYMOUS.

THE GREENWOOD SHRIFT.

GEORGE III. AND A DYING WOMAN IN WINDSOR FOREST.

OUTSTRETCHED beneath the leafy shade
Of Windsor forest's deepest glade,
    A dying woman lay;
Three little children round her stood,
And there went up from the greenwood
    A woful wail that day.

"O mother!" was the mingled cry,
"O mother, mother! do not die,
    And leave us all alone."
"My blessèd babes!" she tried to say,
But the faint accents died away
    In a low sobbing moan.

And then, life struggled hard with death,
And fast and strong she drew her breath,
    And up she raised her head;
And, peering through the deep wood maze
With a long, sharp, unearthly gaze,
    "Will she not come?" she said.

Just then, the parting boughs between,
A little maid's light form was seen,
   All breathless with her speed;
And, following close, a man came on
(A portly man to look upon),
   Who led a panting steed.

" Mother!" the little maiden cried,
Or e'er she reached the woman's side,
   And kissed her clay-cold cheek,—
" I have not idled in the town,
But long went wandering up and down,
   The minister to seek.

" They told me here, they told me there,—
I think they mocked me everywhere;
   And when I found his home,
And begged him on my bended knee
To bring his book and come with me,
   Mother! he would not come.

" I told him how you dying lay,
And could not go in peace away
   Without the minister;
I begged him, for dear Christ his sake,
But O, my heart was fit to break,—
   Mother! he would not stir.

" So, though my tears were blinding me,
I ran back, fast as fast could be,
   To come again to you;
And here—close by—this squire I met,
Who asked (so mild) what made me fret;
   And when I told him true,—

" ' I will go with you, child,' he said,
' God sends me to this dying bed,'—
   Mother, he 's here, hard by."
While thus the little maiden spoke,
The man, his back against an oak,
   Looked on with glistening eye.

The bridle on his neck hung free,
With quivering flank and trembling knee,
   Pressed close his bonny bay;
A statelier man, a statelier steed,
Never on greensward paced, I rede,
   Than those stood there that day.

So, while the little maiden spoke,
The man, his back against an oak,
   Looked on with glistening eye
And folded arms, and in his look
Something that, like a sermon-book,
   Preached,—" All is vanity."

But when the dying woman's face
Turned toward him with a wishful gaze,
   He stepped to where she lay;
And, kneeling down, bent over her,
Saying, " I am a minister,
   My sister! let us pray! "

And well, withouten book or stole,
(God's words were printed on his soul!)
   Into the dying ear
He breathed, as 't were an angel's strain,
The things that unto life pertain,
   And death's dark shadows clear.

He spoke of sinners' lost estate,
In Christ renewed, regenerate,—
   Of God's most blest decree,
That not single soul should die
Who turns repentant, with the cry
   " Be merciful to me."

He spoke of trouble, pain, and toil,
Endured but for a little while
   In patience, faith, and love,—
Sure, in God's own good time, to be
Exchanged for an eternity
   Of happiness above.

Then, as the spirit ebbed away,
He raised his hands and eyes to pray
   That peaceful it might pass;
And then—the orphans' sobs alone
Were heard, and they knelt, every one,
   Close round on the green grass.

Such was the sight their wandering eyes
Beheld, in heart-struck, mute surprise,
   Who reined their coursers back,
Just as they found the long astray,
Who, in the heat of chase that day,
   Had wandered from their track.

But each man reined his pawing steed,
And lighted down, as if agreed,
   In silence at his side;
And there, uncovered all, they stood,—
It was a wholesome sight and good
   That day for mortal pride.

For of the noblest of the land
Was that deep-hushed, bareheaded band;
And, central in the ring,
By that dead pauper on the ground,
Her ragged orphans clinging round,
Knelt their anointed king.

ROBERT AND CAROLINE SOUTHEY.

THE REVENGE.

A BALLAD OF THE FLEET.

I.

At Flores in the Azores Sir Richard Grenville lay,
And a pinnace, like a fluttered bird, came flying
from far away :
"Spanish ships of war at sea ! we have sighted fifty-
three ! "
Then sware Lord Thomas Howard : " 'Fore God I am
no coward ;
But I cannot meet them here, for my ships are out
of gear,
And the half my men are sick. I must fly, but follow quick.
We are six ships of the line ; can we fight with fifty-
three ? "

II.

Then spake Sir Richard Grenville : " I know you are
no coward ;
You fly them for a moment to fight with them
again.
But I 've ninety men and more that are lying sick
ashore.

I should count myself the coward if I left them, my
　　Lord Howard,
To these Inquisition dogs and the devildoms of
　　Spain."

III.

So Lord Howard past away with five ships of war
　　that day,
Till he melted like a cloud in the silent summer
　　heaven ;
But Sir Richard bore in hand all his sick men from
　　the land
Very carefully and slow,
Men of Bideford in Devon,
And we laid them on the ballast down below ;
For we brought them all aboard,
And they blest him in their pain, that they were
　　not left to Spain,
To the thumbscrew and the stake, for the glory of
　　the Lord.

IV.

He had only a hundred seamen to work the ship
　　and to fight,
And he sailed away from Flores till the Spaniard
　　came in sight,
With his huge sea-castles heaving upon the weather
　　bow.
" Shall we fight or shall we fly ?
Good Sir Richard, tell us now,
For to fight is but to die !
There 'll be little of us left by the time this sun be set."
And Sir Richard said again : " We be all good Eng-
　　lish men.

Let us bang these dogs of Seville, the children of
    the devil,
For I never turned my back upon Don or devil yet."

V.

Sir Richard spoke and he laughed, and we roared a
    hurrah, and so
The little Revenge ran on sheer into the heart of
    the foe,
With her hundred fighters on deck, and her ninety
    sick below ;
For half of their fleet to the right and half to the
    left were seen,
And the little Revenge ran on thro' the long sea
    lane between.

VI.

Thousands of their soldiers looked down from their
    decks and laughed,
Thousands of their seamen made mock at the mad
    little craft
Running on and on, till delayed
By their mountain-like San Philip, that, of fifteen
    hundred tons,
And up-shadowing high above us with her yawning
    tiers of guns,
Took the breath from our sails, and we stayed.

VII.

And while now the great San Philip hung above us
    like a cloud
Whence the thunderbolt will fall
Long and loud,
Four galleons drew away
From the Spanish fleet that day,

And two upon the larboard and two upon the starboard lay,
And the battle-thunder broke from them all.

VIII.

But anon the great San Philip, she bethought herself and went
Having that within her womb that had left her ill
content;
And the rest they came aboard us, and they fought
us hand to hand,
For a dozen times they came with their pikes and
musqueteers,
And a dozen times we shook 'em off as a dog that
shakes his ears
When he leaps from the water to the land.

IX.

And the sun went down, and the stars came out far
over the summer sea,
But never a moment ceased the fight of the one and
fifty-three.
Ship after ship, the whole night long, their high-
built galleons came,
Ship after ship, the whole night long, with her
battle-thunder and flame;
Ship after ship, the whole night long, drew back
with her dead and her shame.
For some were sunk and many were shattered, and
so could fight us no more—
God of battles, was ever a battle like this in the
world before?

x.

For he said "Fight on! fight on!"
Tho' his vessel was all but a wreck ;
And it chanced that, when half of the short summer
 night was gone,
With a grisly wound to be drest he had left the
 deck,
But a bullet struck him that was dressing it sud-
 denly dead,
And himself he was wounded again in the side and
 the head,
And he said "Fight on! fight on!"

xi.

And the night went down, and the sun smiled out
 far over the summer sea,
And the Spanish fleet with broken sides lay round
 us all in a ring ;
But they dared not touch us again, for they feared
 that we still could sting,
So they watched what the end would be.
And we had not fought them in vain,
But in perilous plight were we,
Seeing forty of our poor hundred were slain,
And half of the rest of us maimed for life
In the crash of the cannonades and the desperate
 strife ;
And the sick men down in the hold were most of
 them stark and cold,
And the pikes were all broken or bent, and the
 powder was all of it spent ;
And the masts and the rigging were lying over the
 side ;
But Sir Richard cried in his English pride,

" We have fought such a fight for a day and a night
As may never be fought again !
We have won great glory, my men !
And a day less or more
At sea or ashore,
We die—does it matter when ?
Sink me the ship, Master Gunner—sink her, split
  her in twain !
Fall into the hands of God, not into the hands of
  Spain ! "

XII.

And the gunner said " Ay, ay," but the seamen made
  reply :
" We have children, we have wives,
And the Lord hath spared our lives.
We will make the Spaniard promise, if we yield, to
  let us go ;
We shall live to fight again and to strike another
  blow."
And the lion there lay dying, and they yielded to
  the foe.

XIII.

And the stately Spanish men to their flagship bore
  him then,
Where they laid him by the mast, old Sir Richard
  caught at last,
And they praised him to his face with their courtly
  foreign grace ;
But he rose upon their decks, and he cried :
" I have fought for Queen and Faith like a valiant
  man and true ;
I have only done my duty as a man is bound to do :

With a joyful spirit I Sir Richard Grenville die ! "
And he fell upon their decks, and he died.

XIV.

And they stared at the dead that had been so valiant
    and true,
And had holden the power and glory of Spain so
    cheap
That he dared her with one little ship and his
    English few ;
Was he devil or man ? He was devil for aught they
    knew,
But they sank his body with honor down into the
    deep,
And they manned the Revenge with a swarthier
    alien crew,
And away she sailed with her loss and longed for
    her own ;
When a wind from the lands they had ruined awoke
    from sleep,
And the water began to heave and the weather to
    moan,
And or ever that evening ended a great gale blew,
And a wave like the wave that is raised by an earth-
    quake grew,
Till it smote on their hulls and their sails and their
    masts and their flags,
And the whole sea plunged and fell on the shot-shat-
    tered navy of Spain,
And the little Revenge herself went down by the
    island crags
To be lost evermore in the main.

ALFRED, LORD TENNYSON.

ENGLAND.

FROM " KING JOHN," ACT V. SC. 7.

THIS England never did, nor never shall,
Lie at the proud foot of a conqueror,

. . . . .

Come the three corners of the world in arms,
And we shall shock them. Nought shall make us
    rue,
If England to itself do rest but true.

SHAKESPEARE.

JOCK JOHNSTONE THE TINKLER.

" O, CAME ye ower by the Yoke-burn Ford,
    Or down the King's Road o' the cleuch?*
Or saw ye a knight and a lady bright,
    Wha ha'e gane the gate they baith shall rue? "

" I saw a knight and a lady bright
    Ride up the cleuch at the break of day;
The knight upon a coal-black steed,
    And the dame on one of a silver-gray.

" And the lady's palfrey flew the first,
    With many a clang of silver bell:
Swift as the raven's morning flight
    The two went scouring ower the fell.

" By this time they are man and wife,
    And standing in St. Mary's fane;
And the lady in the grass-green silk
    A maid you will never see again."

* Dell.

" But I can tell thee, saucy wight,—
  And that the runaway shall prove,—
Revenge to a Douglas is as sweet
  As maiden charms or maiden's love."

" Since thou say'st that, my Lord Douglas,
  Good faith some clinking there will be;
Beshrew my heart but and my sword,
  If I winna turn and ride with thee!"

They whipped out ower the Shepherd Cleuch,
  And doun the links o' the Corsecleuch Burn;
And aye the Douglas swore by his sword
  To win his love, or ne'er return.

" First fight your rival, Lord Douglas,
  And then brag after, if you may;
For the Earl of Ross is as brave a lord
  As ever gave good weapon sway.

" But I for ae poor siller mork,
  Or thirteen pennies and a bawbee,
Will tak in hand to fight you baith,
  Or beat the winner, whiche'er it be."

The Douglas turned him on his steed,
  And I wat a loud laughter leuch he:
" Of a' the fools I have ever met,
  Man, I ha'e never met ane like thee.

" Art thou akin to lord or knight,
  Or courtly squire or warrior leal?"
" I am a tinkler," quo' the wight,
  " But I like croun-cracking unco weel."

When they came to St. Mary's kirk,
　The chaplain shook for very fear;
And aye he kissed the cross, and said,
　" What deevil has sent that Douglas here!

" He neither values Book nor ban,
　But curses all without demur;
And cares nae mair for a holy man
　Than I do for a worthless cur."

" Come here, thou bland and brittle priest,
　And tell to me without delay
Where have you hid the lord of Ross
　And the lady that came at the break of day."

" No knight or lady, good Lord Douglas,
　Have I beheld since break of morn;
And I never saw the lord of Ross
　Since the woful day that I was born."

Lord Douglas turned him round about,
　And looked the Tinkler in the face;
Where he beheld a lurking smile,
　And a deevil of a dour grimace.

" How 's this, how 's this, thou Tinkler loun?
　Hast thou presumed to lie on me?"
" Faith that I have!" the Tinkler said,
　" And a right good turn I have done to thee;

" For the lord of Ross and thy own true-love,
　The beauteous Harriet of Thirlestane,
Rade west away, ere the break of day;
　And you'll never see the dear maid again;

" So I thought it best to bring you here,
  On a wrang scent, of my own accord;
For had you met the Johnstone clan,
  They wad ha'e made mince-meat of a lord."

At this the Douglas was so wroth
  He wist not what to say or do;
But he strak the Tinkler o'er the croun,
  Till the blood came dreeping ower his brow.

" Beshrew my heart," quo' the Tinkler lad,
  " Thou bear'st thee most ungallantlye!
If these are the manners of a lord,
  They are manners that winna gang doun wi'
    me."

" Hold up thy hand," the Douglas cried,
  " And keep thy distance, Tinkler loun!"
" That will I not," the Tinkler said,
  " Though I and my mare should both go
    doun!"

" I have armor on," cried the Lord Douglas,
  " Cuirass and helm, as you may see."
" The deil me care!" quo' the Tinkler lad;
  " I shall have a skelp at them and thee."

" You are not horsed," quo' the Lord Douglas,
  " And no remorse this weapon brooks."
" Mine 's a right good yaud," quo' the Tinkler lad,
  " And a great deal better nor she looks.

" So stand to thy weapons, thou haughty lord,
  What I have taken I needs must give;

Thou shalt never strike a tinkler again,
    For the langest day thou hast to live."

Then to it they fell, both sharp and snell,
    Till the fire from both their weapons flew;
But the very first shock that they met with,
    The Douglas his rashness 'gan to rue.

For though he had on a sark of mail,
    And a cuirass on his breast wore he,
With a good steel bonnet on his head,
    Yet the blood ran trickling to his knee.

The Douglas sat upright and firm,
    Aye as together their horses ran;
But the Tinkler laid on like the very deil,—
    Siccan strokes were never laid on by man.

"Hold up thy hand, thou Tinkler loun,"
    Cried the poor priest with whining din;
"If thou hurt the brave Lord James Douglas;
    A curse be on thee and all thy kin!"

"I care no more for Lord James Douglas
    Than Lord James Douglas cares for me;
But I want to let his proud heart know
    That a tinkler 's a man as well as he."

So they fought on, and they fought on,
    Till good Lord Douglas' breath was gone;
And the Tinkler bore him to the ground,
    With rush, with rattle, and with groan.

"O hon! O hon!" cried the proud Douglas,
　" That I this day should have lived to see!
For sure my honor I have lost,
　And a leader again I can never be!

" But tell me of thy kith and kin,
　And where was bred thy weapon hand?
For thou art the wale of tinkler louns
　That ever was born in fair Scotland."

" My name 's Jock Johnstone," quo' the wight;
　" I winna keep in my name frae thee;
And here, tak thou thy sword again,
　And better friends we two shall be."

But the Douglas swore a solemn oath,
　That was a debt he could never owe;
He would rather die at the back of the dike
　Than owe his sword to a man so low.

" But if thou wilt ride under my banner,
　And bear my livery and my name,
My right-hand warrior thou shalt be
　And I 'll knight thee on the field of fame."

" Woe worth thy wit, good Lord Douglas,
　To think I 'd change my trade for thine;
Far better and wiser would you be,
　To live a journeyman of mine,

" To mend a kettle or a casque,
　Or clout a goodwife's yettlin' pan,—
Upon my life, good Lord Douglas,
　You 'd make a noble tinkler-man!

" I would give you a drammock twice a day,
　And sunkets on a Sunday morn,
And you should be a rare adept
　In steel and copper, brass and horn!

" I 'll fight you every day you rise,
　Till you can act the hero's part;
Therefore, I pray you, think of this,
　And lay it seriously to heart."

The Douglas writhed beneath the lash,
　Answering with an inward curse,—
Like salmon wriggling on a spear,
　That makes his deadly wound the worse.

But up there came two squires renowned;
　In search of Lord Douglas they came;
And when they saw their master down,
　Their spirits mounted in a flame.

And they flew upon the Tinkler wight,
　Like perfect tigers on their prey:
But the Tinkler heaved his trusty sword,
　And made him ready for the fray.

" Come one to one, ye coward knaves,—
　Come hand to hand, and steed to steed;
I would that ye were better men,
　For this is glorious work indeed!"

Before you could have counted twelve,
　The Tinkler's wondrous chivalrye
Had both the squires upon the sward,
　And their horses galloping o'er the lea.

The Tinkler tied them neck and heel,
    And many a biting jest gave he:
" O fie, for shame! " said the Tinkler lad;
    " Siccan fighters I never did see! "

He slit one of their bridle reins,—
    O, what disgrace the conquered feels!—
And he skelpit the squires with that good tawse,
    Till the blood ran off at baith their heels.

The Douglas he was forced to laugh
    Till down his cheek the salt tear ran:
" I think the deevil be come here
    In the likeness of a tinkler man! "

Then he has to Lord Douglas gone,
    And he raised him kindly by the hand,
And set him on his gallant steed,
    And bore him away to Henderland:

" Be not cast down, my Lord Douglas,
    Nor writhe beneath a broken bane;
For the leech's art will mend the part,
    And your honor lost will spring again.

" 'T is true, Jock Johnstone is my name;
    I 'm a right good tinkler, as you see;
For I can crack a casque betimes,
    Or clout one, as my need may be.

" Jock Johnstone is my name, 't is true,—
    But noble hearts are allied to me;
For I am the lord of Annandale,
    And a knight and earl as well as thee."

Then Douglas strained the hero's hand,
  And took from it his sword again:
"Since thou art the lord of Annandale,
  Thou hast eased my heart of meikle pain.

"I might have known thy noble form
  In that disguise thou 'rt pleased to wear;
All Scotland knows thy matchless arm,
  And England by experience dear.

"We have been foes as well as friends,
  And jealous of each other's sway;
But little can I comprehend
  Thy motive for these pranks to-day."

"Sooth, my good lord, the truth to tell,
  'T was I that stole your love away,
And gave her to the lord of Ross
  An hour before the break of day;

"For the lord of Ross is my brother,
  By all the laws of chivalrye;
And I brought with me a thousand men
  To guard him to my ain countrye.

"But I thought meet to stay behind,
  And try your lordship to waylay,
Resolved to breed some noble sport,
  By leading you so far astray.

"Judging it better some lives to spare,—
  Which fancy takes me now and then,—
And settle our quarrel hand to hand,
  Than each with our ten thousand men.

"God send you soon, my Lord Douglas,
    To Border foray sound and haill!
But never strike a tinkler again,
    If he be a Johnstone of Annandale."

JAMES HOGG.

LORD ULLIN'S DAUGHTER.

A CHIEFTAIN, to the Highlands bound,
    Cries, "Boatman, do not tarry!
And I 'll give thee a silver pound,
    To row us o'er the ferry."

"Now who be ye, would cross Lochgyle,
    This dark and stormy water?"
"O, I 'm the chief of Ulva's isle,
    And this Lord Ullin's daughter.

"And fast before her father's men
    Three days we 've fled together,
For should he find us in the glen,
    My blood would stain the heather.

"His horsemen hard behind us ride;
    Should they our steps discover,
Then who will cheer my bonny bride
    When they have slain her lover?"

Out spoke the hardy Highland wight,
    "I 'll go, my chief,—I 'm ready:—
It is not for your silver bright;
    But for your winsome lady:

" And by my word! the bonny bird
    In danger shall not tarry:
So, though the waves are raging white,
    I 'll row you o'er the ferry."

By this the storm grew loud apace,
    The water-wraith was shrieking;
And in the scowl of heaven each face
    Grew dark as they were speaking.

But still as wilder grew the wind,
    And as the night grew drearer,
Adown the glen rode armèd men,
    Their trampling sounded nearer.

" O, haste thee, haste!" the lady cries,
    " Though tempests round us gather;
I 'll meet the raging of the skies,
    But not an angry father."

The boat has left a stormy land,
    A stormy sea before her,—
When, O, too strong for human hand,
    The tempest gathered o'er her.

And still they rowed amidst the roar
    Of waters fast prevailing:
Lord Ullin reached that fatal shore,
    His wrath was changed to wailing.

For sore dismayed, through storm and shade,
    His child he did discover:
One lovely hand she stretched for aid,
    And one was round her lover.

"Come back! come back!" he cried in grief,
  "Across this stormy water:
And I 'll forgive your Highland chief,
  My daughter!—O my daughter!"

'T was vain;—the loud waves lashed the shore,
  Return or aid preventing;
The waters wild went o'er his child,
  And he was left lamenting.

                              THOMAS CAMPBELL.

_____

MARMION AND DOUGLAS.

FROM "MARMION," CANTO VI.

Not far advanced was morning day,
When Marmion did his troops array
  To Surrey's camp to ride;
He had safe-conduct for his band,
Beneath the royal seal and hand,
  And Douglas gave a guide:
The ancient Earl, with stately grace,
Would Clara on her palfrey place,
And whispered in an undertone,
"Let the hawk stoop, his prey is flown."
The train from out the castle drew,
But Marmion stopped to bid adieu:—
"Though something I might plain," he said,
"Of cold respect to stranger guest,
Sent hither by your king's behest,
While in Tantallon's towers I stayed,
Part we in friendship from your land,
And, noble Earl, receive my hand."—

But Douglas round him drew his cloak,
Folded his arms and thus he spoke:—
  " My manors, halls, and bowers shall still
  Be open, at my sovereign's will,
  To each one whom he lists, howe'er
  Unmeet to be the owner's peer.
  My castles are my king's alone,
  From turret to foundation-stone,—
  The hand of Douglas is his own;
  And never shall in friendly grasp
  The hand of such as Marmion clasp."—

Burned Marmion's swarthy cheek like fire,
And shook his very frame for ire,
  And—" This to me!" he said,—
" An 't were not for thy hoary beard,
Such hand as Marmion's had not spared
  To cleave the Douglas' head!
And, first, I tell thee, haughty Peer,
He who does England's message here,
Although the meanest in her state,
May well, proud Angus, be thy mate:
And, Douglas, more I tell thee here,
  Even in thy pitch of pride,
Here in thy hold, thy vassals near,
(Nay never look upon your lord,
And lay your hands upon your sword,)
  I tell thee, thou 'rt defied!
And if thou said'st I am not peer
To any lord in Scotland here,
Lowland or Highland, far or near,
  Lord Angus, thou hast lied!"—
On the Earl's cheek the flush of rage

O'ercame the ashen hue of age:
Fierce he broke forth,—" And dar'st thou then
To beard the lion in his den,
  The Douglas in his hall?
And hop'st thou hence unscathed to go?
No, by St. Bride of Bothwell, no!
Up drawbridge, grooms,—what, Warder, ho!
  Let the portcullis fall."—
Lord Marmion turned,—well was his need!—
And dashed the rowels in his steed;
Like an arrow through the archway sprung;
The ponderous grate behind him rung:
To pass there was such scanty room,
The bars descending razed his plume.

The steed along the drawbridge flies,
Just as it trembled on the rise;
Not lighter does the swallow skim
Along the smooth lake's level brim;
And when Lord Marmion reached his band,
He halts, and turns with clenchèd hand,
And shout of loud defiance pours,
And shook his gauntlet at the towers.
" Horse! horse!" the Douglas cried, " and chase!"
But soon he reined his fury's pace:
" A royal messenger he came,
Though most unworthy of the name.

.   .   .   .   .

Saint Mary, mend my fiery mood!
Old age ne'er cools the Douglas blood,
I thought to slay him where he stood.
'T is pity of him too," he cried;

" Bold can he speak, and fairly ride:
I warrant him a warrior tried."
With this his mandate he recalls,
And slowly seeks his castle halls.

SIR WALTER SCOTT.

FITZ–JAMES AND RODERICK DHU.

FROM " THE LADY OF THE LAKE," CANTO V.

" I AM by promise tried
To match me with this man of pride:
Twice have I sought Clan-Alpine's glen
In peace; but when I come again,
I come with banner, brand, and bow,
As leader seek this mortal foe.
For lovelorn swain, in lady's bower,
Ne'er panted for the appointed hour,
As I, until before me stand
This rebel Chieftain and his band."

" Have, then, thy wish!"—He whistled shrill,
And he was answered from the hill;
Wild as the scream of the curlew,
From crag to crag the signal flew.
Instant, through copse and heath, arose
Bonnets and spears and bended bows;
On right, on left, above, below,
Sprung up at once the lurking foe;
From shingles gray their lances start,
The bracken bush sends forth the dart,
The rushes and the willow-wand
Are bristling into axe and brand,
And every tuft of broom gives life

To plaided warrior armed for strife.
That whistle garrisoned the glen
At once with full five hundred men,
As if the yawning hill to heaven
A subterranean host had given.
Watching their leader's beck and will,
All silent there they stood, and still.
Like the loose crags whose threatening mass
Lay tottering o'er the hollow pass,
As if an infant's touch could urge
Their headlong passage down the verge,
With step and weapon forward flung,
Upon the mountain-side they hung.
The Mountaineer cast glance of pride
Along Benledi's living side,
Then fixed his eye and sable brow
Full on Fitz-James: " How say'st thou now?
These are Clan-Alpine's warriors true;
And, Saxon,—I am Roderick Dhu! "

Fitz-James was brave;—though to his heart
The life-blood thrilled with sudden start,
He manned himself with dauntless air,
Returned the Chief his haughty stare,
His back against a rock he bore,
And firmly placed his foot before:—
" Come one, come all! this rock shall fly
From its firm base as soon as I."
Sir Roderick marked,—and in his eyes
Respect was mingled with surprise,
And the stern joy which warriors feel
In foemen worthy of their steel.

Short space he stood,—then waved his hand:
Down sunk the disappearing band;
Each warrior vanished where he stood,
In broom or bracken, heath or wood:
Sunk brand and spear, and bended bow,
In osiers pale and copses low:
It seemed as if their mother Earth
Had swallowed up her warlike birth.
The wind's last breath had tossed in air
Pennon and plaid and plumage fair,—
The next but swept a lone hillside,
Where heath and fern were waving wide;
The sun's last glance was glinted back,
From spear and glaive, from targe and jack,—
The next, all unreflected, shone
On bracken green, and cold gray stone.

Fitz-James looked round,—yet scarce believed
The witness that his sight received;
Such apparition well might seem
Delusion of a dreadful dream.
Sir Roderick in suspense he eyed,
And to his look the Chief replied:
" Fear naught—nay, that I need not say—
But—doubt not aught from mine array.
Thou art my guest;—I pledged my word
As far as Coilantogle ford:
Nor would I call a clansman's brand
For aid against one valiant hand,
Though on our strife lay every vale
Rent by the Saxon from the Gael.
So move we on;—I only meant
To show the reed on which you leant,

Deeming this path you might pursue
Without a pass from Roderick Dhu."
They moved;—I said Fitz-James was brave,
As ever knight that belted glaive;
Yet dare not say that now his blood
Kept on its wont and tempered flood,
As, following Roderick's stride, he drew
That seeming lonesome pathway through,
Which yet, by fearful proof, was rife
With lances, that, to take his life,
Waited but signal from a guide,
So late dishonored and defied.
Ever, by stealth, his eye sought round
The vanished guardians of the ground,
And still, from copse and heather deep,
Fancy saw spear and broadsword peep,
And in the plover's shrilly strain
The signal whistle heard again.
Nor breathed he free till far behind
The pass was left; for then they wind
Along a wide and level green,
Where neither tree nor tuft was seen,
Nor rush nor bush of broom was near,
To hide a bonnet or a spear.

The Chief in silence strode before,
And reached that torrent's sounding shore,
Which, daughter of three mighty lakes,
From Vennachar in silver breaks,
Sweeps through the plain, and ceaseless mines
On Bochastle the mouldering lines,
Where Rome, the Empress of the world,
Of yore her eagle wings unfurled.

And here his course the Chieftain stayed,
Threw down his target and his plaid,
And to the Lowland warrior said:
" Bold Saxon! to his promise just,
Vich-Alpine has discharged his trust.
This murderous Chief, this ruthless man,
This head of a rebellious clan,
Hath led thee safe through watch and ward,
Far past Clan-Alpine's outmost guard.
Now, man to man, and steel to steel,
A Chieftain's vengeance thou shalt feel.
See, here, all vantageless I stand,
Armed, like thyself, with single brand;
For this is Coilantogle ford,
And thou must keep thee with thy sword."

The Saxon paused: " I ne'er delayed,
When foeman bade me draw my blade;
Nay more, brave Chief, I vowed thy death:
Yet sure thy fair and generous faith,
And my deep debt for life preserved,
A better meed have well deserved:
Can naught but blood our feud atone?
Are there no means?" " No, Stranger, none;
And hear,—to fire thy flagging zeal,—
The Saxon cause rests on thy steel;
For thus spoke Fate, by prophet bred
Between the living and the dead:
' Who spills the foremost foeman's life,
His party conquers in the strife.' "
" Then, by my word," the Saxon said,
" The riddle is already read.
Seek yonder brake beneath the cliff,—

There lies Red Murdock, stark and stiff.
Thus Fate hath solved her prophecy,
Then yield to Fate, and not to me.
To James, at Stirling, let us go,
When, if thou wilt be still his foe,
Or if the King shall not agree
To grant thee grace and favor free,
I plight mine honor, oath, and word,
That, to thy native strengths restored,
With each advantage shalt thou stand,
That aids thee now to guard thy land."

Dark lightning flashed from Roderick's eye.
" Soars thy presumption, then, so high,
Because a wretched kern ye slew,
Homage to name to Roderick Dhu?
He yields not, he, to man nor fate!
Thou add'st but fuel to my hate:—
My clansman's blood demands revenge.
Not yet prepared?—By Heaven, I change
My thought, and hold thy valor light
As that of some vain carpet knight,
Who ill deserved my courteous care,
And whose best boast is but to wear
A braid of his fair lady's hair."
" I thank thee, Roderick, for the word!
It nerves my heart, it steels my sword;
For I have sworn this braid to stain
In the best blood that warms thy vein.
Now, truce, farewell! and ruth, begone!—
Yet think not that by thee alone,
Proud Chief! can courtesy be shown;
Though not from copse, or heath, or cairn,

Start at my whistle clansmen stern,
Of this small horn one feeble blast
Would fearful odds against thee cast.
But fear not—doubt not—which thou wilt—
We try this quarrel hilt to hilt."
Then each at once his falchion drew,
Each on the ground his scabbard threw,
Each looked to sun and stream and plain,
As what they ne'er might see again;
Then, foot and point and eye opposed,
In dubious strife they darkly closed.

Ill fared it then with Roderick Dhu,
That on the field his targe he threw,
Whose brazen studs and tough bull-hide
Had death so often dashed aside;
For, trained abroad his arms to wield,
Fitz-James's blade was sword and shield.
He practised every pass and ward,
To thrust, to strike, to feint, to guard;
While less expert, though stronger far,
The Gael maintained unequal war.
Three times in closing strife they stood,
And thrice the Saxon blade drank blood:
No stinted draught, no scanty tide,
The gushing floods the tartans dyed.
Fierce Roderick felt the fatal drain,
And showered his blows like wintry rain;
And, as firm rock or castle-roof
Against the winter shower is proof,
The foe, invulnerable still,
Foiled his wild rage by steady skill;
Till, at advantage ta'en, his brand

Forced Roderick's weapon from his hand,
And, backwards borne upon the lea,
Brought the proud Chieftain to his knee.
" Now yield thee, or, by Him who made
The world, thy heart's blood dyes my blade! "
" Thy threats, thy mercy, I defy!
Let recreant yield, who fears to die."
Like adder darting from his coil,
Like wolf that dashes through the toil,
Like mountain-cat who guards her young,
Full at Fitz-James's throat he sprung;
Received, but recked not of a wound,
And locked his arms his foeman round.
Now, gallant Saxon, hold thine own!
No maiden's hand is round thee thrown!
That desperate grasp thy frame might feel
Through bars of brass and triple steel!
They tug, they strain! down, down they go,
The Gael above, Fitz-James below.
The chieftain's gripe his throat compressed,
His knee was planted in his breast;
His clotted locks he backward threw,
Across his brow his hand he drew,
From blood and mist to clear his sight,
Then gleamed aloft his dagger bright!
But hate and fury ill supplied
The stream of life's exhausted tide,
And all too late the advantage came,
To turn the odds of deadly game;
For, while the dagger gleamed on high,
Reeled soul and sense, reeled brain and eye.
Down came the blow! but in the heath
The erring blade found bloodless sheath.

The struggling foe may now unclasp
The fainting Chief's relaxing grasp;
Unwounded from the dreadful close,
But breathless all, Fitz-James arose.

He faltered thanks to Heaven for life,
Redeemed, unhoped, from desperate strife;
Next on his foe his look he cast,
Whose every gasp appeared his last;
In Roderick's gore he dipped the braid,—
" Poor Blanche! thy wrongs are dearly paid.
Yet with thy foe must die, or live,
The praise that faith and valor give."
With that he blew a bugle note,
Undid the collar from his throat,
Unbonneted, and by the wave
Sat down his brow and hands to lave.
Then faint afar are heard the feet
Of rushing steeds in gallop fleet;
The sounds increase, and now are seen
Four mounted squires in Lincoln green;
Two who bear lance, and two who lead,
By loosened rein, a saddled steed;
Each onward held his headlong course,
And by Fitz-James reined up his horse,—
With wonder viewed the bloody spot,—
" Exclaim not, gallants! question not,—
You, Herbert and Luffness, alight,
And bind the wounds of yonder knight;
Let the gray palfrey bear his weight,
We destined for a fairer freight,
And bring him on to Stirling straight;
I will before at better speed,

To seek fresh horse and fitting weed.
The sun rides high;—I must be boune
To see the archer-game at noon;
But lightly Bayard clears the lea.
De Vaux and Herries, follow me."

SIR WALTER SCOTT.

FITZ–JAMES AND ELLEN.

FROM "THE LADY OF THE LAKE," CANTO VI.

A FOOTSTEP struck her ear,
And Snowdoun's graceful Knight was near.
She turned the hastier, lest again
The prisoner should renew his strain.
"O welcome, brave Fitz-James!" she said;
"How may an almost orphan maid
Pay the deep debt"—"O, say not so!
To me no gratitude you owe.
Not mine, alas! the boon to give,
And bid thy noble father live;
I can but be thy guide, sweet maid,
With Scotland's King thy suit to aid.
No tyrant he, though ire and pride
May lead his better mood aside.
Come, Ellen, come; 't is more than time,
He holds his court at morning prime."
With beating heart and bosom wrung,
As to a brother's arm she clung.
Gently he dried the falling tear,
And gently whispered hope and cheer;
Her faltering steps half led, half stayed,
Through gallery fair and high arcade,

Till, at his touch, its wings of pride
A portal arch unfolded wide.

Within 't was brilliant all and light,
A thronging scene of figures bright;
It glowed on Ellen's dazzled sight,
As when the setting sun has given
Ten thousand hues to summer even,
And from their tissue fancy frames
Aerial knights and fairy dames.
Still by Fitz-James her footing stayed;
A few faint steps she forward made,
Then slow her drooping head she raised,
And fearful round the presence gazed:
For him she sought who owned this state,
The dreaded prince whose will was fate!
She gazed on many a princely port
Might well have ruled a royal court;
On many a splendid garb she gazed,—
Then turned bewildered and amazed,
For all stood bare; and in the room
Fitz-James alone wore cap and plume.
To him each lady's look was lent,
On him each courtier's eye was bent,
Midst furs and silks and jewels sheen
He stood, in simple Lincoln green,
The centre of the glittering ring,—
And Snowdoun's Knight is Scotland's King!

As wreath of snow, on mountain breast,
Slides from the rock that gave it rest,
Poor Ellen glided from her stay,
And at the Monarch's feet she lay;

No word her choking voice commands:
She showed the ring, she clasped her hands.
O, not a moment could he brook,
The generous prince, that suppliant look!
Gently he raised her, and the while
Checked with a glance the circle's smile;
Graceful, but grave, her brow he kissed,
And bade her terrors be dismissed:—
"Yes, fair; the wandering poor Fitz-James
The fealty of Scotland claims.
To him thy woes, thy wishes bring;
He will redeem his signet-ring.
Ask naught for Douglas; yester even
His prince and he have much forgiven:
Wrong hath he had from slanderous tongue,
I, from his rebel kinsmen, wrong.
We would not to the vulgar crowd
Yield what they craved with clamor loud;
Calmly we heard and judged his cause,
Our council aided and our laws.
I stanched thy father's death-feud stern,
With stout De Vaux and gray Glencairn;
And Bothwell's Lord henceforth we own
The friend and bulwark of our Throne.
But, lovely infidel, how now?
What clouds thy misbelieving brow?
Lord James of Douglas, lend thine aid;
Thou must confirm this doubting maid."

Then forth the noble Douglas sprung,
And on his neck his daughter hung.
The Monarch drank, that happy hour,
The sweetest, holiest draught of Power,—

When it can say, the godlike voice,
Arise, sad Virtue, and rejoice!
Yet would not James the general eye
On nature's raptures long should pry:
He stepped between—" Nay, Douglas, nay,
Steal not my proselyte away!
The riddle 't is my right to read,
That brought this happy chance to speed.
Yes, Ellen, when disguised I stray
In life's more low but happier way,
'T is under name which veils my power,
Nor falsely veils,—for Stirling's tower
Of yore the name of Snowdoun claims,
And Normans call me James Fitz-James.
Thus watch I o'er insulted laws,
Thus learn to right the injured cause."
Then, in a tone apart and low,
" Ah, little trait'ress! none must know
What idle dream, what lighter thought,
What vanity full dearly bought,
Joined to thine eye's dark witchcraft, drew
My spell-bound steps to Benvenue,
In dangerous hour, and all but gave
Thy Monarch's life to mountain glaive!"
Aloud he spoke,—" Thou still dost hold
That little talisman of gold,
Pledge of my faith, Fitz-James's ring;
What seeks fair Ellen of the King?"

Full well the conscious maiden guessed,
He probed the weakness of her breast;
But with that consciousness there came
A lightening of her fears for Græme,

And more she deemed the monarch's ire
Kindled 'gainst him, who, for her sire,
Rebellious broadsword boldly drew;·
And, to her generous feeling true,
She craved the grace of Roderick Dhu.
" Forbear thy suit; the King of kings
Alone can stay life's parting wings.
I know his heart, I know his hand,
Have shared his cheer, and proved his brand.
My fairest earldom would I give
To bid Clan-Alpine's Chieftain live!—
Hast thou no other boon to crave?
No other captive friend to save? "
Blushing, she turned her from the King,
And to the Douglas gave the ring,
As if she wished her sire to speak
The suit that stained her glowing cheek.
" Nay, then, my pledge has lost its force,
And stubborn justice holds her course.
Malcolm, come forth! "—And, at the word,
Down knelt the Græme to Scotland's Lord.
" For thee, rash youth, no suppliant sues,
From thee may Vengeance claim her dues,
Who, nurtured underneath our smile,
Hast paid our care by treacherous wile,
And sought, amid thy faithful clan,
A refuge for an outlawed man,
Dishonoring thus thy loyal name,—
Fetters and warder for the Græme! "
His chain of gold the King unstrung,
The links o'er Malcolm's neck he flung,
Then gently drew the glittering band,
And laid the clasp on Ellen's hand.

SIR WALTER SCOTT.

MUCKLE–MOU'D MEG.

"Oh, wha hae ye brought us hame now, my
  brave lord,
    Strappit flaught ower his braid saddle-
    bow?
Some bauld Border reiver to feast at our board
    An' herry our pantry, I trow.
He 's buirdly an' stalwart in lith an' in limb:
  Gin ye were his master in war
The field was a saft eneugh litter for him—
    Ye needna hae brought him sae far;—
Then saddle an' munt again, harness an' dunt
  again,
An' when ye gae hunt again, strike higher
    game."—

"Hoot, whist ye, my dame, for he comes o' gude
  kin,
    An' boasts o' a lang pedigree;
This night he maun share o' our gude cheer
  within,
    At morning's gray dawn he maun dee.
He 's gallant Wat Scott, heir o' proud Harden
  Ha',
    Wha ettled our lands clear to sweep;
But now he is snug in auld Elibank's paw,
    An' shall swing frae our donjon-keep.
Though saddle an' munt again, harness an' dunt
  again,
I 'll ne'er when I hunt again strike higher
    game."—

"Is this young Wat Scott? an' wad ye rax his
  craig,
  When our daughter is fey for a man?
Gae, gaur the loun marry our muckle-mou'd Meg,
  Or we 'll ne'er get the jaud aff our
  han'!"—
"'Od, hear our gudewife! she wad fain save your
  life:—
  Wat Scott, will ye marry or hang?"
But Meg's muckle mou set young Wat's heart
  agrue,
  Wha swore to the woodie he'd gang.
Ne'er saddle nor munt again, harness nor dunt
  again,
Wat ne'er shall hunt again, ne'er see his hame.

Syne muckle-mou'd Meg pressed in close to his
  side,
  An' blinkit fu' sleely and kind;
But aye as Wat glowered on his braw proffered
  bride,
  He shook like a leaf in the wind.
"A bride or a gallows; a rope or a wife!"
  The morning dawned sunny and clear:
Wat boldly strode forward to part wi' his life,
  Till he saw Meggy shedding a tear;
Then saddle an' munt again, harness an' dunt
  again,
Fain wad Wat hunt again, fain wad he hame.

Meg's tear touched his bosom—the gibbet
  frowned high—
  An' slowly Wat strode to his doom;

He gae a glance round wi' a tear in his eye,—
    Meg shone like a star through the gloom.
She rushed to his arms; they were wed on the
        spot,
    An' lo'ed ither muckle and lang.
Nae bauld border laird had a wife like Wat Scott:
    'T was better to marry than hang.
So saddle an' munt again, harness an' dunt again,
Elibank hunt again, Wat 's snug at hame.

                JAMES BALLANTINE.

THE HEART OF THE BRUCE.

It was upon an April morn,
    While yet the frost lay hoar,
We heard Lord James's bugle-horn
    Sound by the rocky shore.

Then down we went, a hundred knights,
    All in our dark array,
And flung our armor in the ships
    That rode within the bay.

We spoke not as the shore grew less,
    But gazed in silence back,
Where the long billows swept away
    The foam behind our track.

And aye the purple hues decayed
    Upon the fading hill,
And but one heart in all that ship
    Was tranquil, cold, and still.

The good Lord Douglas paced the deck,
And O, his face was wan!
Unlike the flush it used to wear
When in the battle-van.—

" Come hither, come hither, my trusty knight,
Sir Simon of the Lee;
There is a freit lies near my soul
I fain would tell to thee.

" Thou know'st the words King Robert spoke
Upon his dying day:
How he bade take his noble heart
And carry it far away;

" And lay it in the holy soil
Where once the Saviour trod,
Since he might not bear the blessèd Cross,
Nor strike one blow for God.

" Last night as in my bed I lay,
I dreamed a dreary dream:—
Methought I saw a Pilgrim stand
In the moonlight's quivering beam.

" His robe was of the azure dye,
Snow-white his scattered hairs,
And even such a cross he bore
As good Saint Andrew bears.

" ' Why go ye forth, Lord James,' he said,
' With spear and belted brand?
Why do you take its dearest pledge
From this our Scottish land?

" ' The sultry breeze of Galilee
 Creeps through its groves of palm,
The olives on the Holy Mount
 Stand glittering in the calm.

" ' But 't is not there that Scotland's heart
 Shall rest, by God's decree,
Till the great angel calls the dead
 To rise from earth and sea!

" ' Lord James of Douglas, mark my rede!
 That heart shall pass once more
In fiery fight against the foe,
 As it was wont of yore.

" ' And it shall pass beneath the Cross,
 And save King Robert's vow;
But other hands shall bear it back,
 Not, James of Douglas, thou!'

" Now, by thy knightly faith, I pray,
 Sir Simon of the Lee,—
For truer friend had never man
 Than thou hast been to me,—

" If ne'er upon the Holy Land
 'T is mine in life to tread,
Bear thou to Scotland's kindly earth
 The relics of her dead."

The tear was in Sir Simon's eye
 As he wrung the warrior's hand,—
" Betide me weal, betide me woe,
 I 'll hold by thy command.

" But if in battle-front, Lord James,
   'T is ours once more to ride,`
Nor force of man, nor craft of fiend,
   Shall cleave me from thy side!"

And aye we sailed and aye we sailed
   Across the weary sea,
Until one morn the coast of Spain
   Rose grimly on our lee.

And as we rounded to the port,
   Beneath the watch-tower's wall,
We heard the clash of the atabals,
   And the trumpet's wavering call.

" Why sounds yon Eastern music here
   So wantonly and long,
And whose the crowd of armèd men
   That round yon standard throng? "

" The Moors have come from Africa
   To spoil and waste and slay,
And King Alonzo of Castile
   Must fight with them to-day."

" Now shame it were," cried good Lord James,
   " Shall never be said of me
That I and mine have turned aside
   From the Cross in jeopardie!

" Have down, have down, my merry men all,—
   Have down unto the plain;
We 'll let the Scottish lion loose
   Within the fields of Spain!"

" Now welcome to me, noble lord,
    Thou and thy stalwart power;
Dear is the sight of a Christian knight,
    Who comes in such an hour!

" Is it for bond or faith you come,
    Or yet for golden fee?
Or bring ye France's lilies here,
    Or the flower of Burgundie? "

" God greet thee well, thou valiant king,
    Thee and thy belted peers,—
Sir James of Douglas am I called,
    And these are Scottish spears.

" We do not fight for bond or plight,
    Nor yet for golden fee;
But for the sake of our Blessèd Lord,
    Who died upon the tree.

" We bring our great King Robert's heart
    Across the weltering wave,
To lay it in the holy soil
    Hard by the Saviour's grave.

" True pilgrims we, by land or sea,
    Where danger bars the way;
And therefore are we here, Lord King,
    To ride with thee this day! "

The King has bent his stately head,
    And the tears were in his eyne,—
" God's blessing on thee, noble knight,
    For this brave thought of thine!

" I know thy name full well, Lord James;
    And honored may I be,
That those who fought beside the Bruce
    Should fight this day for me!

" Take thou the leading of the van,
    And charge the Moors amain;
There is not such a lance as thine
    In all the host of Spain!"

The Douglas turnèd towards us then,
    O, but his glance was high!—
" There is not one of all my men
    But is as bold as I.

" There is not one of all my knights
    But bears as true a spear,—
Then onward, Scottish gentlemen,
    And think King Robert 's here!"

The trumpets blew, the cross-bolts flew,
    The arrows flashed like flame,
As spur in side and spur in rest,
    Against the foe we came.

And many a bearded Saracen
    Went down, both horse and man;
For through their ranks we rode like corn,
    So furiously we ran!

But in behind our path they closed,
    Though fain to let us through,

For they were forty thousand men,
　And we were wòndrous few.

We might not see a lance's length,
　So dense was their array,
But the long fell sweep of the Scottish blade
　Still held them hard at bay.

"Make in! make in!" Lord Douglas cried—
　" Make in, my brethren dear!
Sir William of St. Clair is down;
　We may not leave him here!"

But thicker, thicker grew the swarm,
　And sharper shot the rain,
And the horses reared amid the press,
　But they would not charge again.

" Now Jesu help thee," said Lord James,
　" Thou kind and true St. Clair!
An' if I may not bring thee off,
　I 'll die beside thee there!"

Then in his stirrups up he stood,
　So lion-like and bold,
And held the precious heart aloft,
　All in its case of gold.

He flung it from him, far ahead,
　And never spake he more,
But—" Pass thou first, thou dauntless heart,
　As thou were wont of yore!"

The roar of fire rose fiercer yet,
   And heavier still the stour,
Till the spears of Spain came shivering in,
   And swept away the Moor.

"Now praised be God, the day is won!
   They fly, o'er flood and fell,—
Why dost thou draw the rein so hard,
   Good knight, that fought so well?"

"O, ride ye on, Lord King!" he said,
   "And leave the dead to me,
For I must keep the dreariest watch
   That ever I shall dree!

"There lies, above his master's heart,
   The Douglas, stark and grim;
And woe is me I should be here,
   Not side by side with him!

"The world grows cold, my arm is old,
   And thin my lyart hair,
And all that I loved best on earth
   Is stretched before me there.

"O Bothwell banks, that bloom so bright
   Beneath the sun of May!
The heaviest cloud that ever blew
   Is bound for you this day.

"And Scotland! thou mayst veil thy head
   In sorrow and in pain,

The sorest stroke upon thy brow
  Hath fallen this day in Spain!

" We 'll bear them back unto our ship,
  We 'll bear them o'er the sea,
And lay them in the hallowed earth
  Within our own countrie.

" And be thou strong of heart, Lord King,
  For this I tell thee sure,
The sod that drank the Douglas' blood
  Shall never bear the Moor!"

The King he lighted from his horse,
  He flung his brand away,
And took the Douglas by the hand,
  So stately as he lay.

" God give thee rest, thou valiant soul!
  That fought so well for Spain;
I 'd rather half my land were gone,
  So thou wert here again!"

We bore the good Lord James away,
  And the priceless heart we bore,
And heavily we steered our ship
  Towards the Scottish shore.

No welcome greeted our return,
  Nor clang of martial tread,
But all were dumb and hushed as death
  Before the mighty dead.

We laid our chief in Douglas Kirk,
  The heart in fair Melrose;
And woful men were we that day,—
  God grant their souls repose!

WILLIAM EDMUNDSTOUNE AYTOUN.

BARCLAY OF URY.

Up the streets of Aberdeen,
By the kirk and college green,
  Rode the laird of Ury;
Close behind him, close beside,
Foul of mouth and evil-eyed,
  Pressed the mob in fury.

Flouted him the drunken churl,
Jeered at him the serving-girl,
  Prompt to please her master;
And the begging carlin, late
Fed and clothed at Ury's gate,
  Cursed him as he passed her.

Yet with calm and stately mien
Up the streets of Aberdeen
  Came he slowly riding;
And to all he saw and heard
Answering not with bitter word,
  Turning not for chiding.

Came a troop with broadswords swinging,
Bits and bridles sharply ringing,
  Loose and free and froward:

Quoth the foremost, " Ride him down!
Push him! prick him! through the town
　Drive the Quaker coward!"

But from out the thickening crowd
Cried a sudden voice and loud:
　" Barclay! Ho! a Barclay!"
And the old man at his side
Saw a comrade, battle-tried,
　Scarred and sunburned darkly;

Who, with ready weapon bare,
Fronting to the troopers there,
　Cried aloud: " God save us!
Call ye coward him who stood
Ankle-deep in Lutzen's blood,
　With the brave Gustavus?"

" Nay, I do not need thy sword,
Comrade mine," said Ury's lord;
　" Put it up, I pray thee.
Passive to his holy will,
Trust I in my Master still,
　Even though he slay me.

" Pledges of thy love and faith,
Proved on many a field of death,
　Not by me are needed."
Marvelled much that henchman bold,
That his laird, so stout of old,
　Now so meekly pleaded.

" Woe 's the day," he sadly said,
With a slowly shaking head,
　And a look of pity;

" Ury's honest lord reviled,
Mock of knave and sport of child,
    In his own good city!

" Speak the word, and, master mine,
As we charged on Tilly's line,
    And his Walloon lancers,
Smiting through their midst, we 'll teach
Civil look and decent speech
    To these boyish prancers!"

" Marvel not, mine ancient friend,—
Like beginning, like the end!"
    Quoth the laird of Ury;
" Is the sinful servant more
Than his gracious Lord who bore
    Bonds and stripes in Jewry?

" Give me joy that in his name
I can bear with patient frame,
    All these vain ones offer;
While for them he suffered long,
Shall I answer wrong with wrong,
    Scoffing with the scoffer?

" Happier I, with loss of all,—
Hunted, outlawed, held in thrall,
    With few friends to greet me,—
Than when reeve and squire were seen
Riding out from Aberdeen
    With bared heads to meet me;

" When each goodwife, o'er and o'er,
Blessed me as I passed her door;
    And the snooded daughter,

Through her casement glancing down,
Smiled on him who bore renown
  From red fields of slaughter.

" Hard to feel the stranger's scoff,
Hard the old friends' falling off,
  Hard to learn forgiving;
But the Lord his own rewards,
And his love with theirs accords
  Warm and fresh and living.

" Through this dark and stormy night
Faith beholds a feeble light
  Up the blackness streaking;
Knowing God's own time is best,
In a patient hope I rest
  For the full day-breaking! "

So the laird of Ury said,
Turning slow his horse's head
  Towards the Tolbooth prison,
Where, through iron gates, he heard
Poor disciples of the Word
  Preach of Christ arisen!

Not in vain, confessor old,
Unto us the tale is told
  Of thy day of trial!
Every age on him who strays
From its broad and beaten ways
  Pours its seven-fold vial.

Happy he whose inward ear
Angel comfortings can hear,
  O'er the rabble's laughter;

And, while hatred's fagots burn,
Glimpses through the smoke discern,
Of the good hereafter.

Knowing this,—that never yet
Share of truth was vainly set
In the world's wide fallow;
After hands shall sow the seed,
After hands from hill and mead
Reap the harvests yellow.

Thus, with somewhat of the seer,
Must the moral pioneer
From the future borrow,—
Clothe the waste with dreams of grain,
And, on midnight's sky of rain,
Paint the golden morrow!

JOHN GREENLEAF WHITTIER.

THE FIGHT OF THE "ARMSTRONG" PRIVATEER.

TELL the story to your sons
Of the gallant days of yore,
When the brig of seven guns
Fought the fleet of seven score,
From the set of sun till morn, through the long
September night—
Ninety men against two thousand, and the ninety
won the fight
In the harbor of Fayal the Azore.

Three lofty British ships came a-sailing to Fayal:
One was a line-of-battle ship, and two were frigates
tall;

Nelson's valiant men of war, brave as Britons ever
    are,
Manned the guns they served so well at Aboukir
    and Trafalgar.
Lord Dundonald and his fleet at Jamaica far away
Waited eager for their coming, fretted sore at their
    delay.
There was loot for British valor on the Mississippi
    coast
In the beauty and the booty that the Creole cities
    boast ;
There were rebel knaves to swing, there were pris-
    oners to bring
Home in fetters to old England for the glory of the
    King !

At the setting of the sun and the ebbing of the
    tide
Came the great ships one by one, with their portals
    opened wide,
And their cannon frowning down on the castle and
    the town
And the privateer that lay close inside ;
Came the eighteen-gun Carnation, and the Rota,
    forty-four,
And the triple-decked Plantagenet an admiral's
    pennon bore ;
And the privateer grew smaller as their topmasts
    towered taller,
And she bent her springs and anchored by the
    castle on the shore.

Spake the noble Portuguese to the stranger : " Have
    no fear ;
They are neutral waters these, and your ship is
    sacred here
As if fifty stout armadas stood to shelter you from
    harm,
For the honor of the Briton will defend you from
    his arm."
But the privateersman said, " Well we know the
    Englishmen,
And their faith is written red in the Dartmoor
    slaughter pen.
Come what fortune God may send, we will fight
    them to the end,
"And the mercy of the sharks may spare us then."

" Seize the pirate where she lies ! " cried the Eng-
    lish admiral :
"If the Portuguese protect her, all the worse for
    Portugal ! "
And four launches at his bidding leaped impatient
    for the fray,
Speeding shoreward where the Armstrong, grim and
    dark and ready, lay.
Twice she hailed and gave them warning ; but the
    feeble menace scorning,
On they came in splendid silence, till a cable's
    length away—
Then the Yankee pivot spoke ; Pico's thousand
    echoes woke ;
And four baffled, beaten launches drifted helpless
    on the bay.

Then the wrath of Lloyd arose till the lion roared
    again,
And he called out all his launches and he called five
    hundred men ;
And he gave the word " No quarter ! " and he sent
    them forth to smite.
Heaven help the foe before him when the Briton
    comes in might !
Heaven helped the little Armstrong in her hour of
    bitter need ;
God Almighty nerved the heart and guided well the
    arm of Reid.

Launches to port and starboard, launches forward
    and aft,
Fourteen launches together striking the little craft.
They hacked at the boarding-nettings, they swarmed
    above the rail ;
But the Long Tom roared from his pivot and the
    grape-shot fell like hail :
Pike and pistol and cutlass, and hearts that knew
    not fear,
Bulwarks of brawn and mettle, guarded the priva-
    teer.
And ever where fight was fiercest, the form of Reid
    was seen ;
Ever where foes drew nearest, his quick sword fell
    between.
    Once in the deadly strife
    The boarders' leader pressed
    Forward of all the rest
    Challenging life for life ;
    But ere their blades had crossed,

A dying sailor tossed
His pistol to Reid, and cried,
" Now riddle the lubber's hide! "
But the privateersman laughed, and flung the
weapon aside,
And he drove his blade to the hilt, and the foeman
gasped and died.
Then the boarders took to their launches laden with
hurt and dead,
But little with glory burdened, and out of the
battle fled.

Now the tide was at flood again, and the night was
almost done,
When the sloop of-war came up with her odds of
two to one,
And she opened fire ; but the Armstrong answered
her, gun for gun,
And the gay Carnation wilted in half an hour of sun.

Then the Armstrong, looking seaward, saw the
mighty seventy-four,
With her triple tier of cannon, drawing slowly to
the shore.
And the dauntless captain said : " Take our wounded
and our dead,
Bear them tenderly to land, for the Armstrong's
days are o'er ;
But no foe shall tread her deck, and no flag above
it wave—
To the ship that saved our honor we will give a
shipman's grave."

So they did as he commanded, and they bore their
 mates to land
With the figurehead of Armstrong and the good
 sword in his hand.
Then they turned the Long Tom downward, and
 they pierced her oaken side,
And they cheered her, and they blessed her, and
 they sunk her in the tide.

  Tell the story to your sons,
   When the haughty stranger boasts
  Of his mighty ships and guns
   And the muster of his hosts,
How the word of God was witnessed in the gallant
 days of yore
When the twenty fled from one ere the rising of
 the sun,
  In the harbor of Fayal the Azore !

       JAMES JEFFREY ROCHE.

DRIFTED OUT TO SEA.

Two little ones, grown tired of play,
Roamed by the sea, one summer day,
Watching the great waves come and go,
Prattling, as children will, you know,
Of dolls and marbles, kites and strings ;
Sometimes hinting at graver things.

At last they spied within their reach
An old boat cast upon the beach ;
Helter-skelter, with merry din,
Over its sides they scrambled in,—

Ben, with his tangled, nut-brown hair,
Bess, with her sweet face flushed and fair.

Rolling in from the briny deep,
Nearer, nearer, the great waves creep,
Higher, higher, upon the sands,
Reaching out with their giant hands,
Grasping the boat in boisterous glee,
Tossing it up and out to sea.

The sun went down, 'mid clouds of gold;
Night came, with footsteps damp and cold;
Day dawned; the hours crept slowly by;
And now across the sunny sky
A black cloud stretches far away,
And shuts the golden gates of day.

A storm comes on, with flash and roar,
While all the sky is shrouded o'er;
The great waves, rolling from the west,
Bring night and darkness on their breast.
Still floats the boat though driving storm,
Protected by God's powerful arm.

The home-bound vessel, " Sea-bird," lies
In ready trim, 'twixt sea and skies:
Her captain paces, restless now,
A troubled look upon his brow,
While all his nerves with terror thrill,—
The shadow of some coming ill.

The mate comes up to where he stands,
And grasps his arm with eager hands.
" A boat has just swept past," says he,
" Bearing two children out to sea;

'T is dangerous now to put about,
Yet they cannot be saved without."

" Nought but their safety will suffice!
They must be saved ! " the captain cries.
" By every thought that 's just and right,
By lips I hoped to kiss to-night,
I 'll peril vessel, life, and men,
And God will not forsake us then."

With anxious faces, one and all,
Each man responded to the call;
And when at last, through driving storm,
They lifted up each little form,
The captain started, with a groan:
" My God is good, they are my own ! "

ROSA HARTWICK THORPE.

INDEX: AUTHORS AND TITLES.

INDEX OF AUTHORS AND TITLES.

For occupation, nativity, etc., of Authors and the American publishers of American poetical works, see General Index of Authors, Volume X.

ALDRICH, THOMAS BAILEY.   PAGE.
Guilielmus Rex 53
Tennyson 83

ARNOLD, MATTHEW.
Memorial Verses 72

AYTOUN, WILLIAM EDMONSTOUNE.
Broken Pitcher, The 325
Heart of the Bruce, The 420

BALLANTINE, JAMES.
Muckle-Mou'd Meg 418

BARHAM, RICHARD HARRIS (*Thomas Ingoldsby, Esq.*)
City Bells (*Lay of St. Aloy's*) 147

BARNES, WILLIAM.
Castle Ruins, The 213

BENTON, MYRON B.
Mowers, The 249

BOKER, GEORGE HENRY.
Prince Adeb 308

BONER, JOHN HENRY.
Poe's Cottage at Fordham 94

BOWEN, SIR CHARLES.
Fall of Troy, The (*Latin of Virgil*) 261

BROOKS, CHARLES TIMOTHY.
Nobleman and the Pensioner, The (*German of Pfeffel*). 303

BROWNE, FRANCES.
" O, the pleasant days of old " 206

443

BROWNING, ELIZABETH BARRETT.   PAGE.
George Sand 40
Portrait of Wordsworth, On a 69
That England (*Aurora Leigh*) 200
View across the Roman Campagna, A 187

BROWNING, ROBERT.
Glove, The 332
Hervé Riel 341
House 108
How they brought the Good News 349
Lost Leader, The 70
Memorabilia 58

BRYANT, WILLIAM CULLEN.
Hurricane, The 151

BURNS, ROBERT.
Bard's Epitaph, A 113

BYRON, GEORGE NOEL GORDON, LORD.
Coliseum, The (*Childe Harold*) 178
Napoleon (*Childe Harold*) 9
Orient, The (*The Bride of Abydos*)............... 164
Pantheon, The (*Childe Harold*) 181
Rhine, The (*Childe Harold*) 169
Saint Peter's at Rome (*Childe Harold*) 186
Thomas Moore, To 57

CAMPBELL, THOMAS.
Lord Ullin's Daughter 399
Napoleon and the British Sailor 347

CHAUCER, GEOFFREY.
Canterbury Pilgrims, The (*The Canterbury Tales*).. 363

CLEVELAND, JOHN.
Memory of Ben Jonson, To the 46

CLOUGH, ARTHUR HUGH.
Gondola, The 191

COLERIDGE, HARTLEY.
Shakespeare 52

CORNWELL, HENRY SYLVESTER.
Sunset City, The 158

COSTELLO, LOUISE STUART.
Mary Stuart, To (*French of De Ronsard*).......... 4

DAVIDSON, JOHN.
London 230

DAVIES, SIR JOHN.   PAGE.
Spring, To the (*Hymnes of Astræa*)...   3

DAY, THOMAS FLEMING.
Coasters, The 153

DOBSON, [HENRY] AUSTIN.
Longfellow 107

DOWDEN, EDWARD.
Leonardo's " Monna Lisa " 152

DRYDEN, JOHN.
Under the Portrait of John Milton 54

DUNBAR, PAUL LAWRENCE.
Harriet Beecher Stowe 105

ELLIOTT, EBENEZER.
Burns 63

FAIRFAX, EDWARD.
Erminia and the Wounded Tancred (*Italian of
Tasso*) 319

FERGUSON, SIR SAMUEL.
Forging of the Anchor, The 234

FIELD, MICHAEL.
Burial of Robert Browning, The 89

GILDER, RICHARD WATSON.
Life-Mask of Lincoln, On the (*Five Books of Song*). 29

GOLDSMITH, OLIVER.
Deserted Village, The 214
England (*The Traveller*) 199

GOSSE, EDMUND [WILLIAM].
February in Rome 185
Hans Christian Andersen 43

GREENE. ALBERT GORTON.
Baron's Last Banquet, The 300

HALLECK, FITZ-GREENE.
Joseph Rodman Drake 91
Weehawken and the New York Bay (*Fanny*)....... 244

HARRISON. S. FRANCES (*Seranus*).
Château Papineau 253

HARTE, [FRANCIS] BRET.
Dickens in Camp 80

HERBERT, W. PAGE
Thor recovers his Hammer (*Icelandic of Sœmund*) .. 284

HERRICK, ROBERT.
Ben Jonson, Ode to 47
Delight in Disorder 135

HEYWOOD, THOMAS.
Hierarchy of Angels 53

HOGG, JAMES.
Jock Johnstone, the Tinkler 390

HOLMES, OLIVER WENDELL.
Daniel Webster 20

HOUGHTON, RICHARD MONCKTON MILNES, LORD.
Thackeray, To 83

HUGO, VICTOR MARIE.
Napoleon (*Translation*) 8

HUNT, LEIGH.
Glove and the Lions, The 330
Mahmoud 305
Nile, The 160
On Hearing a little Music-Box 139

JAPP, ALEXANDER HAY (*H. A. Page*).
Shelley 58

JOHNSON, DR. SAMUEL.
Charles XII. (*Vanity of Human Wishes*) 7
Shakespeare 51

JONSON, BEN.
Freedom in Dress (*Epicœne; or the Silent Woman*). 131
Memory of Shakespeare, To the 48
Portrait of Shakespeare, On the 48

KEATS, JOHN.
Benjamin Robert Haydon, To 69
Grecian Urn, Ode on a 136

KIPLING, RUDYARD.
Christmas in India 161

LANDOR, WALTER SAVAGE.
Art Criticism 110
Macaulay as Poet 61
Robert Browning 89

LANG, ANDREW.
Scythe Song 248

LANIER, SIDNEY.   PAGE.
Song of the Chattahoochee 242

LAZARUS, EMMA.
Chopin 114

LEWIS, MATTHEW GREGORY (*Monk Lewis*).
Alonzo the Brave and the Fair Imogine........... 321

LONGFELLOW, HENRY WADSWORTH.
Carillon 166
Hawthorne 104
Old Bridge at Florence, The 174
Skeleton in Armor, The 295

LOWELL, JAMES RUSSELL.
Abraham Lincoln 32
Henry Wadsworth Longfellow, To 106
In a Copy of Omar Khayyám 39
Lowell on Himself (*A Fable for Critics*).......... 100
Washington 15
William Lloyd Garrison 22

MACKAIL, JOHN WILLIAM.
Etruscan Ring, An 149

MACAULAY, THOMAS BABINGTON, LORD.
Horatius at the Bridge 265

MAHONY, FRANCIS SYLVESTER (*Father Prout*).
Bells of Shandon, The 145

MILTON, JOHN.
Adam and Eve (*Paradise Lost*).................. 124
Epitaph on Shakespeare 51
Lord-General Cromwell, To the 5

MISTRAL, FRÉDÉRIC.
Ballad of Guibour, The (*Preston's Translation*)..... 327

MONTREUIL, MATHIEU DE.
Madame de Sevigné, To.......................... 40

MOORE, THOMAS.
" O, breathe not his name " 6
" Those evening bells " 141
Vale of Cashmere, The (*The Light of the Harem*)... 165

MOULTON, LOUISE CHANDLER.
Laus Veneris 138

O'BRIEN, FITZ-JAMES.
Kane 120

PARSONS, THOMAS WILLIAM.   PAGE
  Bust of Dante, On a   41

PFEFFEL, GOTTLIEB CONRAD.
  Nobleman and the Pensioner, The (*Brooks' Transla-
    tion*) 303

PHELPS, CHARLES HENRY.
  Henry Ward Beecher   24

POE, EDGAR ALLAN.
  Bells, The 141

POLLOK, ROBERT.
  Byron (*The Course of Time*)....................   59

POPE, ALEXANDER.
  Poet's Friend, The 112
  Toilet, The (*Rape of the Lock*) 135

PRAED, WINTHROP MACKWORTH.
  Camp-Bell   56

PRESTON. HARRIET WATERS.
  Ballad of Guibour, The (*Provençal of Mistral*).... 327

PROCTOR, EDNA DEAN.
  Brooklyn Bridge, The 247

QUEVEDO Y VILLEGAS, FRANCISCO DE.
  Rome, To (*Wiffen's Translation*)................. 177

READ, THOMAS BUCHANAN.
  Drifting 195

ROCHE, JAMES JEFFREY.
  Fight of the " Armstrong " Privateer, The 433

ROGERS, SAMUEL.
  Naples (*Italy*) 194
  Venice (*Italy*) 189

RONSARD, PIERRE DE.
  Mary Stuart, To (*Costello's Translation*).........   4

ROYDEN, MATTHEW.
  Sir Philip Sidney (*Elegy on a Friend's Passion*).... 45

SÆMUND, SIGFUSSON.
  Thor recovers his Hammer (*Herbert's Translation*) .. 284

SCHUYLER, MONTGOMERY.
  Carlyle and Emerson 97

SCOTT, SIR WALTER. PAGE.
Fitz-James and Ellen (*Lady of the Lake*) 413
Fitz-James and Roderick Dhu (*Lady of the Lake*) .. 404
Knight, The (*Marmion*) 201
Marmion and Douglas (*Marmion*) 401
Melrose Abbey (*Lay of the Last Minstrel*) 208
Old Time Christmas, An (*Marmion*) 210

SHAKESPEARE, WILLIAM.
Cleopatra (*Antony and Cleopatra*) 127
England (*King John*) 390
Seven Ages of Man (*As You Like It*) 126

SHARP, WILLIAM.
White Peacock, The (*Sospiri di Roma*) 175

SHELLEY, PERCY BYSSHE.
Ianthe, Sleeping, To (*Queen Mab*) 129
Ozymandias of Egypt 161
Venice (*View from the Euganean Hills*) 192

SHENSTONE, WILLIAM.
Village Schoolmistress, The (*The Schoolmistress*) ... 231

SIMMONS, BARTHOLOMEW.
Memory of Thomas Hood, To the 62

SOUTHEY, CAROLINE ANNE BOWLES.
Cuckoo Clock, The (*The Birthday*) 148
Greenwood Shrift, The 379

SOUTHEY, ROBERT.
Cataract of Lodore, The 170
Greenwood Shrift, The 379

STEDMAN, EDMUND CLARENCE.
Cousin Lucrece 131
Hand of Lincoln, The 30
Hawthorne 103

STEIN, EVALEEN.
In Mexico (*One Way to the Woods*) 257

STERLING, JOHN.
Louis XV. 339

STOWE, HARRIET BEECHER.
Day in the Pamfili Doria, A 182

STREET, ALFRED BILLINGS.
Settler, The 240

STRONG, WILLIAM.
Frithiof at the Court of Angantyr (*Swedish of Tegnér*). 289

SWINBURNE, ALGERNON CHARLES.   PAGE.
Deaths of Carlyle and Eliot, On the 96
Dickens 82
Monument erected to Mazzini, On the 13
Walter Savage Landor, In Memory of 75

SYMONDS, JOHN ADDINGTON.
Venice 188

TASSO, TORQUATO.
Erminia and the Wounded Tancred (*Fairfax's
Translation*) 319

TAYLOR, TOM.
Abraham Lincoln 25

TEGNÉR, ESAIAS.
Frithiof at the Court of Angantyr (*Strong's Translation*) 289

TENNYSON, ALFRED LORD.
Albert, Prince Consort of England 34
Godiva 361
Mort D'Arthur 352
Revenge, The 383
Victor Hugo, To 41
Virgil, To 37

THOREAU, HENRY DAVID.
Mist 153
Smoke 156

THORPE, ROSE HARTWICK.
Drifted out to Sea 438

TUCKERMAN, HENRY THEODORE.
Newport-Beach 239

VENABLE, WILLIAM HENRY.
Welcome to " Boz," A (*Saga of the Oaks and Other
Poems*) 77

VIRGIL — PUBLIUS VERGILIUS MARO.
Fall of Troy, The (*Bowen's Translation*) 261

WATSON, WILLIAM.
Lachrymæ Musarum 84
" Wordsworth's Grave," From 74

WHITMAN, SARAH HELEN POWER.
Still Day in Autumn, A ....: 157

WHITMAN, WALT.   PAGE.
  Mannahatta 245
  Myself (*Song of Myself*) 102
  " O Captain! my Captain " 28
  " Out from behind this mask " (*Wound-Dresser*)... 100

WHITTIER, JOHN GREENLEAF.
  Barclay of Ury 429
  Burns 64
  Fitz-Greene Halleck 92
  Prayer of Agassiz, The 116

WIFFEN, BENJAMIN B.
  To Rome (*Spanish of De Quevedo*)................ 177

WILLIS, NATHANIEL PARKER.
  Leper, The 315

WILSON, JOHN (*Christopher North*).
  Evening Cloud, The 156

WOOLSEY, SARAH CHAUNCEY (*Susan Coolidge*).
  Emerson 97

WORDSWORTH, WILLIAM.
  Departure of Sir Walter Scott, On the 61
  Milton, To 54
  Sonnet: " Earth has not anything ".............. 229
  Sonnet, The 55
  Walton's Book of Lives (*Ecclesiastical Sonnets*).... 55

ANONYMOUS.
  Anne Hathaway 110
  George Washington 15
  Lord Lovel 373
  Robin Hood and Allan-a-Dale 375